THE CAGED PHOENIX

THE CAGED PHOENIX

CAN INDIA FLY?

Dipankar Gupta

PENGUIN
VIKING

VIKING
Published by the Penguin Group
Penguin Books India Pvt. Ltd, 11 Community Centre, Panchsheel Park,
New Delhi 110 017, India
Penguin Group (USA) Inc., 375 Hudson Street, New York, New York 10014, USA
Penguin Group (Canada), 90 Eglinton Avenue East, Suite 700, Toronto,
Ontario, M4P 2Y3, Canada (a division of Pearson Penguin Canada Inc.)
Penguin Books Ltd, 80 Strand, London WC2R 0RL, England
Penguin Ireland, 25 St Stephen's Green, Dublin 2, Ireland
(a division of Penguin Books Ltd)
Penguin Group (Australia), 250 Camberwell Road, Camberwell,
Victoria 3124, Australia (a division of Pearson Australia Group Pty Ltd)
Penguin Group (NZ), 67 Apollo Drive, Rosedale, North Shore 0632,
New Zealand (a division of Pearson New Zealand Ltd)
Penguin Group (South Africa) (Pty) Ltd, 24 Sturdee Avenue, Rosebank,
Johannesburg 2196, South Africa

Penguin Books Ltd, Registered Offices: 80 Strand, London WC2R 0RL, England

First published in Viking by Penguin Books India 2009

Copyright © Dipankar Gupta 2009

10 9 8 7 6 5 4 3 2 1

ISBN 9780670082728

Typeset in Bell MT by SÜRYA, New Delhi
Printed at Replika Press Pvt. Ltd, Kundli, Haryana

To Dipayan

'You are the only man of all men whom I would wish would surpass me in all things'

—as Cicero said to his son

CONTENTS

PREFACE AND ACKNOWLEDGEMENTS

This book was written under the very generous hospitality of the Woodrow Wilson International Center for Scholars (WWICS) in Washington DC. I spent a term there in the fall of 2007 and it will remain one of the pleasantest months I have enjoyed in a long, long time. As I remarked to Dr Robert Hathaway, my immediate host at WWICS, the period I spent there was like a 'working holiday'. I have no doubt that other scholars too share a similar opinion about the Center because of its convivial and non-invasive institutional structure.

I must thank all my friends in WWICS not only for allowing me to have a wonderful time, but also for helping me to put this book together. The presentations I made at the Center under Dr Hathaway's stewardship certainly went a long way in lending finesse to many of my arguments. Dr Joe Brinley was also a great source of help in this regard and constantly encouraged me, gently yet persuasively, to get on with the volume.

Neil Kumar proved a sterling research assistant, his drive and enthusiasm for my project often shaming me into action. He was always generous with his time, and even in the worst Washington DC weather drove up to the Center to help me in a myriad ways. He traced books and articles for me and also drew my attention to literature I might have otherwise overlooked. In sum, a truly wonderful intellectual partner.

Janet Spikes made research work so easy and visiting the Center's library a most pleasurable experience. Under her directions books came to my table almost instantly, whether from the Center's library holding or from the Library of Congress. As far as I am concerned, Janet Spikes is the ultimate librarian. I also learnt how difficult, technical and supportive a librarian's role can be. Indeed, from now on I will always be more than kind to librarians, though I am sure there will be nobody else who will measure up to her abilities.

Arlyn Charles attended to every hair-brained request I made, from finding living quarters to obtaining advance payments, to working out how to get my insurance papers processed in a hurry. Had all of this not been handled so efficiently by her I would have spent at least an extra month fretting over these details. Lindsay Collins was always ready to help with a smile and it was a great feeling to enter the premises of WWICS and be greeted by her. I have lost count of the number of times I have bothered her without even considering whether I could have accomplished the task myself by mildly exerting myself. That is how spoilt one gets at WWICS.

I am not at all certain that this book could have been written, warts and all, were I anywhere else. For this I must also thank the gentle clock on Q Street that kept time for me.

While I was in Washington DC, I took the opportunity of testing my views and findings with a larger audience in different universities. A roadshow seemed the best way to accomplish this so I took my intellectual baggage to New York, Baltimore, Maryland, Illinois, and New Jersey and learnt a lot from my discussions there. These excursions were quite satisfying because I was encouraged by those to whom I presented my arguments and data, to press on with the writing of this book. In this connection I must particularly thank Sumit Guha, Indrani Chatterjee, Pradeep Dhillon, John Echeverry Gent, Sonalde Desai, Smita Jassal, and Harold Gould. Mary Anne Weaver, whose term at Woodrow Wilson International Center for Scholars (WWICS) coincided with mine, was a great source of encouragement, friendship, and flattery. She buoyed up my spirits before and after every academic encounter I had at the

WWICS and is also responsible for the title of this book. Her advice was to keep it simple and short. As for the text, she has done what she could to improve my communicative skills. Sunil Nehru made things uncomfortable for me from time to time by bringing inconvenient facts and stylistic shortcomings to my notice. My wife, Harmala, helped me to sharpen my ideas by contesting every one of them in this book. I must also acknowledge Amrita Mishra for carefully checking the references and lapses in the text. *And*, thank you, Adil, for going over the manuscript so carefully, and making such a difference. I know you don't like sentences beginning with 'and' but I had to sneak this one in.

Before I left for Washington DC, I packed in a lot of data and information from a variety of Indian sources. I had mounds of tables, data sheets, and even scraps of paper with precious material scrawled on them strewn all over my office in Jawaharlal Nehru University. Nanda Dulal Das is partly responsible for doggedly adding to this heap virtually every day, but he also helped me sift through the pile and cull out the kind of information I would need for the book. What surprises me most is the good cheer with which he undertook all this.

I have been meaning to write this book for a long time. I was somewhat piqued that many travelling intellectuals shoot off a book on India with such ease and success while the university scholar is still examining and cross-checking fundamental data with caution and rigour. The end product of such an exercise is of course unreadable except to a very few, while the popular, cleverly and breezily conjured books run away with all the laurels! I wanted, therefore, to write about India, bearing in mind my years of working in different areas and bringing them together in such a way that the material would both satisfy a university scholar's critical scrutiny and yet be accessible to a well-informed and willing-to-be-informed general readership.

In attempting to appeal to both the scholar and the intelligent layperson I may have fallen between two styles, but that is the risk I felt I must take. There are many pages with numbers, but I hope they will not scare away readers habituated to reading more pleasurable prose. I did not want to altogether bypass these important figures but I have attempted to soften them by positioning them within a textual format in order to cushion their hard, cold, and hospital-bed-like contours. I can only hope I have succeeded to a degree. Sometimes I wish I had a literary agent and guide to help me along. But even so, I've done well with Heather Adams by my side, correcting and sharpening my sentences to give them a just-crispated look. Archana Shankar made enough room for me, even at the last minute, without losing her sense of editorial judgement. So, I ask myself, why should I need anyone else?

I hope the reader stays with me while I work out my peeve against various forms of culture-laden explanations for things Indian. It may sometimes sound a touch obsessive, but I believe such points of view periodically surface very spontaneously, especially when a good factual answer is difficult to come by. What really gets to me most is that while this tendency is kept somewhat in abeyance when discussing issues in Western societies, there is no such censor at work when it comes to the Indian subcontinent.

Over the past years our economy has been growing impressively, touching 9 per cent in the financial year 2007-08. Some analysts were quite confident that growth would touch double digits in the period 2008-09, but that has not happened. Instead, in recent months, the figure has come down to 6-7 per cent. Though there are good reasons for this, many of us were earlier unprepared to even entertain the suggestion that this could be a possibility. Even today, in the face of this sudden slowing down of the economy, the matter still remains untheorized. In the light of what has happened it is all the more imperative to ask why our economic growth was not as self-sustaining as it promised to be? Alongside, we must also know why our economic engines are still powered by cheap labour and low domestic demand? In this book I have tried to provide a categorical answer to both these pressing questions, not by setting them apart from each other, but by seeing them as obverse sides of the same process.

Should we await the long term so that the end results eventually trickle down once every reservoir is full? Or should we intervene in this process through normatively guided policies that should be expected from a liberal democratic society? Does the economic realm have an autarkic explanatory character, or does it require to be buttressed by sociological facts to make better sense? Is it possible for a class to get rich and richer because there are so many poor around? And what does culture have to do with all of this?

Well, let us see!

1

INTRODUCTION
THE CAGED PHOENIX

When India became Independent in 1947 it was a tremendous feat; the phoenix had truly risen from the ashes. Till then, India was not only economically undeveloped, its cultural blinkers were so closed that for all practical purposes she was still in the Dark Ages. At the time the West was celebrating the Enlightenment, India was toiling with superstitions, caste prejudices and mindless rituals which often lasted for days. From Karl Marx to Richard F. Burton, to Thomas Macaulay to Raja Ram Mohan Roy, and later Rabindranath Tagore, regardless of one's intellectual pedigree, great people looked at India as if it were a mental black hole. What is more, they also worried about whether India would ever come out of this time warp and step into the light.

With Independence, casteism, untouchability and feudalism were legally abolished and India was suddenly a much brighter place to be in. These scourges did not give way because of the logic of history, but rather because there were big people in big places who threw aside the veils and dispelled the darkness. Mahatma Gandhi was not just a fakir politician who believed in mud packs and vegetarianism, Jawaharlal Nehru was not just an Etonian waylaid by socialists, but they, and people like them,

1

forced India into a liberal dawn. Consequently, India drew up a Constitution that the best democracies in the world both envy and emulate.

Though the old held on, the advances made by the national, anti-colonial movement made tradition quite wobbly. In the sixty years and more since Independence, India has had a much-respected President of the Republic from a caste that was once considered untouchable. This would have been unthinkable even a few decades back. We have had Muslims, Sikhs and Christians in high places, and they were not always minority trophies on display. Urbanization today has made it almost impossible for anyone to entertain caste taboos regarding inter-dining and occupational choices, at least outside the village.

Indian independence also promised great advances in education and scholarship. Its first-generation leaders were not satisfied with just economic sovereignty, they wanted intellectual and economic independence too. Accordingly, universities and institutes of science and technology were set up with the highest standards in mind. The results of these efforts were quick to materialize. It happened so fast that it encouraged the view that Brahmannical culture and ancient traditions of learning provided propitious conditions for the emergence of modern knowledge. Jawaharlal Nehru, India's first prime minister, wanted the old religious temples to be replaced by new ones where science, technology and public welfare would be welded together. This was the stuff of which our early dreams were made. By all accounts the phoenix was ready to fly.

But that take off did not quite happen. The phoenix was caged in again because India lost its will to push ahead with those enlightened policies that Gandhi, Nehru and their contemporaries had in mind. Instead, latter-day Indian politicians, and those in public office, gave in to the dull logic of the everyday. There was also a change of guard at the top. Politics was no longer about statesmanship and vision, but about satisfying token representatives who were unconcerned about delivery. This enabled Indian politicians to separate themselves as a class, compelling the ordinary voter to choose only among political bosses. As the long view was bartered away for a myopic one, the cage fell heavily on the phoenix, just as it was testing its wings.

Perhaps in countries where development and equity are yesterday's news, a run-of-the-mill politician is adequate. But in places like India where there is so much to be done before the night falls again, extraordinary efforts are required by extraordinary leaders. India is a very new nation-state but it has turned tired and haggard in just six decades. Obviously, this is not a flattering picture. As if to compensate, Indians please themselves by pointing only to those features that have held firm, though everything in between sags with gravity.

Standards have been so lowered at home that ambitious Indians are often forced to realize their potential abroad. Indians are doing well in USA, UK and Europe as software experts, doctors and scientists. I was told by a senior executive of a multinational company in London that whenever they have to sell a proposal they take a brown face along to impress their clients. While Indian professionals have a great reputation abroad for their competence, they do not shine in the same way in their motherland. There are many reasons for this, but most importantly intellectuals are generally uncomfortable with political graft and craft. What came as a surprise to me is that the actual amount allocated by the State to Research and Development has come down over the years. Naturally, the best and the brightest are tempted to leave for foreign shores, and can we blame them? Instead of asking why such skilled professionals head westwards, every time a non-resident Indian does well abroad, it is happy hour at home.

Now that India is prospering in the software business, all eyes are focused on it. Our export earnings from the Information Technology Enabled Services (ITES) have grown significantly over the last decade. But how can we forget that there is very little cutting edge technology that Indian ITES enterprises are engaged in. They are generally doing the kind of hack work that Western companies find too dull and unrewarding. We need also to keep in mind that the ITES sector employs only three million people. No doubt their jobs are financially rewarding, but 72 per cent of Indians live on less than US$2 a day, and roughly 35 per cent on less than US$1 a day.

Agriculture is going through a ruinous time, prompting millions to search for jobs outside the village, at whatever wages. This has encouraged the informalization of labour and a phenomenal rise in sweat shops. The predominance of cheap labour makes Indian commodities, from software to clothing, internationally competitive. But this unpleasant fact is kept out of view by concentrating on growth statistics and not human development. It is not surprising then that education, health, energy and transport do not reach a majority of our population in ways they should. But the bulk of our intellectuals, and practically every political leader, have no time for these concerns.

The idea of being an independent economic and intellectual power has lost its steam. In fact, nobody talks about it any more. They take refuge from these uncomfortable issues by likening the need for excellence at home as a variant of red rhetoric. This is where they go wrong, and this is where they should learn from the West. All Western societies took special care to make sure that they did not lag behind, either intellectually or materially, when they were climbing to the top. They insured this by making public goods available to the public at quality levels. Further, they prompted domestic capital to temper its pure profit motives and contribute to social good as well. Also, privatization grew in the social service sectors in Europe, even USA, once the majority in these countries had attained a certain level of prosperity. They now had the means to choose between competing products with competing prices. Till then, the State stood as guarantor.

It was not easy to achieve this in Europe or America, but strangely enough, extraordinary men appeared in these continents in the nineteenth century who strove to create a public of equal citizens based on access to health, education and other public goods. This is what gave Western democracies their strong foundation. In spite of the fillip that our nationalist leaders gave us at the time of our Independence, we failed to forge ahead in the way we should have. It is true that more

Indian villages have electricity, schools and hospitals now than they did in the past. These facts however lose their shine the moment we enquire into the quality of their delivery. We have the knowledge, we have skilled human resources, we have people willing to serve, but the system has not harnessed these attributes adequately.

In the very long run things will probably get better, but in that case what use is democracy? The idea of democracy is to make a difference here and now by putting in place normative policies that act as catalytic agents. A democratic state needs to quicken the pace and buck the trend and not just to mind the store. The conditions in India do not allow the State the luxury to leisurely roll back and look out of the window. A lot needs to be accomplished before the day is done.

I have tried to sound a warning bell, hoping that at least intellectuals and members of the concerned public will take a second look at the Indian growth story. What we need to ask is why this growth is not translating into development? We must also critically enquire why our once vaunted human resource prowess is not taking us towards excellence. We should not overlook either the ugly warts on our industrial profile even as we are impressed by what the IT, communications and assorted service-sectors have accomplished.

India's backwardness has a cultural ring about it because such extremes and contraries inhabit this country. This naturally prompts cultural-based theories to explain not just India's poverty, but also its *undelivering* democracy. Through every page I have argued against such culturological positions for, I believe, they only entrench the status quo. Caste, religious differences and even a multi-ethnic State do not by themselves create conditions inimical to development. What harms democracy most is when we ignore the fact that wealth can grow on a sustained basis, and the rich can get richer, only after the poor are out of their poverty. This is where the West can really teach us a lesson or two. We should learn from the development experiences of Europe and America, it is always instructive to observe how other mountaineers have scaled peaks before we set off on our own climb.

2

CONNECTING THE RICH TO THE POOR
STRUCTURAL ALTERNATIVES TO CULTURAL ANSWERS

India is viewed in many quarters the world over as a fast-paced success story and most people just can't wait to reach the end. Indeed, America, which till quite recently viewed India as a country it loved to hate has reversed its earlier attitude of scorn and scepticism to one of admiration and affection. This has naturally warmed the hearts of Indians worldwide and it has ushered in a new era of Indo–US relations that could not have been imagined a decade and a half ago.

With America changing its views on India, the rest of the developed world too has become enthusiastic about what happens here. The huge growth-rate figures, the possibility of the world's largest middle-class in the world's largest democracy, and the remarkable aptitude that Indian computer entrepreneurs have demonstrated have added a veneer of glamour to everything in this subcontinent. Even Galerie LaFayette, the hub of French fashion display in Paris, held a full-scale India Week, larded with Bollywood kitsch in full frontal display, and people loved it.

When the Indian growth-rate was sluggish prior to the introduction of liberalization in 1990, it was widely believed that Hindu culture was partly responsible for it as it inherently despised business. Lofty, otherworldly Brahmanism had nothing in common with crass trade, and indeed found this occupation and those who practised it not quite *au fait.* In spite of India's status today as an economic powerhouse, Hindu culture still retains its exotic persuasive power. It is still summoned to account for this or that aspect of social life, often in a disaggregated way. Sometimes it is the Hindu tilt towards otherworldliness that is centralized; on other occasions it could be the caste order and its 'obsession with minor differences'; and in some cases it could well be earthy sentiments rising from the imagined village. What remains the same is the preeminence of culture, in one form or another, to explain secular life in India. Occasionally, the aptitude Indians have demonstrated in Information Technology is attributed to the Hindu preference for mental over manual work, an idea with a Brahmanical tinge[1]. It is also argued that the mathematical skills required in IT enterprises come easily to Brahmans, as astrology was part of their traditional occupation.

On a negative note, but still staying with culture, India's caste system and its unwieldy multicultural and multilinguistic nation-state are held responsible for holding up her maturity as a world-class economic power. Thus, if there are the rich and the poor there are customized cultural explanations at each level. Even when there is little self-conscious attempt at using culture as an explanatory device, it makes its way in the moment one attempts to explain the whole. As the empirical interlinkages between classes are never quite emphasized, culture comes in to fill the gap and complete the circle. Soon such cultural explanations assume a life of their own, and we tend to forget that it all began with a descriptive lapse.

Interlinked Contraries

As I look around me I cannot help but see contradictory realities. I am impressed by the huge surge in consumerism and in affluent lifestyles. It is not uncommon for professional and higher-salaried families to have more than one car in their garage and an air-conditioner in every bedroom. In contrast to this, it is impossible to overlook the extent of poverty that is in your face as it characterizes such huge sections of the society, beginning right at your doorstep. It is something of a conundrum how people can ignore this glaringly obvious reality when they write about India's tremendous economic success. The lives of the poor, particularly those in villages, have hardly had the occasion to ride on India's phenomenal growth charts. However, a tweedy leftish attitude that takes in only this side of the picture might fail to note the changing visage of poverty in both villages and towns. Landlordism is no longer the principal cause of rural poverty, nor is exploitation by big capital the reason for urban deprivation.

In this book I intend to understand the nature of India's growth and why large sections of the population have still not experienced development. The difference between growth and development is, as we all know, central to the well being of a democratic society. Growth can be statistically quite impressive but it need not reflect development because large sections of the society might still be in situations of abysmal poverty. True democracy, on the other hand, pays attention to social development and not just to sectoral growth. Only when this economic and social uplift occurs across the board do numbers in growth figures actually start adding up to development.

My experiences in villages and factories, in cottage manufactories and urban slums lead me to believe that growth, such as we know it to be in the Indian case, is not independent of the poverty that still characterizes a majority of our population. The tendency in many circles is to separate the two, but this is incorrect in my view. Of course, it could be argued that what I see as separate is actually not so because within the span of a few generations prosperity will seep down to the lowest quarters. I am not particularly warm to this idea for two reasons. The rich in India depend on cheap labour in a variety of ways to stay on top. This is not only reflected in their business successes but also in their lifestyles. This is a harsh judgement, but we must squarely address it for the sake of development. It might of course be argued that there is no point in being in an unseemly rush. As time rolls by, today's sweatshop worker will be tomorrow's computer geek, or at least, a close kin. But where is the evidence? What have we done to upgrade the skills of the working poor? The Cabinet set up a Rs 15,000 crore Skill Development Centre, but we are still waiting for it to stir. So far, not a single rupee has been spent. Where is the public delivery of public goods happening at quality levels? Must industrial Research and Development (R&D) beat ever so faintly that we might leave it for dead? Should we also not realize that waiting for growth to morph unhurriedly into development over generations is inimical to the democratic spirit? In a democratic society we are supposed to plan normative interventions that enable citizens in general, and not a class here and a profession there, to experience lifestyle benefits during their lifetimes.

Now that we have the vote, we should all be in a hurry. Democracy enjoins us not to be ostrich-like, nor to place uncritical trust in the beneficial effects of the long run. Democracy makes one impatient, and the need to see progress and a betterment of one's life situation cannot be postponed to succeeding generations. The voters want action now! Besides, it is possible only in a democratic system to raise contrary voices and to look at facts for what they are without being constrained by an objective epistemology, or thought system, originating from above, whether from the church or the State. It is therefore crucially important that normative interventions be contemplated without allowing them to descend to pure administrative expediency.

Facts will be merged with democratic concerns in order to prepare the ground somewhat for substantive normative interventions. My concerns with ethnocentrism and with the relationship between town and country and between caste, class, and nation-state proceed from my background as a professional sociologist. The critical feature of any serious sociological study is to be as independent as consciously possible from the interests of this or that power wielder, real or imagined.

That should not however mean that we have to become abusive, for academics, properly understood, are never perched on an ivory tower. In this investigative process one tends to be over-critical, but that is still preferable to being credulous and easy to please.

The truth is that this remarkable growth-rate in India is accompanied by poverty, by ethnic tensions, and by identity politics. The multinational corporate boardroom has nothing in common with sweat shops and diminishing farm returns. The squabbling fields of caste and ethnic rivalries seem remote from these elevated quarters, as if they belong to another world. And yet all of these are not just contemporaneous but are hyperlinked: click on one and the whole lot rolls out. The character of economic growth, the Indian village, the state of public goods delivery, caste, and ethnic conflict interpenetrate one another in ways that escape our attention if viewed from a single lens. I believe that there is an alternative, and it need not be an exotic optic. It is with this conviction that I have written this book.

Normalizing India

The task then is to figure out how prosperity can coexist with poverty, and how service sector growth can live side by side with a failed agrarian system. Though some of the earlier signature features of Indian society no longer remain the same, for we see great changes from caste to village to urban growth, and yet for the most part prosperity has not yet touched the lives of millions; anything between a third to about half the population. This is not a statistic that should bring comfort to any democratic society, and yet the big story today is only about India's prospering classes. Indeed, when India falters the well-to-do dynamic agents are not culpable, and no fingers are pointed at them. Instead, the blame falls on caste politics, regional passions, or excessive rootedness in the village, all projected as mass sentiments. Therefore the reliance on culture-based explanations has not yet become obsolete in the Indian context. It has only added a low-lying annexe to its established living quarters in Brahmanical heights.

This explains why you either love or hate India and Indians, nothing in between. However, through all of this a sense of incomprehensible wonderment remains, compelling scholars, commentators, tourists, and stay-at-home intellectuals in the West to view India in a way that they would never do for their own society. They find it easier to separate one aspect of India from its other and then ignore it, or at best explain the two separately. Either of these positions actually favour culture-based explanations, and it is necessary to recognize this aspect at the very outset of our endeavours.

The perception of high Hindu traditions as the seedbed that prepares Indians to excel in the knowledge and IT sector does not actually make for a flattering account. In such renditions the successful, privileged Indians tend to be viewed as quirky one-sided brainiacs and not quite normal people. But beyond this basic competence they really have to be led by the hand, well meaning though they may be. As it is their tradition that gives them the edge in a highly partial manner within the knowledge sector, they are still seen as creatures of the past. Undoubtedly in this case tradition is manifesting itself differently, but it still lurks within. That is why India cannot be like the rest of the developed world. When not locked into their villages and in their closed economies, Indians can at best be accentuated specialists. They can, nevertheless, be quite charming once the lights are adjusted and their images airbrushed.

I vividly realized this side of patronizing Western ethnocentrism quite by chance. It was not long ago, around the closing years of the last century, when I happened to be a visiting scholar at a quaint university town in the West, which shall remain unnamed. I met a charming senior professor there who immediately took a shine to me. I later discovered that he was in fact an India lover and his house was a veritable caravanserai for passing Indians of all descriptions. Some of them had broken wings, many were short of funds, and some others just exploited his hospitality with utter cynicism.

My colleague nonetheless remained the ultimate gracious host. He took me to his bosom too and invited me frequently to his home to sup with his wife and whoever else was passing by from India. I soon realized that he was a compulsive collector of Indians, but as it was working out rather well for me, I did not object.

Quite without warning, our warm relationship suddenly turned frigid one fateful afternoon. I must say it was probably all my fault. We were having lunch in the faculty lounge of the university and my host (yet again) was telling me of the Indians he had met over the years, and how much he had gained from them. They were 'spiritual', 'beautiful', 'gracious', 'charming', 'colourful', and so on. It was almost as if India was teeming with only wonderful people who were all cute, brown, soft and cuddly. Just when he was about to conclude his list I heard myself asking him why he had not met a single 'intelligent' person from amongst all those wonderful people from India he had befriended? Was there no Indian of his acquaintance, if not exactly a friend, who was bright, clever, smart, and may have occasionally taken his pants off in a debate? Our friendship died almost instantly. We kept up pretenses but the magic had vanished.

My attempt here is to 'normalize' India and provide an explanation of how the rich and the poor, the IT and the tired village, live in the same time frame; how technological training and caste and religious bigotry can express themselves with equal felicity in the same society. This would first lead us to examine why the economic miracle that IT and some service-sector industries have brought to India has been so limited in its scope.

Of course not many Indians and consumer-market advocates will accept this story. They believe that the current high growth rate will rise exponentially and by 2050 or even 2020 India will become the world's most powerful and affluent economy[2]. The highly respected *McKinsey Report* had in fact a big story with the telling and vivid title 'The Bird of Gold'[3] on the subject of India's fantastic rate of growth. This is, of course, assuming, among other things, that the rest of the world is stagnant and blinded by India's brilliance.

Every society is unique after a fashion, but this is rarely conceded when it comes to Europe or the United States. Instead, terms like American exceptionalism, British exceptionalism, even European exceptionalism, are used to overcome specific aspects of the social order that appear recalcitrant to generalization. It is almost as if there is a gigantic all-purpose swill that is sloshing around the continents, to which only local flavours need to be added in measured spoons.

Yet, one rarely talks of Indian exceptionalism. This is because the subcontinent is supposedly so unique that one needs special faculties to savour it. The high mountains to the north and the deep seas to the south have blocked the natural tendency of the swill to flow down to the lower reaches. As everything about India is unique, a simple standby condiment like exceptionalism is too dull for the task.

This view has been encouraged by legions of prolix politicians and writers, past and present, dead and alive. By subordinating every person's fact to elitist fiction they have succeeded in pushing India beyond the credibility barrier. Whether we talk of caste, or the nation-state, or the so-called economic miracle post-liberalization in 1991, we are never rid of a sense of awe.

With caste the question is: how can the vast majority accept such an obvious system of inequality? With the nation-state, the issue is: how long can India last, given its myriad religious and linguistic features? The much-discussed economic miracle in the service sector is attributed to the Brahmanical streak in our cultural make-up. This last obviously implies that those of us in India who do not belong to this cultural heritage are outside these growth charts and probably have only themselves to blame.

Such concerns acquire greater meaning today as we are faced with a situation that is widely accepted as being paradoxical. If India is steaming ahead with a growth rate of roughly seven to nine per cent, why is the countryside still poor, and caste and ethnic politics so rampant? Why is India shining on some fronts but not on others? One way out would be to concentrate only on the high-tech sectors such as the knowledge industries and feel satisfied that the percolation effect will soon make a difference by the year 2020, or 2040, take your pick. The other is to deny advance altogether and argue that nothing has really changed; and perhaps India is worse off than before. This too however does not quite square up with what we see around us. Clearly, there is a need for a sociological analysis that is sensitive to the urgencies of normative interventions.

Paradoxes and Dilemmas

On the one hand there is little doubt that India has a lot going for it, and on the other, it does not seem to be able to take off: as if an incubus from the past is sitting heavily on it. Is it a trapped phoenix or, as McKinsey reports, a 'golden bird'? I believe that India is rising from the ashes of its past, like the phoenix, but cannot yet spread its wings. Instead of seeing this incapacity as an effect of traditional culture, I would rather see it as the conjoint effect of status differentials, extreme scarcity at the lower levels, and inaccessibility to institutions of democratic governance.

We should be on guard at this point against the argument that India's stasis is because Jawaharlal Nehru's Brahmanical background led him to advocate a socialist/planned economy, leading to our sorry plight. The argument could be that our commercial unproductivity is because of traditional caste prejudice against commerce. Poverty in India then supposedly prevails because it emanates from popular culture and from those of our leaders who are themselves part of this system rather than the kinds of constraints mentioned above. So the conclusion is often that caste, and not the underdevelopment of industrial capital, is hugely responsible for India's impoverished reality.[5]

Although village, caste, and ethnic relations, appear to be in the eternal culture bind, they have changed appearances, although they remain as dishevelled as ever. The villagers continue to be poor, but are now looking beyond the traditional hand-me-down occupations to better options, but rarely with success. Village schools are still dysfunctional and yet there is a growing appreciation for education among the people who have not yet had a shot at literacy. Rough people from the village with earth in their fingernails are finding jobs in factories, but continue to live at abysmal levels, sometimes below the poverty line. On the face of it, rural poverty can be written about without taking into account the development in industry, and, indeed, the reverse is also equally compelling. Explanations of poverty yield to a temptation to rely on cultural stereotypes. In the case of industry, the constraints on and character of economic growth are overlooked in order to project a roseate image. True, there is spectacular growth in some favoured industries, but the largest chunk of our economy is still underdeveloped. The village appears stagnant, but is churning at the bottom. As I am painfully aware of this reality I cannot help but question our economic miracle and place it alongside other features with which it coexists, even correlates. After all, the village is very near the city, just beyond the last traffic light.

Then there are villagers in metros and small towns rubbing shoulders with people with different levels of urban depth. Their cultural horizons don't merge under the same canopy and yet they participate in each other's lives for reasons of the economy. Surely all of this must have an impact on urban structures as they must have on caste and village. Without appreciating these other cohorts of India's growth rate we will never understand the specifics of our contemporary economic scenario. In particular we need to know why the phoenix that is India is unable to take wing.

India not only assaults the senses but it also appears to leave a deep impress on the intellect, perhaps even confounding it. Not just the dilettante who tends to hit and write, but also those who have spent a lifetime working on India often confess, without embarrassment, that they know so little about this country. After all, India is stubbornly and impenetrably exotic. The commentators extenuate their indolence and lack of analytical rigour by labelling Indians as strange and inscrutable folks. They are not open, normal, and rational like normal people. Hence, the eager confession, made with a self-deprecatory and disarming smile, that nobody can really understand India, this is the best you will get, and it will not account for all that you see.

Surely, specialists on America or Europe cannot claim complete knowledge about everything in their area of study? Yet they never feel pressured in the same way as Indian scholars, to baldly, and gladly confess their analytical ineptitude regarding the whole. An occasional node that is awkwardly positioned can be excised as an 'exceptional' circumstance, but what if, as in India, every node bears this feature? Doesn't that make the whole society mysterious?

Can we dare to go against such a dominant stream of thought and argue that India is not really exotic? Can we ask our readers to brain up and not suspend judgment when they come to Indian shores? Dare we posit India as a normal society amenable to universal categories of analysis? I realize that all this militates against years of indoctrination and received wisdom about India. At the same time there is no better way of doing justice to a quarter of humankind than to acknowledge that they are not exotic fare, but just a little tastier than that all-purpose swill that is said to be the basic staple elsewhere in the world.

For a Sociology and Not Culturology of India

It is said that you are stuck with the face with which you are born for the first twenty years of your life, and then you get the face you deserve. Indian intellectuals certainly deserve the status of second-hand orientalists for they do the job of exoticizing and prettifying their fellow people from within. Up to a point one could place the blame on colonialism, which is often made out to be fount of all misery, but we cannot take recourse to it all the time for all our petty traits.

In today's world of highly brittle sensitivities, when terms like 'gollywog' and rhymes like 'eenie, meenie, minah, moe, catch a nigger by his toe . . .' are taboo in the West, foreign scholars in America or Europe have to be very careful about what they say about people in developing countries. Terms like the 'dark continent' or the 'inscrutable Orient' are out. Naturally, it would now be grossly politically incorrect for them to remark negatively about Indians: about how they revel in dirt, or their inherent incapacity to deal with democracy, secularism, and for that matter, any impersonal, formal institution. As they cannot pronounce all this themselves, they are subconsciously relieved when they find Indians who can do the job for them. This unleashes a chain reaction and soon a long line of eager 'native' orientalists forms to decry their own people as incorrigibly 'culture laden', in order to win recognition first in the West, and then, as is to be expected, even at home.

If these matters appear to be gigantic puzzles, irresolvable by routine methods, it is simply because we don't want to believe that India can indeed offer simple solutions. Why should every issue in India be drenched in idiosyncratic history, tradition, mindsets, and folklore? Yet it is the common presumption that without such an elaborate marinade, no institution in India can be brought to the table, and if a simple answer exists to any elaborate question, we must instinctively distrust it. Everything in India is about culture, and can be examined only as a cultural phenomenon. It is like reading a detective novel backwards: 'of course the butler did it'.

It is not my intention to blanche the peculiarities of the subcontinent, but to caution my readers against yielding too readily to culture-based explanations that demand extreme doses of relativism. This relativist attitude calls out for special tastes and faculties that are supposedly either innate or need to be cultivated over a long period of time to understand anything Indian. This superficially gracious and sympathetic view is actually intellectually specious as it is based on a careful separation between 'us' and 'them'.

Let us begin to instead adopt a universalistic sociological mode and start with the hopeful assumption of the possibility of some good, upright, and utterly 'normal' explanation for things that appear different in India. This, I believe, is the kernel of the sociological approach. Can we not see parallels between Indian institutions, even caste, with those we have elsewhere in the world? At this point I am not just thinking about apartheid or the shrouded practice of untouchability in Japan, but of institutions and practices that are routine and normal in Western societies. Should we not resist cultural typification that treats only the West as 'normal' and everybody else as an obstinate riddle?

It is not as if this intellectual tendency to fantasize everything Indian is a characteristic Western trait. Many Indians, some of the best-known ones, do the same and derive a lot of mileage from it. Dr S. Radhakrishnan, who was also the second President of India, was probably the first Indian of repute who legitimized this 'exotic India' approach that separated the East from the West. He believed Europe, and indeed the rest of the world, should learn from India where '[b]oth in life and in philosophy the spiritual motive is a predominant one'.[6] For him religion was something the Hindu lived and breathed and everything they did in their mundane world was informed by a spiritual urge.

> '[A] characteristic view of Indian philosophy is the belief in the intimate relationship of philosophy and life. This attitude of the practical application of philosophy to life is found in every school of Indian philosophy ... Every Indian system seeks the truth, not as academic knowledge, but to learn the truth to make men free ... The goals of life which are accepted by Hindus are righteousness or obedience to the moral law [*dharma*].'[7]

This was not so hard for the Hindus to accomplish for, the 'spiritual motive dominates life in India ... The Gita and the Upanishads are not remote from popular belief'.[8] Calmly ignoring both the inter-faith bloodshed of 1947 and the centuries of caste oppression in the country, Radhakrishnan could still write that 'religion in India is not dogmatic',[9] and that the 'Aryans and the Dravidians, the Hindus and the Buddhists, the Jains and the Christians, the Zoroastrians and the Muslims, were all received with open hospitality by the Indian people and their systems of thought and practice were enabled to develop according to natural genius'.[10] With such a lofty and empyrean view of the Hindus, he could argue that 'practically all of Indian philosophy, from its beginning in the Vedas to the present day, has striven to bring about a socio-spiritual reform in the country'.[11] It is this indomitable spiritualism of Hindus that enabled them to survive the ravages of time [read Muslim invasions] and the 'accidents of history'.[12]

An exotic rendition of Indians such as this obviously endeared Radhakrishnan to the West and, on the rebound, to Indians too. One wonders where he saw these Indians that he was writing about? Certainly not in the killing fields that separated India and Pakistan, certainly not in the villages where caste atrocities were a way of life, certainly not in the hungry pursuit of power and prestige that consumes the elite in this country. Perhaps, following on the footsteps of some of the best-known European Indologists before him, Radhakrishnan too believed that the best Indians were the dead ones who lived wondrously aeons ago.

Amartya Sen argues that the major reason for W.B. Yeats and Ezra Pound falling out with India's greatest modern poet and Nobel laureate, Rabindranath Tagore, was that they could not fit him in the 'narrow box' of Orientalism. Yeats let out his frustration quite openly when he wrote his essay 'Damn Tagore'. Tagore was too much of a modernist inspite of his wizard-like appearance. It was difficult to exoticize him and he refused to be exoticized as if the River Ganges flowed in his veins.[13]

The making of Gandhi by the West is, however, a successful example of how India is mystified. The most capricious aspects of Gandhian thought are elevated over those other issues such as universal franchise and minority rights, for which he fought consistently throughout his life. Even his advocacy of non-violence had a very modern content and was not wrapped up in mystery, or in an ascetic, otherworldly Hindu disposition. What escapes notice in this stylization of Gandhi, the archetypal and caricatured Hindu, is his insistence that non-violence was primarily a democratic weapon. It was meant to encourage democratic debates in a modern setting and not simply because it was godlike to be truthful. As Gandhi would argue, only those who cannot win a rational argument would rather resort to force to settle issues. Bertrand Russell also believed in something very similar for he wrote: 'If an opinion contrary to your own makes you angry, that is a sign that you are sub-consciously aware of having no good reason for thinking as you do'.[14] Gandhi's non-violence embraced truth in this critical sense, and not for any other artful reason. Although theorists of the Frankfurt School later championed this democratic modality, or operational key, nobody calls them spiritual. Interestingly, however, Gandhi is never mentioned in these Frankfurt School texts, for that would make him a modernist, and hence of no use to the exotica-hunting Western imagination.

Gandhi was no mystic with his head in incense clouds. Had there been no Gandhi I am sure India would not have been a democratic nation-state, howsoever flawed this may appear by classical standards. The Constitution of the Indian Republic is replete with Gandhian thinking, from giving dignity to the individual, enshrining non-discrimination, outlawing untouchability, protecting political and cultural minorities, and gender equality. Habermas could not have done better even after so many years. It is quite likely that without Gandhi India may have become Independent of British rule earlier. It may have also survived as a sovereign nation-state as it does now. But it would have certainly found it hard to work up any enthusiasm for democracy.

I am not sure if many Western lovers of Gandhi are aware of his huge impact in the making of a modern, liberal, and democratic India? If truth were told, Gandhi is idolized and revered in the West for all the wrong reasons. His highly sensationalized fasts-unto-death and his celebrations of non-violence, vegetarianism, celibacy, village life, and mud packs as a panacea, most catch our attention. Would Attenborough have made a film on Gandhi if this aspect of Gandhi were not regnant in the Western mind? Clearly, nobody in the fable-churning world of Hollywood would ever think of making a motion picture on Jawaharlal Nehru, for he was such a transparent, one-dimensional modernist. He had no fads and hence no colour and was much too much like any Western stalwart. If such a film were made it would shrivel in its trudge to Western theatres. Ironically, Nehru was Gandhi's choice as India's first prime minister. You wouldn't expect this from a Gandhi who was all fakir and oriental mendicant. By wiping out the modern and modernizing Gandhi, the West was able to cast him as a quaint throwback from the past and thus ideally suited to be an Indian icon. However why should we blame only the West: was this not also Radhakrishnan's view of the Indian?

Even the fascination Indians have with cricket has been approached in cultural–religious terms. Now what could be more convincing than this to show how nothing Indian can be left on its own and judged on its own terms? Played in Pakistan, Bangladesh, the West Indies, England, and Australia, only in India is cricket treated as a cultural phenomenon rubbing shoulders with the religious rather than in a secular, no-nonsense fashion.

For example, the five-day cricket test matches are viewed as another expression of the Hindus yearning for eternity, calmly ignoring the fact that this mode of contestation was invented by the British and not by Indians. Ashis Nandy actually began his book entitled *The Tao of Cricket* with the comment: 'Cricket [test matches] is an Indian game accidentally discovered by the British.'[15] Another example of an Indian scholar succumbing to orientalist pressures and internalizing them. The truth is that India has taken to one-day quick-time cricket with the same enthusiasm as UK or Australia.

It is interesting that sociologists who write about their own society place culture in its context, and anthropologists who write about 'other' societies tend to place culture in the text. Consequently, the burden of 'culture' as a variable changes from locale to locale. In one case, culture is the effect, and in another case the cause. For Western scholars writing about their own societies which are thoroughly normal, culture-based explanations are not entertained, but anthropologists are given the license to do so as they are writing about other people who are not really normal, but 'lovely', 'gracious', 'spiritual', 'beautiful', and so on.

I once asked a close friend, Professor Milton Israel, why North Americans are so excited about certain Indian scholars who were not very distinguished till they were discovered by Western academia? Milton's answer was characteristically blunt. He said in plain words: 'because they tell us that you are different. Why should I pay return airfare to you if you are going to announce that Indians are as normal as the rest of us?'

Around the same time I also asked another American academic, who I shall not name for reasons that will soon be obvious, why tourists from New York, Helsinki or Vienna nearly always make it a point to visit Varanasi? His answer was also blunt for he knew that I wanted an honest opinion. Without hesitation he said that 'people from my country and Europe find Varanasi attractive for it confirms our superiority over you'. His words stunned me though I was half-expecting it. They were just so true!

For most Indians who don't live in Varanasi, though many local residents would disagree, it is a stinking, dirty pile of earth and bricks, with temples at every street corner that are equally filthy. Yet, as foreigners are crowding this place many Indians have begun to find virtues in Varanasi. They too come to this city as tourists, and not as they used to earlier, just to die by the Ganges and go straight up without further mediation.

From a Daughter/Wife to Goddess

The cultural lore about India is truly fascinating, and not easy to overlook. The rope trick and the fakir napping on a bed of nails may be figments of imagination, but there are so many other empirically ascertained facts about India that truly astound the untrained eye. Indians spontaneously create filth wherever they go though they are personally fastidiously clean; the best mathematicians among them are also astrologers; they see God in stones and trees; they fast at the drop of a hat but make a great to-do about castes they can eat with and accept water from.

Though phenomena similar to these can be found elsewhere, if one were to do a comparative study through time and space, it is because all these features and more are present here and now in India that makes this country and its people so incredible. Other countries also have women leaders, but when Indira Gandhi became India's prime minister there were a slew of articles that likened her to Goddess Durga (no less) and as an embodiment of the feminine principle of *shakti*, or pure power. India's Picasso, M.F. Husain, painted in those years a portrait of Indira Gandhi, astride a tiger, slaying demons. Only later did the irony surface when it was clear she wanted to get off the tiger but could not. At any rate, it is almost as if Indians were culturally nudged to appoint her prime minister. Indira Gandhi's accession to this high office raised the cultural banner, in a way that did not happen with Benazir Bhutto in Pakistan, Khaleda Zia and Hasina Wajed in Bangladesh, or Aung San Suu Kyi in Myanmar.

The truth is that it is only in the developing countries, with their great gender disparities, that women rise politically by riding on the legacy of their dead ancestors or husbands. Interestingly, sons inherit tangible property while wives and daughters are left holding the bag of political heritage. This anomaly is striking enough and should be quizzed further, but without recourse to mystical symbols of Durga or *Shakti*. Once we rub our eyes clean of such orientalist explanations, what strikes us immediately is that daughters and widows of powerful men become politically significant only in patriarchal societies in Asia (particularly South Asia) which are democratic, or harbour democratic pretensions.

In a patriarchal, backward society, but with an aspiring democratic polity, a female relative of the late hero is pushed to take his place because she is seen as an empty signifier with no worthwhile qualities of her own. In a male-dominated society this makes perfect sense, which is why there is a demotic drive to install the departed hero's female relatives and not his son. A woman escapes comparison with the male figure as she can only represent him and not herself. What does she have to call her own except for her ties with her late, and much admired, male relative?

A son, on the other hand, is considered to have independent worth unlike his sister or mother. Therefore, he is subject to comparisons with his father and falls short. This inhibits him from becoming a natural choice as successor. Once he is positioned man-to-man against his father all his faults come to light. A female relative escapes this kind of comparison because she is not expected to have any worthwhile attributes, which is why she is such a useful flag. This explains the initial rise of Indira Gandhi, Benazir Bhutto, the warring begums of Bangladesh, Sirimavo Bandaranike, Megawati Sukarnoputri, and Aung San Suu Kyi. This phenomenon is thus a much more general one and cannot be explained simply by relying on Hindu symbols like Durga or Shakti. Of course, once these women become powerful they adroitly marginalize all others, but it is the first step that is crucial. They should thank patriarchy and an underdeveloped democracy for that.

Before we accept the idea that patriarchy is just an oriental phenomenon it is worth remembering that in Britain a wife could not run away from home to escape an abusive and violent husband till the verdict of the *Regina* v. *Jackson* case was delivered in 1891.[16] In European tradition too a husband was allowed to beat his wife so long as the cane was no thicker than the thumb. This is the origin of the phrase 'rule of thumb'. Even so, the extent of patriarchy in the West today is nowhere as oppressive as in countries of South Asia. Contrast Margaret Thatcher with Indira Gandhi or Benazir Bhutto. This Conservative prime minister of Britain came to the top by scratching, clawing, and outwitting every other contender, just as men do in politics. She was not handed leadership on a platter.

The Exotic as Stupid

Exoticization works also in studies whose subject matter is boringly mundane. The way to achieve it is to insert a little cultural twist here and deliberately overlook a detail there and a precious research project can be erected. The website of the World Wide Fund For Nature (WWF), which has won millions of hearts, and dollars, courtesy of the Chinese panda, carried the slogan 'Cotton is a thirsty crop' in order to get large sums of money for a project of its own. Strangely, in spite of the absurdity of this proposition the project garnered considerable funding. This could only happen because donor agencies assumed that South Asian farmers needlessly despoil the environment for they are too stupid to learn from experience.

Everybody has known for centuries that cotton grows only in semi-arid regions; so how can it be thirsty? Here we are treated to the 'silly farmer' stereotype. According to the WWF, most South Asian farmers, even though they may have been cultivating cotton for years, have to be taught the basics on how to grow cotton with less water. The first baby step is to perform an easy test to make sure that it is time to irrigate his crop. Instead of wastefully letting his cotton field be inundated by scarce water he must first pick up a handful of earth and squeeze it to test whether any remnant of moisture remains. If the earth is still damp then the farmer is advised to stay away from irrigating the fields for that would be a waste of water. As a measure of abundant caution, as farmers are prone to flooding their cotton fields quite recklessly, they are advised to sow cotton seed in ridges to protect the crop from receiving excess water. The aim of the project throughout is to protect the cotton crop from the farmer himself.

When I met cotton farmers in India and Pakistan, I asked them if they believed that cotton was a thirsty crop. They said, of course it was not, which is why they grew it in semi-arid regions. Somewhat chastised I enquired if they flooded the cotton fields with water. They said, in response, that this must be some kind of cynical joke. There was not enough water anyway, so how could they squander it? I then probed whether they learnt how to squeeze earth to make out if it is time to irrigate the cotton fields. They replied that they could tell from the appearance of the plant when it needed water. A Punjabi farmer in India responded somewhat graphically: 'Does a mother have to kick a baby in the stomach to make out if it is hungry?' The assembled farmers agreed. As I looked around me at the standing crop of cotton I realized that they were all growing on an elevated ridge. I asked the farmers who had taught them to do this, half expecting them to say: 'WWF.' Instead they replied that this was the way they had always grown cotton.

I now understand that after 2005 the WWF has removed from its website the claim that cotton is a thirsty crop. I think I must take some credit for that, but money was already pouring in and many of these funding agencies were not even aware that the WWF had surreptitiously dropped the claim that cotton was a thirsty crop. Call it cognitive dissonance or whatever, a functionary of a North European agency, which is a major source of funds for this project, continued to argue with me on this matter well after the deletion had taken place, insisting that cotton was a thirsty crop. She fully endorsed the view that South Asian farmers needed to be taught this truth and urged to grow something less demanding instead. I tried hard to impress upon her that villagers do not have their heads tilted to the 'other world' but were always learning from experience. These villagers may be unlettered and poor, but they are also eminently practical.

With things Indian, a village setting is not the only thing to be exoticized. Even the current economic good fortune that India is said to be experiencing has cultural ifs and buts to it. Mark Tully, arguably one of the Commonwealth's most loved radio and TV broadcasters, argues that although Indians now have fatter wallets and want to empty them before sunset hits the malls, they are also torn by a religious upbringing that leaves them patently schizophrenic. They alternate between the spiritual and the material and are seemingly caught in between. Thus, in his view, Indians might hanker for material wealth but they cannot also help reaching out to religion.[17] Mark Tully could have paused mid-sentence for a moment and asked why does all this appear so strange? Is this phenomenon not common elsewhere in the world? Has affluence, which is much more widespread in the West, killed religion and the search for spiritual solace there? If this does not raise issues related to cultural schizophrenia in America or Europe, why should it be termed so in India? Incidentally, what proportion of Indians are we really talking about? It is just a tiny fraction whose incomes have grown in the last few years, because the multitudes are generally where they were. The rising prosperity of the ITES (Information Technology Enabled Services) should not blind us to the other Indias, which are not equally fortunate.

We willingly suspend rational judgment and the secular, comparative approach when it comes to looking at what happens in India. So from Indira Gandhi to cricket to cotton farms to civil society, India ostensibly gives each of these otherwise universally comprehensible social facts a cultural wrinkle that both ages them and distinguishes them from cognate phenomena elsewhere. Too often we tend to forget that Hippocratic and traditional Hindu systems of medicine have much in common. When these systems were initiated they were all for anatomy and surgery, but as time went on, practitioners of both these schools gradually distanced themselves from touching the human body. Anatomy was out, and the surgeon's skills were only good enough for barbers to practise. In India this turnabout is explained in terms of caste-related taboos, but how would they use this tack to account for the abhorrence that Hippocratic doctors displayed towards cutting up the human body to take a look inside, let alone to perform surgery?

Absurdities in the history of Western thought abound but are carefully screened away from view when contemporary European or American scholars draw their philosophical heritage from the Greeks. Some of the things that Plato and his star disciple Aristotle have said could easily match if not outdo the irrationalities of any Eastern soothsayer, guru or mendicant. Plato once argued, almost in a karmic vein, that men who do not pursue a life of knowledge were doomed to be born as women in the next life. Aristotle advised all expectant mothers to have their children in winter when the northerly winds blow; and if they married too young they would only have daughters. Aristotle was also convinced that a woman's blood was blacker then that of men, and they also had fewer teeth than men.[18] Had an Indian said any of this, Orientalists would immediately have picked it up as another example of the other-worldly (karmic), male-preferring, non-empirical Hindu mind. But as this is an important part of the Western heritage, they ignore these statements and concentrate on the more intelligent things the Greeks had said. Would that they applied the same yardstick when discussing Indian thought and philosophy.

Thomas Sydenham, Thales of Miletos, and Hippocrates before him, much like the ayurveds, also believed in humoural theory.[19] For them, the body goes out of whack when it loses its rhythm with the cosmos and the natural elements around. So a good doctor would bring the *milieu intérieur* in sync with the *milieu extérieur*, and voila, all would be well. When the Portuguese came to India in the sixteenth century, Akbar, the great Mughal emperor, was pleased with their doctors, if with no one else. This was because their worldview was so close to those of his palace hakims and of the other native medical specialists. When therefore these Portuguese men of medicine advised Akbar to smoke a strange weed, which proved to be tobacco, the great monarch willingly acquiesced. All this fraternal interaction between Arabic, Hippocratic, Chungi, and Ayurvedic systems ceased once germ theory became regnant. This was the point that clearly separated Western, not Hippocratic, medicine from the rest. It is important to make this point for, in many textbook notions, Western medicine today has emerged unproblematically from the original source, i.e. Hippocrates himself.

The exoticization of India is so complete that most people who practise this low art never realize that they are promoting a variant of cultural degradation. When the tsunami of 2004 hit Car Nicobar Islands, south of the coast of Kerala, Indian journalists fabricated a charming story of how tribals in that region were able to save themselves because they were such close observers of nature. Even before the tidal waves hit the shores of Car Nicobar islands the animals sensed something was amiss and headed for higher ground. As tribals and animals are always in such close proximity they took off too and headed for the hills with the beasts. Thus while the 'civilized' world perished in the floods, animals and their closest human allies, the tribals, were saved.

There is not a shred of evidence that anything like this occurred, yet, the *Times of India* went to the extent of reporting that many tribals even saved themselves by 'hanging to trees' like animals.[20] The truth is that tribals suffered like the rest. Over 45 per cent of those who died in the tsunami tragedy were tribals. Regardless, urban journalists concocted and circulated an exoticized story about their cultural 'other' in the island forests of Car Nicobar. It does not always take a non-Indian to exoticize India.

News items of this sort stoke curiosity that leads to well-funded research projects and other intellectual ventures. The sad truth is that nothing talks like money, and this prompts many, otherwise reasonable, intellectuals to drop everything and run after projects that have this folksy, community-participatory character where a hefty monetary endowment should be taken as read. Over the years this has had a deleterious impact on research and thinking about India, even within India. As exoticizing India has a certain cachet and readily wins applause and supporters in the West, it stimulates research in a certain direction that primarily suits Western sensibilities.

That this traditional cultural perspective on India is widely shared can also be demonstrated by apparently harmless publications on Indian tradition and its sources. In such enterprises, the authors rarely discuss classical Indian treatises on aesthetics, literature, love, warfare, governance, or even good manners, and nobody seems to mind. These books give such issues a wide berth and concentrate instead on arcane matters concerning Hindu textual traditions. One of the best-selling books of this kind, very serious and scholarly, is edited by Ainslee Embree.[21] The sources of Indian tradition are entirely religious or quasi-religious in character and all of them can be eventually tracked down to sacerdotal texts. There are chapters on Hindu other-wordliness, devotional ecstasy, and even Islamic mysticism. Can any society survive, as India did for centuries, on such exotica alone? Even so, lesser books of the same genre are printed every year and flood the shelves of railway and airport bookstores as well as the libraries of recognized savants.

Such a presentation would have been offensive had it been about the sources of Western tradition, but for India it is part for the course. Can you imagine a work on British tradition that only talks about the High Anglican Church and not about Shakespeare, Chaucer or Oliver Cromwell? Can you find a publisher for American tradition that does not detail the contributions of hardy farmers and fur-trappers, of William Penn and those who sailed out from inhospitable conditions in the land of their birth? Of course, the witchhunts in Salem would figure, so would the specifics of American religious denominations, and Billy Graham and Jerry Falwell would be duly acknowledged, but there would also be cowboys and Indians, playboys and red-necks, Henry Ford and the Amish, all rubbing shoulders within the covers of such a volume. Why is such a line of treatment unthinkable for a book on Indian tradition?

Is there a way out? There probably is, but it is not going to be easy.

3

INTELLECTUAL CAPITAL AND MERCHANT CAPITAL

WHO IS MAKING WHOM RICH BY DOING WHAT?

For a passing tourist, India is a great destination: buy one ticket and get at least another India free. There are places in this country that would make some of the world's richest nervously shine their shoes on the back of their trousers. Property prices in Delhi and Mumbai put New York in the shade. A single-floor apartment, with a built-up area that is no more than 400 square metres in South Delhi would cost about $7 million. One could acquire a lovely house in a wooded area with all the modern amenities for that price anywhere in the eastern seaboard of America. In Delhi or Mumbai, however, it's just an apartment, and only the utterly filthy rich with cakes of unwashed sins can afford to live a technicoloured life in them.

For a black-and-white version of India one does not have to go very far from these spiffy quarters. In this other India, tens of millions live in hovels when not actually on the streets. There are over 72,000 slums in India and shockingly, roughly 15 per cent of urban India lives in them.[1] Notwithstanding diverse consumption patterns, aesthetics, and ambitions, the super rich and the very poor live in close physical proximity. That is why both wealth and poverty in India appear so vulgar

31

to the untropicalized eye. What often softens the harshness is the presence of the intermediate strata, from small shopkeepers to petty clerks with pencils in their ears. They perforate the distance between the class extremities allowing for minor seepages.

As the rich and the poor differ on virtually every lifestyle axis, it is easy to overlook their interconnectedness. On the face of it they live in different solitudes, but in reality there are noisy, fractious relations between them, frequently, as can be imagined, in contravention of the law. In most cases, one can easily assume that the poor get the short end of the stick in such transactions. Therefore, while there are two or more Indias (we have not come to the villages yet), it is not as if they are actually unrelated. This is what makes this country so incomprehensible: a single tree apparently fruits both apples and oranges.

When I read about 'resurgent India', 'India on the move', or the 'Indian economic miracle', or the 'golden bird', I wonder whether it is the same India that I know from my village studies, and from the fieldwork with contract and migrant workers in small and large towns. It is not as if the growth story is a lie. In recent decades rich Indians are getting richer in quick time, their 'animal spirits unleashed' by liberalization[2], but there is the other Indian too. Are the two related in some way or do they lead hermetically sealed lives?

The Poor-seeking Rich

The Indian affluents like to believe that they are not just a world apart from the grime around them, but in fact, world class. This belief has been sponsored by the World Bank and by almost every other high-tech enterprise that is looking to invest in India. The encomiums have been so consistent that the factual bases for such accolades are rarely contested. Like water, praise too is a fugitive that constantly seeks lower levels to fill out. Now even politicians and assorted think-tank specialists have bobbed to the top swollen with unconcealed pride. How the other half, and then some, live is not immediately relevant for any of them. This constitutes the blind side of our social awareness.

I am sure this line of reasoning would also have swayed me as I am a natural connoisseur of the mediocre. However, my field experiences in factories and villages sound alarm-bells in my head. I have seen persistent poverty although official figures claim a huge drop in the percentage of the poor. I have seen sweatshops that make millions for their owners but where workers toil in subhuman conditions. Recently, the American media has exposed the sweatshops from where Victoria's Secret and Gap outsource their goods. I have also seen the mad scramble to exit agriculture as if rural India had been torpedoed at the hull. Some of these escapees have sighted a paradise in distant cities, but only a few make it there given the infrastructural constraints. They try nevertheless; and like all struggles to stay alive, each such effort is like an epic saga.

The attraction cities have for the poor is bound to disappoint the romantic, but the benefits to them are real. While in the late 1990s roughly 28 per cent in India were officially below the poverty line, this figure is only 14 per cent for the same period for the urban population.[3] As only 30 per cent of India is urban, the poverty statistic in villages by themselves will obviously exceed 40 per cent. This would mean that nearly every other person in rural India lives below the poverty line and cannot afford the bare caloric requirements. They are just about alive but far from well.

Naturally, the number of migrants from the countryside to the cities resembles a mass exodus. Between 1994 and 2000 about 3.09 million people left agriculture, which is more than double the number of people who left in the preceding decade. The pace has gathered momentum to that degree in recent times. These figures are staggering enough, but this is only the official picture limited to those who could be enumerated. My experience tells me that the figure is probably ten times higher. I have been to a large number of villages where there are only a few able-bodied men between the ages of twenty to forty. The others have all upped and left for the cities hoping for a life of dignity and not, as most romantics would have us believe, just for bright lights, or to lead dissolute double lives.

So how real is the story of India's economic miracle? Does this miracle take within its sweep the poor, and even the not so poor? How does the relationship between different classes affect the nature of our economic growth and our political judgement? By putting these issues together and juxtaposing their problems, we derive a more comprehensive understanding of India's growth trajectory and its constraints. India is like a phoenix. It has risen, undoubtedly, but it is also trapped and unable to take wing. Why should this be so?

The Cage of the Phoenix

On the face of it India should just take off. In comparison to most other poor countries, India's manpower is diversified, technically qualified, and, from the starched white-collar to the dirty white-collar to the blue-collar class, English is not really alien to India. This is a tremendous resource base, particularly as English is today the most-used international language. In hindsight, we acquired this gift at considerable expense by ceding to the British in virtually every encounter during the eighteenth and nineteenth centuries. However, at the end of the day, we have not only acquired proficiency in English but have also artfully Indianized it.

This should not however take away from the efforts made after Independence to raise the standards of higher education in India. Institutes of technology, medical colleges, universities and research centres were set up all over India in the hope that India would also become a knowledge hub. It did not quite happen that way but it was nevertheless not an entirely wasted exercise.

Even a quick glance at the Information Technology (IT) sector and the giant high-end service industry would confirm this. This is where I find intellectual capital at its best. Not surprisingly, this is also the destination for the bulk of foreign investments that head towards India. If India can do so well in the high-end IT sector why can't it get itself up and going when it comes to other aspects of its economy? Why are its social services so abysmally poor? Why can't we do something about poverty? These questions come tumbling out fast and furious but there are no immediate answers, other than the quick ones that draw on stereotypes.

If our manpower is so vibrant and technologically savvy, why is the boom limited to only a few sectors leaving out the rest? Can we ignore the remainder as if does not exist? Alternatively, should we wait for prosperity to trickle down in the fullness of time? Or again, as is most often the case, this prosperous economic sector is seen as an anomalous phenomenon that somehow got away when exotic India was not paying attention. IT and financial experts wriggled out of antique cracks, leaving the rest of society roughly where it was.

To answer these big questions it is best to begin by looking at a close-up of the Indian economic boom. The magnified picture makes it easier to see the sociological cohorts of this boom, principally, agriculture, education, migration, caste, ethnicity, and the Indian state. This enables us to understand the significance of their interrelations and how thoughtless it would be to separate one aspect from the others. Each of these issues has been discussed at great length elsewhere and with enviable competence. However, by seeing them together in a single perspective I hope to bring all the sub-plots in touch with each other within a larger narrative that can credibly relate the story of the caged phoenix.

We also need to admit here that while most sociologists and anthropologists recognize the profound changes at all institutional levels, such as caste, religion, village life, and the like, they retreat into niche specializations and in-house gossip when it comes to theorizing about the whole. Regardless of narrow specialist inclinations, a focus on caste, village, or community ties cannot singly accomplish the task of theorizing about India. Further, these institutions no longer function as they supposedly did in tradition. Culture and text must give way to practice and context if we want to enliven the many variables that support or constrain economic growth and social development in India.

In other words, and the truth must emerge, we plan a sociological study of India's economy in order to demonstrate the salience of putting things in relation and not as stand-alone phenomena. This is a perfectly legitimate methodological position. Society comes well before the market[4]. This should also act as a corrective to a large number of specialists who believe that these other institutional neighbours of the economy are pure riff-raff, and it is best to shake them off before the party begins.

Even those who are impressed with the nine per cent growth-rate picture cannot but ask why the infrastructural facilities do not work and cannot be made to work. It is not just the hypercritical eye that seizes upon problems such as these, but they are all so easily visible. Even so, there is a clear reluctance on the part of these economic commentators to go the distance and incorporate contradictory aspects of the social order in terms of universalistic categories.

Their reason for good cheer is that if our growth rate is high as it is now and that of the advanced world is a mere two to three per cent, then surely before long (2020? 2050?), we will surge ahead while the others choke on our dust. The idea is that the West will stand still while we are in overdrive. However if that were to happen our growth would slow down perceptibly, for so much of it is dependent on America and Europe. India does not have the purchasing power within to grow autarkically, unaffected by the ups and downs around it. This is what hinders the phoenix. However, the greatest assumption of such optimists is in their argument that growth will naturally permeate down the line and the will of the market will set things right. The shocks of 2008 in terms of inflation and the bearish stock market might induce a sense of reality to these roseate projections. According to a recent report, about US$5.3 billion in terms of FII left the stock market in 2008 alone.[5] Certainly not encouraging news!

Whilst it is true that in 2007 India officially recorded a staggering growth-rate of nine per cent, even if you believe the figures, it is not as if everyone's incomes are growing at that level. Obviously, some sectors are doing better than others; and some jobs are getting better paid than others. Before we examine some of these complications it is worthwhile taking a broader view first to identify the issues that need to be watched closely if we want to sustain this growth trajectory.

To begin with, the big story:

- Agriculture in India is not growing, or only growing very slowly. It registered a growth of 2.3 per cent in 2005.[6] Its share of GDP is down to 21 per cent in 2002.[7] A large number of villagers are now engaged in rural, non-farm employment.
- The service sector is very buoyant and, paradoxically, manufacturing is way behind. The service sector contributes 48.5 per cent of the GDP and manufacturing roughly 15 per cent.[8] Services constituted 52 per cent in 2004.[9]
- Traditional merchandise export items are still very strong. The merchandise export growth-rate fluctuates between 24–26 per cent per annum.[10]
- Strong growth in small-scale industries and unorganized sector.[11]
- Employment is stagnant in the organized sector and may have even shrunk.[12]
- In terms of human development indicators, India is still very low on the international scale. Even Bangladesh appears to have a lower infant-mortality rate than India.[13]

Together the above summary should alert us to the following:

- The buoyancy of the service sector, if seen alongside the stagnant numbers of workers in the organized sector, indicates that this growth has not translated in terms of employment. This implies that the prosperity is severely limited to a certain stratum.

- If the small-scale and unorganized sectors are growing in terms of numbers and workforce does this mean that the unemployed are finding adequate jobs here or is their poverty being exploited?
- This is not too startling a hypothesis given that public health and educational standards are still abysmally low.
- If 70 per cent of India lives in villages and if agricultural growth is not taking place then something is amiss somewhere. If rural non-farm employment is growing is this because agricultural occupations can no longer sustain the village population? Are these rural poor, untrained and in poor health, the workforce for the small-scale and unorganized sectors?

Once spelt out, none of these issues are trivial.

The Golden Bird or the Service Sector

First the happy story.

The growth in the service sector is at the heart of India's miracle story. The contribution of IT and ITES to the country's GDP has grown from a mere 1.2 per cent in the entire decade 1989–99 to an impressive 4.8 per cent in 2005-06. Its export performance is spectacular and was approximately US$23.4 billion in 2005-06, i.e. up by 32 per cent in one year.[14] This figure is obviously rising by the nano-second. Software production for domestic consumption is Rs 196 million but it earns Rs 782 million, or four times that amount, through exports.[15]

Now for the bad news.

For all its growth and development, the ITES sector employs *only* 3 million people in India. Even if one were to admit that each person in ITES adds four more to the numbers employed[16] that means, in a population of one billion only 12 million, benefit from the expansion in the ITES sector. We should also bear in mind that these additional 12 million are not paid nearly as well as the proper ITES professionals.

Not surprisingly, FDI (foreign direct investment) flows are

mostly to the service sector. Electronics (17.54 per cent), financial and non-financial service sectors (12.69 per cent), and the telecommunications industry (10.39 per cent) are some of the major beneficiaries of FDI in India.[17] This is in terms of the share of cumulative inflows in percentage terms from August 1991 to September 2006.

Electrical equipment including computer software and electronics leads the pack of small-scale industries in terms of FDI by attracting 26.84 per cent of the total that flows into this sector.[18] Consultancy services receive about 8.0 per cent and telecommunications 4.12 per cent. In sum, 40 per cent of FDI locates itself in just these limited areas of the service sector. Clearly, foreign investors know where it is most profitable to put in their money. Even so, it has been noticed that in contrast to China, the flow of foreign exchange to India is primarily for short-term portfolio investments.[19]

The most attractive aspect of India's offshore operations is the low-cost services of the IT sector here—between 40 to 50 per cent of its cost in the West.[20] Given that much of what the ITES does is to export cheap white-collar labour, it is not surprising that providers of these services do not pay attention to the domestic market or seek to expand their 'verticals' from just banking, financial services and telecom, which is where they are now concentrated.[21] This sector is so far not interested in specializing in high-end jobs, because by Indian standards they are making quite a killing by successfully exporting white-collar coolie work.

This exacerbates the anomaly that arises when the service sector of an economy is well ahead of manufacturing. An unhappy trend that will, in all probability, adversely affect general growth over the long run.[22] The service sector boom in India has not only not led to an employment boom, but also, only in India as compared to the other seven fast-growing economies of the developing world, does the service sector outpace manufacturing.[23] For a quick comparative picture, we may take the instance of China where, in contrast to India, the employment in the organized sector is about 50 million and growing. There is an additional 100 million, or thereabouts, if we also consider the town and village enterprises there.[24]

It is not just in the service sector, as in ITES, where the numbers employed are low. The entire organized sector employs about 27 million workers, and this figure has remained practically unchanged over the past two decades. There has been a slight rise in the organized private sector from 7.58 million in 1990 to 8.24 million in 2004. This is largely because the number of women employed in these enterprises has gone up by about 700,000 in the past fifteen years.[25] The real increase in employment in the private sector is in areas such as finance and insurance, and in community, social, and personal services. However, these together account for only 2.2 million people as of 2004.[26] In terms of total employment, the organized sector has shrunk, and has at best been stagnant, between 1987 and 2003. However, what furthers the illusion of prosperity is that the wages in this sector are up three times and the value of their output has risen roughly seventy-one times.[27] Can these figures be correct? Be that as it may, what is indisputable is that second- and third-generation labourers in the organized sector are much better off than their predecessors. But the question still remains: what are the other avenues of employment?

The decline in daily employment of registered working factories is a persistent, and I daresay, a worrisome feature.[28] The number of daily workers in these registered factories decreased from 10.78 million in 1988 to 10.20 million in 2000[29] with a similar decrease in the number of such factories.[30] Who would have believed this while the economic miracle sagas were being narrated? Indeed, employment is also down in the favoured state sectors such as in the railways, in mines, and in central government services.[31]

Where then are the rural migrants and those in non-farm employment finding jobs?

Small-scale and Informal Sector

Perhaps the absorption is taking place in informal units[32] and in micro and small enterprises[33] where the accent is typically on making profits by using cheap labour: largely unskilled or semi-skilled. Not surprisingly, the earnings of the small scale sector in terms of exports have risen, registering an increase of 27.4 per cent in 2005-06.[34] It is truly phenomenal that such a leap was accomplished in a single year.

In addition there is a huge expansion of unregistered units that clearly fall under the ambit of the informal sector. What makes the situation more complex is that a large number of small-scale-sector units farm out their jobs to these informal enterprises. Incidentally, this is something that big establishments do as well, but not as rampantly. This informalization of labour often misses scrutiny, but it is the surest way of keeping prices low and beating trade union laws. This is what adds to our global competitiveness.

These informal units are our modern sweatshops, from which some of the largest international brands source goods. In clear contrast to the sluggish organized sector, employment in small-scale and in unorganized/informal enterprises has grown at a lively pace of a little over 4 per cent per annum since 2000. In conformity with our statement about merchant producers, the number of unregistered units has also grown at a faster pace than those that are registered. There are roughly seven times more unregistered than registered units in general.[35]

Let us look at the question in another way. The cotton-textile industry was, till not very long ago, an important index of the Indian economy. Undoubtedly it no longer occupies the position that it once did as the pacesetter of industrialization in Mumbai, and by extension, in the rest of India. Today, the cotton and textile industry excites interest largely because the huge expansion of its production capacity has actually occurred in the small-scale sector and not in the traditional mills. In 1980-81 this industry produced only six billion square metres of cloth (both cotton and synthetic), but this number crossed twenty-five billion square metres by 2006.[36] In the past year alone the value of exports of this sector increased by 8.2 per cent,[37] and in the period 1995-96 to 2002-03 by over a 100 per cent, i.e. from Rs 1.48 trillion to Rs 3.12 trillion.[38] The export of ready-made garments, woollen clothes, and knitwear account for almost a third of all exports from the largely unsung registered small-scale sector.[39] Given the fact that the contribution of small-scale industries to total export is about 35 per cent,[40] it is indeed surprising that such an important aspect of our economy today should escape the attention of those who write about the 'golden bird'.

All this was accomplished even though the number of mills has remained stagnant over the years, and the production of cloth in them has actually declined. Power-looms in the small-scale sector now produce over 80 per cent of all fabrics manufactured, and even handlooms have a greater share than mill-produced cloth.[41] Besides, in terms of the index of industrial production one finds that the greatest increase[42] has been in cotton textiles, wool and silk, man-made fibres, jute fibre, textile and apparel, leather, fur products, and paper.[43] The overwhelming majority of production of these items is in the small-scale sector. This trend indicates a growing predominance of micro- and small enterprises.

Gems and jewellery, another traditional merchant capitalist segment, continues to maintain its impressive position in terms of exports. In 2005-06 it contributed 15 per cent of India's total merchandise export and corners about 8 per cent of the world's exports in this commodity. Almost the entire production of these items is in the small scale and informal sectors, the latter is perhaps more predominant. The export of carpets and floor coverings is also impressive with almost 11 per cent of the world market coming from India.[44] Even public sector banks seem to prefer small-scale industries, obviously because they show greater growth potential. From a mere 51,000 thousand accounts of small-scale industries in public sector banks in 1960 this has grown to 1,729,000 in 2006.[45] No other set of account-holders anywhere else has grown nearly as rapidly.

If we now turn to the informal sector we find an indication of its growth from the fall in the contribution of main workers to the economy and the phenomenal rise of marginal workers. Marginal workers suit operations akin to sweatshops and unregulated industrial conditions as they do not enjoy security of tenure and can be hired and fired at will. This is why bidi[46] rolling moved over entirely from the formal to the informal sector. It is now produced in thousands of household-level enterprises. Workers in these units do not even work for the full eight-hour period, but on some days they may work for eighteen hours at a stretch. Between 1991 and 2001 there has actually been a decrease of -1.11 per cent in the participation rate of main workers, *but* the participation rate for marginal workers has increased by 11.98 per cent to 9.85 per cent of the total workforce. This is a big jump when compared to the figures for 1981–91 when marginal workers grew at only 2.78 per cent.

What is equally, if not more, striking is that whilst non-agricultural units employing less than ten persons has grown by 110.8 per cent between 1980–2005; in the short period between 2000 and 2005 alone the increase was 35 per cent.[47] Ninety-three per cent of India's workforce, including hired agricultural labour, appears to be employed in the unorganized sector;[48] and 83 per cent of all non-agricultural workers are employed in units that are unorganized and informal in character. In addition, 90 per cent of manufacturing and construction workers find jobs in this sector too.[49] Together, the informal sector contributes 59 per cent of India's Net Domestic Product:[50] certainly not an amount to be sneezed at. In 2005-06 there were roughly 17.07 million unorganized manufacturing units.[51]

While the general impression, and expectation, is that the educational status of workers is rising, unfortunately the facts tell us otherwise. Over the years, from 1997-08 and from 1999-2000, while the proportion of literates has risen from 45.1 to 61.4 per cent, the percentage of those with middle- and high-school degrees has fallen.[52] This reflects a progressive downgrading or, at best, a stagnation of skills required to qualify for a working-class job. This explains to a considerable degree why the informal sector, which in the main exploits cheap labour, has grown so steadily over the years.

Though it is not quite de rigeur to use the 'C' word, I

cannot help but comment that the export picture of our neighbour, China, is quite different from ours. It may sell a lot of gimracks and gizmos to the Western world but one-third of its exports are classified as 'high technology'. What is more, $40 billion of America's trade deficit with China is on account of these 'high technology' items.[53]

Towards Merchant Production

As a preamble it is necessary to bear the following in mind:

- The characterization of native capitalists morphing from merchant tycoons to precocious monopolists after the departure of the British does not help very much in understanding the contemporary Indian economy.[54] The leading players in India's growth story are not from traditional industrial families or houses, but are first-generation entrepreneurs. The service sector of the Indian economy is replete with instances of first generation entrepreneurs. When some of them come from established business or commercial backgrounds they reinvent themselves and virtually start afresh. In this process they take their earlier fortunes well beyond what would have been their traditional limits.
- Regardless of this difference in category, the gap between the rich and the poor, not just in terms of wealth, but also tastes, aspirations, and lifestyles, continues to be vast.
- In my view this holds back the full development of industrial capitalism as the temptation towards exploiting cheap labour, pure and simple, is very strong.

I characterize merchant production as any tendency that profits by producing cheap and selling dear. Unlike the traditional merchants who profit from circulation, the merchant producers in India today profit from the sphere of production. The former prospered on account of price markups on the finished goods brought to the market and the latter prospers by exploiting cheap labour to produce goods for sale. In both cases, the key factor is the exploitation of what is cheap. This might appear an idiosyncratic definition, but I find it to be extremely useful in understanding India, particularly if we want to release the phoenix. In a society dominated by the ethos of merchant production the emphasis will always be on cheap and compliant labour as a way of scoring over competitors.

That is why even as we talk about fast-growing enterprises we cannot take our eyes off the stagnant nature of the rural economy. This is not only to bemoan why our growth rates could not be higher, or why inflation tends to rise because of poor agricultural productivity, but primarily to underline the abundance of cheap labour ready for hire for anything. One must bear in mind that in India approximately 34 per cent of the population survives on less $1 a day.[55] Let me also add as a cautionary note that I do not wish to turn back the clock on economic competition. However, I would advocate a sustainable growth strategy that could act as a model for development. What we need is a proactive all-round development *strategy*, and not one that happens by default in which the merchant producer holds the key. Export dependence is a risky matter.

In this context it is important to factor in the decline of agriculture and agriculturists. Most of the poor come from rural India, a fact that allows merchant producers to aggrandize themselves by exploiting cheap labour. Rural India can hardly be ignored if, as is suggested, about 60 per cent (maybe more) are dependent on some form, and to some degree, on agriculture for their livelihood.

The implications of this are several but never fully exposed. I will explicate them primarily from my own field experiences. To begin with, a majority of the very poor are in non-agrarian occupations that are *not capacity enhancing*. They perform a variety of jobs; both in town and country, but these are not of the kind that can be leveraged for significantly better career options in the future. Notwithstanding that, the rural poor would rather obtain non-farm employment for then they actually know how much they are likely to earn at the end of the day. Working on somebody else's family farm is chancy. For one, wages need to be constantly fought over as both sides are at different levels of vulnerability. Also, family farms need hired hands only for short periods, primarily during the harvesting season.

Second, traditional crafts are not nearly as popular with rural artisans as they were once thought to be. I have interviewed over two hundred carpet weavers in the carpet belt of east Uttar Pradesh and found that they would rather have an urban job for themselves and their children and not have to depend on the vagaries of the contractors who hire them. That is why education figures very prominently in their list of aspirations.

Merge the falling standards of agriculture and of rural artisanry and it is easy to imagine why hordes of migrants are seeking jobs across the country at throwaway wages. This is why it is so tempting to be a merchant producer. Remember, 60 per cent of India is between the ages fifteen and fifty-nine and, more significantly, about 50 per cent of the population is below twenty-five years old. This means that the labour market is teeming with the unemployed. In the last twenty years the workforce has increased by nearly 65 per cent but organized employment, as we mentioned earlier, remains stagnant.[56] This gives a merchant producer greater room for manoeuvre in terms of hiring cheap labour.

The unhappy status of health and education in India also helps the merchant producer's style of functioning, for large masses of employed and potentially employable are low on the human development index. Merchant producers also prosper from the vulnerability of the poor in terms of health and education. Human development reports indicate how slowly, if at all, we are progressing in these areas.[57] The government does not seem very interested either. In India the State bears only 17.3 per cent of all health care expenses. Further, according to the 2004 figures, only 1.3 per cent of GDP is directed towards health. This puts India in the same league as Myanmar, Guinea, Burundi, and Congo. In comparison, the US government contributes as much as 44.7 per cent of the total health expenditure in the country and the figure for Britain is 86.3 per cent.[58] This explains the booming private hospital business in India. Over 20,000 private hospitals operate in India. This is an increase of 75 per cent in the past ten years[59] but there is just one hospital bed for as many as 1,123 potential patients.[60] This also explains the appalling health status of India's poor for whom the diagnosis of a serious illness is like a death sentence. This too adds to the power of the merchant capitalists.

When we come to education the picture is no better. Only 10.7 per cent of government expenditure in India is on education, whereas the US puts in 15.2 per cent of its total expenditure on education.[61] The number of non-functioning schools is scandalous, as also are the numbers of absentee teachers. Over 50 per cent of the children who enter school do not complete basic education and only 35.6 per cent of boys and 19.75 of girls finish middle school.[62] The dropout rate in India is 53 per cent; even Bangladesh and Nepal score better with dropout rates of 35–38 per cent.[63]

What can we conclude from the above?

- The poor in India are extremely vulnerable in terms of basic human indicators.
- Some sectors of the economy, namely the service sector, are faring very well, with computer and telecom services as leaders in the field. We however also know that in terms of total employment the numbers are not very high. ITES together has only 3 million professionals.
- The number of marginal workers is increasing, as is the number of small and micro-enterprises. This is reflected, for example, in garment, cotton and textile production. The contribution of mills is stagnant and dipping, but it is the informal sector, manned by merchant capitalists, that is feverishly active.
- Agriculture releases a large number of people because it is no longer sustainable. This increases the availability of a cheap workforce, which is something that works in favour of merchant producers.
- Education and health need to be strengthened. The

growth in infrastructure is very low and this increases the vulnerability of the poor. Altogether, India spends only 4 per cent of its GDP on infrastructure whereas China puts in more than double that, i.e. 9 per cent. In actual US $ terms, China spends seven times more than India does.[64]

We are now primed to examine how merchant producers function and how their stratagems either violate the law or shave it really very close.

4

HOW MERCHANT PRODUCERS OPERATE
A NEED FOR CORPORATE SOCIAL RESPONSIBILITY

The Small Scale Industries (SSI) and the unorganized sectors, where the merchant producer dominates, are very closely related. A single hosiery unit probably gets its fabric dyed elsewhere, or its embroidery executed in a cottage-based unit where wages are low and hours long. The reality is that a large number of organized sector industries are also closely linked to the unorganized sector and SSIs from where they outsource a range of goods and services that embellish the finished products they put out for sale bearing their label. Very often some of the best-known companies primarily check goods made elsewhere only to ensure that they match the specifications, and then stamp them with their brand names.[1]

This is really how a large number of export-oriented industries profit. Their advantage is that they can produce goods and services at rates much lower than the international price. This is not just true of ITES services, where three quarters of the production is destined for exports. When it comes to sundry other goods as well, the purchasing power of the ordinary Indian is far too low to constitute a robust internal market.

As most of these SSIs are dependent on consumers outside

India, their relation with international trade cannot be overlooked. Today, this link is known by the term 'globalization'. But globalization is more than just that. The manner in which SSIs and the unorganized sectors have flourished leads us to conclude that a strong antipathy towards trade unions is also an important feature of globalization. The days when organized labour could threaten captains of industry are gone. The advantage in dealing with labour in SSIs and in the unorganized sector is that there is hardly any scope for workers' representation in these units, with trade unions having been effectively defanged.

These unorganized industries profit not so much by improving productivity through greater rationalization of the means of production as by simply depending on cheap labour. In this sense these enterprises operate on the merchant logic of buying cheap and selling dear. The difference between the true merchant producer and those who operate India's small-scale and micro-industries is that the former profits from circulation of goods, and the latter by employing cheap labour in the production process. Upgrading skills or technologies of production are of minimal consequence in these fast-growing units in India. That is why it is appropriate to term the entrepreneur of these units as 'merchant producers' and the activity they pursue with such profit as 'merchant production'.

One would have generally expected merchant producerism to characterize early capitalism, or a society which is somewhat autarkic in its economic policy. In the Indian case, however, both these presuppositions do not hold. Merchant producers are at the forefront of the export sector and, as even government records suggest, employment growth too is taking place primarily in these units. But if export falls, jobs do too.

In the light of the prominence that merchant producers have attained in India it is advisable to stay with the concept of 'globalization'. Yet, globalization does not deserve the favourable press it has received from many because it has done nothing to transform merchant producers. It has made no difference to the way merchant producers organize their production. They continue to thrive on cheap labour and see no point in upskilling their workforce.[2] Twenty-five years of a liberalized economy and periodic rounds of structural adjustments have not prompted the merchant producer to think and act differently.

Favourable trade winds were blowing in the direction of SSIs and the unorganized sector well before the official inauguration of liberalization in 1991 that properly welcomed globalization to Indian shores. Naturally, globalization found a congenial atmosphere in this country and soon made itself quite at home, disregarding the possibilities of a downturn.

Social Auditing of Merchant Capitalists

What is the nature of entrepreneurship that characterizes the new breed of industrialists in contemporary India who generally operate small- and micro-scale industries, for that is the fastest growing sector as we earlier discovered? Whether we are looking at enterprises that make garments, textiles, leather products, carpets, or lamps and other metal furnishings, there is a clear uniformity in their style of functioning. In all these cases, the entrepreneurs of such units are capitalizing on low cost workers, their poor educational and health status, and their inability to voice their views or represent themselves.

In the past ten years or so I have had the opportunity to conduct and oversee social audits of over a thousand units, both large and small, cottage and factory, organized and unorganized. As the small-scale and micro-scale sectors have been the more dynamic growth agents in India, this is of some use in assessing the nature of entrepreneurship that has taken place in these quarters in recent times.

An initial striking impression on entering many of these factories is the mad rush of a mass of labourers trying to flee the units through exit gates that are located at the rear or at the side of the premises. I discovered soon enough that these workers were not on the regular rolls of the company. Therefore the factories had no wage records, or any record, which bore their names, other than the informal, rough-and-ready tally that the management maintained. As one would expect, these workers are paid below minimum wages for long hours of work and have been trained to flee on a signal from the management. They wait at a distance from the factory so that they can be recalled once the coast is clear. Sometimes they receive a wrong signal and the whole plot unfolds in the open.

Unreliable Records

On two occasions I have even found handwritten training manuals to instruct workers on how to answer possible questions from outsiders. I suspect that drills of this kind are held in many of these factories to rehearse answers to questions on wages, leave, bonuses, and other benefits. All this is locked into memory by rote for those who are not the ones asked to flee. Yet the way they respond to the most elementary questions readily reveals that there is something not quite right about their terms of employment, even though there may be a formal record of their job status. As the merchant producers have many ways of ducking the law, it is necessary to understand how exactly these evasions are transacted.

Wage-related documents are systematically fudged by these merchant producers without facing any internal opposition. In a large number of instances we found the existence of dual records (or memo records). These are unofficial records but are in reality the genuine ones. These wage records are important for they tell us about overtime, hours of work, wages paid, different shifts, and entitlements—such as holiday and medical leave. These records are also necessary to determine if differential wages are being paid, and are also important to keep track of retirement benefits and provident fund payments. The books that the factory managers bring forward in neatly bound volumes are nearly always meant for display purposes only.

In almost all the factories I have known, barring two (and both in Tamil Nadu), overtime payments were always fudged. Rather than adhering to the legal stipulation of paying double the amount per hour for overtime work, there was invariably a single rate. I also found while talking to workers that most of them were uncertain about how many hours they had put in as overtime and depended on management records for payments on this account. When these features come to light a distinct air of tension is introduced into the proceedings. Obviously, in these enterprises, workers had not been properly trained on how they should answer questions relating to wages and benefits posed by outsiders. A part of me often wishes that the workers were well-tutored on these matters, for then I would not have to worry whether they would later be persecuted by the management for either being too dumb or too honest. This also shows both how vulnerable these workers are and their low levels of literacy. However, given their conditions of work, would literacy really help? Would they be able to bargain better? I have no clear answer yet.

Contract labourers dominate the workforce of merchant capitalist enterprises. This is because of the widespread, yet erroneous, belief that all difficult questions regarding wages and other issues can be deflected if it can be shown that the workers in the enterprise are employed by contractors and not directly by the factories. I have not come across a single factory with no contract labourers.

There are legal obligations when hiring a contractor, but in most cases these are not taken into account. There is the general belief among most entrepreneurs of the small-scale variety that if they hire a contractor who then organizes labour supply, production, and wages, then they are not responsible for what happens to the workers. This is not, however, according to law, but remains a widespread belief. Rarely are owners of such enterprises held accountable for transgressions that occur on account of what the contractor does.

Then there are different kinds of contractors. Some in fact are dummy-contractors, existing only in name as they are actually old trusted employees of the organization. One of the principal reasons for hiring contractors is the view that if the workers are on the regular rolls they would have a greater propensity to unionism, inevitably resulting in demands for wage increases. There is also the widespread belief that contract workers perform better than regular workers. I have found that, as a rule, contract workers get paid less than regular workers and are often unable to access their provident fund and retirement benefits. In addition, most contract workers are not liable to receive statutory bonuses because they are shifted around at frequent intervals. In some cases workers are hired on a contract basis but are kept on the rolls and marked absent for months together. This gives the impression to a quick reviewer that the factory has only permanent workers, and that the management is very kindly disposed towards labour absenteeism.

It is often argued, incorrectly of course, that many workers prefer contract to permanent work as this affords them the freedom to move to better paying jobs. It is true that with a scarce skill such as glass-blowing, the worker can earn more money by changing jobs and going to the best employer. In most cases however the necessary skill-sets can be acquired within a fortnight. In the dyeing section, apart from the master-dyer, the other workers do not require much training. In stitching again, a month's training is adequate, after which the worker picks up speed on the job.

It is necessary to recall that the work-participation rate for marginal workers is higher than main workers, also signifying the degree to which labour is casualized. Contract labour considerably facilitates this process.

But there is really no pattern regarding where these contractors are to be found. What is more, very often contractors are changed but the workers remain the same. In this way the owners can claim that they do not have old records. This ploy helps, for then they need to manufacture only those records for scrutiny that relate to the past few months or so and it is easier to doctor information for shorter periods of time. I am reminded of the figures discussed earlier regarding the burgeoning numbers of non-agricultural units that employ ten workers or less as many of the contractors in metalwork and garment weaving could qualify as owners of such micro-enterprises.

Contractors and factory owners thus work in tandem. Some large contractors who have connections with a number of enterprises easily shift workers around from one factory to another. As the work within most garment or metal-ware organizations does not vary greatly, labourers can be juggled between factories of a like order without much difficulty at both ends: at the management level and at the level of the workers. In consequence, contract labour is found everywhere. From spinning, painting and buffing in metal industries, to cutting and stitching in garment factories, to weaving, cone-winding, and dyeing in textile factories, to polishing, powder-coating, and fabrication in furniture and home furnishing units, one can find contract labourers in every department.

When a worker's status changes from being a temporary, or contractual labourer, to a regular 'on the rolls' employee then his inclination to take off for long periods for home also changes. It is however very rarely that workers are recipients of such privileges, and most spend their entire working lives under contractors. That is why their commitment to the factory is never wholehearted. This provides the factual basis on which the image of an irresponsible, work-shirking labourer is conjured. Entrepreneurs are happy when this happens for then the general public does not view their many legal transgressions with the merited degree of severity. Exaggeration of the shortcomings of the subaltern people is always the best justification for denying them their basic rights and privileges.

Indeed, the entrepreneur and contractor come to many ingenious arrangements to keep the worker vulnerable. In some cases I have found workers who have worked for long durations in the factory and were interviewed and hired directly by the management presented as contract labourers. All the office records declare them as working for this or that contractor but the worker is completely unaware of this. As far as he is concerned the management has hired him and no middleman is involved.

The invention of the contractor helps the management to cover their tracks and fudge records so that their denial of legal wages and benefits to their workers are both untraced and untraceable. Of course, for the management to pull this off, the labourers in their units have to be supine and never be interviewed directly by other government agents or by auditors.

The absent–present worker is a contradictory term but it captures the manner by which merchant producers try to formally erase the issue of contract labourers without quite changing their operating style. This is how it functions.

In two factories, I was rather foxed when I found workers leaving in large numbers the moment I entered, but paradoxically I also found only records of permanent workers and no contracted worker in sight. As I dug around I soon discovered that there were many workers on record who were absent for periods extending to over 15 months. When I asked the management how they could keep such people on the rolls, in both these factories they said, that they don't want to deny the workers a job should they wish to return. It would simply break their hearts should a worker reappear at their factory gate and they were obliged to turn him back.

All this was too moving to be believable. Soon another piece came unstuck. As far as I could tell from the records of previous months some workers were not just absent for long periods of time, but in fact never resurfaced. I was actually on the point of consulting some labour lawyers when one member of the management inadvertently let the cat out of the bag. In a boastful moment he candidly said that in his line of work he has had people beaten up and workers' records destroyed, for it is either his job on the line or the labourer's. As he argued: 'It is either my children who will be out on the streets or the workers. Life is tough but I cannot kick my children in their stomach (*peit mein laath*).' This vivid imagery was so out of place with the official posture of being ever-kind to workers that it set me thinking, and then the penny dropped!

I suddenly realized that these workers I was puzzling over were not absent but had in fact been fired. They were retained on the attendance registers but were never going to enter the factory premises again. I returned to the unit and I closely looked at the books again and my suspicion proved to be correct. While engaged with this and conducting a fresh round of interviews a worker came up to me in a state of considerable agitation. In a low voice he said that four workers were to be fired the following day and he also gave me their names. I returned a fortnight later and sure enough these workers were marked absent.

This is how these sweatshops are run and this is how the indigenous entrepreneurs and their foreign buyers make money by the sackful. Most European consumers are exercised when it comes to child labour, but they do not worry too much about these other issues concerning conditions of work. Also, while child labour can be proved with a single photograph that will surface repeatedly in newspapers, on TV and the Internet, it takes much longer to demonstrate to the outside world that factory owners have other devious methods to deny their workers their basic rights and dignity. Consequently, these entrepreneurs get away and the workers move from one state of poverty to another— from being impoverished in the villages to being underpaid in the cities.

It is therefore not surprising then that when we talk glowingly about a resurgent India with great rates of growth we never mention these sweatshops and how money is being made in them and what a massive contribution they actually make to our so-called 'economic miracle'. As discussed, small-scale units, particularly the unregistered ones, were showing an impressive rise in numbers, volume, and net export contribution. Now we have a better understanding of why and how this happens.

Migrant workers are a common feature in most merchant producer concerns. There is nothing wrong about that, but it is the way in which they are only too often taken advantage of that is far from ethical. No matter which part of the country I visited, be it Tamil Nadu, Maharashtra, Gujarat, Karnataka, Punjab, Haryana, Rajasthan or UP, there were migrant workers from everywhere. It is not as if these migrants come from nearby regions. In a large number of instances they come from far-flung places. In Punjab there were migrants from West Bengal, in Vapi from Jharkhand, and in Tirupur there were migrants from Bihar. I have come across factories in UP and Gujarat where all the workers were migrants.

In comparison, however, in Tamil Nadu and Karnataka, the two south Indian states I visited for this purpose, the pattern of migration, as I saw it, was largely intra-state and not between states. For textile and carpet weaving, special skills are locally available. Tamil Nadu has a rich tradition of weaving and it also has weavers' cooperatives that are active and run profitable enterprises, and yet for the first time I came across migrants from twenty-four Paraganas in West Bengal and from Madhubani in Bihar and Karur district of Tamil Nadu. This was indeed quite surprising as it has generally been assumed, not without justification, that migrant labourers from the north go everywhere but not to the south of the Vindhya range from where peninsular India begins. Clearly this is no longer true and migration patterns are changing across India.

There are three reasons for this. The first is that in some of these places, such as Panipat, the local people are not skilled in textile weaving. This obviously prompts migration from places like West Bengal where such skills are more easily available. Second, in many instances the local people, particularly certain communities like Jats and Rajputs, refuse to work as labourers, at least not in the proximity of their villages. They have still to come to terms with the fact that they are no longer the proud agriculturists they once were.

The most important reason however is that factory owners actually prefer migrant workers. They have found through experience that these workers, for the duration they are with them, are punctual, as they have fewer domestic responsibilities. Also, these workers from distant places absent themselves to attend trivial festivals and rituals as they would have if home were nearby. In other words, the leave pattern of these migrants is more or less predictable. They usually tend to return home during the harvesting or sowing season and for some special festivals: Diwali for north Indians and Durga Puja for Bengalis.

Consequently, unlike local workers, migrants are happy to put in long hours of work and are quite reconciled to working under contractors. Their aim is to earn as much as they can, often for days without a break. I realize now that it is for all these reasons that migrants are preferred and not, as is often believed, because they are politically subservient. Working class organizations are virtually non-existent in all such units. Nor is there any attempt, as far as I could tell, for workers to seek representation from professional politicians and unionists. I cannot see how a difference can be made to this trade union repelling scenario if local workers were employed. Sometimes, workers' resentment suddenly flashes into a strike, but that does not last very long. Invariably, after workers have returned to their stations the suspected leaders are fired from their jobs. There is no protest after that and a form of medieval peace descends for some time. Workers know that their positions are tenuous. They are aware also that they can rely only on their informal networks and relations, such as these are, with the factory owners and contractors.

Child labour is the only issue that makes merchant producers a touch cautious, but that too only when they are supplying to foreign buyers who are very particular about this matter. That is why the incidence of child labour is not as high as one might imagine in most small-scale industries. Child labourers are rare, though certainly not absent, in these industries. In household-level production units, which may also be called micro-industries, it is difficult to separate child labour from the rest as the working and living areas are common. Even so, the effort of merchant producers to try and keep out child labour is not because of motivations from within but for fear that they might lose their foreign buyer. Before the Iowa Senator Tom Harkin started the move to penalize those who traded in goods made with child labour, the situation was somewhat different. Internationally, the anti-child labour message was never pursued consistently, which is why the Harkin initiative was so important. Eventually, after several revisions, Harkin's proposal was carried and the Child Labour Deterrence Act came into being in the United States in 1999. Well before that, however, awareness about the unconscionable nature of child labour and opposition to it had grown worldwide and Harkin's initiative served only as an accelerator.

Young workers, between fourteen and eighteen years of age, are found most often in small- and medium-scale factories. But I have come across only three instances in over a hundred when the management of these units had age records for these young workers. Here again, there are certain restrictions regarding how many hours these young workers can be employed, and the kind of work they can perform. Indeed, a medical officer is required to testify that these regulations are being followed in each individual case when young workers are hired. When even age records are not maintained for workers in this age group, the question of abiding by the other legal requirements does not really arise. One can link the degree of marginal workers' participation rate to this aspect of employing young workers and child labourers too.

I do not mean to suggest that only small-scale enterprises are susceptible to practices of the kind mentioned above. I have found them to occur in large industries as well, and this picture is representative of a large number of export-oriented enterprises where the monitoring is supposedly better. The major advantage with the larger units is that the paperwork is more efficient. Violations relating to contract labour, young worker, and wages and benefit records exist here too, but they are a little more difficult to ferret out. However, if what we have noted is true for export-oriented industries then things are probably equally, if not more, in need of corrections in the non-exporting units where foreign buyers are not there to turn up the audit heat.

Environmental norms rarely concern merchant producers. This is because, unlike child labour, international buyers hardly pressure them on this score. Given the conditions in which these entrepreneurs operate, why should one expect them to observe this piece of the law at all? However, the way merchant producers handle this issue is hardly surprising and is typical of the recklessness with which they view the law. On many occasions the management gets a private laboratory to certify the environmental fitness of the factory on the plea that the government inspector rarely turns up, if ever. Naturally, the entrepreneurs can manipulate these certificates at will. They only need to show a piece of paper to soothe the foreign buyers who are often finicky about such environmental details.

Re-tooling the Merchant Producer

How long can India capitalize on its low cost advantage? The areas where the majority of low-wage workers find work, such as in textiles, in carpets, in metal- and glass-ware, in rolling *bidis*, and in the production of soft toys, are growing in terms of their export presence even though the workers in their supply chain may be bent over to deliver the promised order in the half-light of their cottages. Surveys by the labour board found that 'only 17% of the workers surveyed had proper lighting'.[3] The best way to raise the bar for the Indian entrepreneur is to put effective state pressure on the management to abide by legal and ethical standards. While this alone may not yield the necessary results, it will certainly do much to put

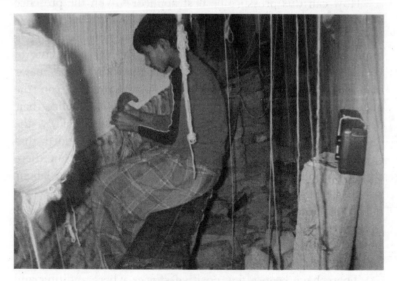

Child carpet-weaver

in place the basic structure of observance. It is only when the merchant producer can realistically be forced to abide by norms of proper bookkeeping, maintaining the integrity of records, of legal hiring, and providing proper conditions of work will they be forced to become true entrepreneurs. As long as they can exploit low wages and worker vulnerability there is little attraction in being anything other than a merchant producer. Child labour is just one of the many disagreeable issues that characterize merchant producerism, but unfortunately Western buyers are most concerned about child labour and are willing to look the other way when other sweatshop conditions prevail in the very units from which they source material. One gets an indication of this bifocality from Clinton–Gore's campaign in 2000–01 against child labour and sweatshops. While the funds for child labour eradication were doubled in one year to a figure of US$92 million in 2001, campaigns against sweatshops received just US$3.9 million in all. The message is clear and the merchant producer can also decipher the difference in emphasis and acts accordingly.

How can this pressure be best applied? Given the presence of foreign investors and the flow of FDI, external business partners can contribute significantly by setting up reliable internal and external audits, and there is also the possibility of standardizing audit procedures for this purpose among major buyers in India. That would put uniform pressure on the merchant entrepreneurs to think in ways that rationalize their organizations and cultivate sustainable skill-sets. Recently, the minister of the department of commerce recommended that child labour monitoring be effected across all units, but there are two problems attached to this. The first is that child labour is one of many issues that plague the small- and micro-sector industries. Second, who is going to enforce these regulations? A third-party monitoring mechanism is worth exploring in this context, with the state conducting random tests on how the units have responded to audit objections.

There have been a few positive stories where auditing and monitoring have helped. The first and the most remarkable case relates to child labour. In all those units where there is systematic monitoring the numbers of children working in factories has fallen significantly. The carpet belt of east Uttar Pradesh is a case in point. The second relates to systematizing the shift system, i.e. converting from two shifts to three, so that the normal working day is eight hours. The third is with reference to training workers in-house in order to upskill them. This would mean that the entrepreneur is investing in a worker and would like to retain the person. As things stand, in most cases worker turnover is of little consequence. To begin with, a chunk of the turnover occurs by management design, as we found with the contract labourers, to escape legal obligations. On occasions when workers leave their jobs voluntarily it is not difficult to find a replacement at that low level of skill.

Finally, formalization of procedures and the insistence that workers must sign for what they receive in terms of emoluments have also made the workers conscious of their entitlements. There is still more that can be done. The resistance towards workers' representation or even setting up a grievance cell is still strong. However, given the beginnings of the successes that external third-party monitoring, instituted by foreign partners in joint ventures, has achieved, there is reason enough to deepen this practice in India.

If it were possible to add these up across the board over a period of time then the industrial profile in India could change for the better. It might encourage long-term FDI rather than short-term ones, as has in the main been the case so far. However, the external agencies and foreign investors can only contribute so much. The government's role in setting up a proper infrastructure and in delivering public goods at quality levels to its citizens cannot be minimized. This will raise the bargaining power of workers, and that will make them less vulnerable. This might induce genuine entrepreneurship and not simply merchant producerism.

Internal and external audits can only grow in strength and efficacy when they are coupled with government-level initiatives in infrastructural and human development. Where educational standards are so low, where an illness can wipe out all the assets of a family, the poor will always remain susceptible and for sheer survival move from one short-term strategy to another. The breakdown of the village economy and the surge of workers willing to trek to factories more readily than the enterprises will have them, make it very tempting to remain a merchant producer.

For now it needs to be said that given the entrepreneurial climate in this low-wage economy, the practices of cooking the books, misusing contract workers, and capitalizing on cheap labour are going to be tremendously tenacious and widespread. Against this background, when the management of a particular unit abides by even the basic legal norms this is viewed as so unusual that it is dressed up and paraded as corporate social responsibility. Doubtless, corporate governance and corporate social responsibility can indeed raise the bar in terms of entrepreneurship in India, but the mere observance of the law does not make for corporate social responsibility.

The Security and Exchange Board of India (SEBI) has now advised all its members to institute grievance cells and the appointment of an ombudsman. These envisaged corporate governance norms also include the nomination of external members to the board of directors of a firm who have the authority to set up separate committees to ensure greater transparency and fiduciary responsibility towards stakeholders. This has already begun in many of the large listed enterprises, though, if the truth be told, much of it is still remains an exercise on paper.

Corporate Social Responsibility

Great potentialities also exist in the recent concern with Corporate Social Responsibility (CSR) that is being voiced among large business houses. Even today CSR is seen as an emblematic badge of good behaviour to be displayed to the external world with little business consequence. However, the fact is being driven home, albeit slowly, that CSR is not just PR cosmetics, philanthropy, or observance of the law.

There are some examples of true CSR in India, but they are few and far between. The best CSR practice will seek sustainability by linking it to business. Otherwise, CSR will remain uncertain and depend on the whims of the CEOs and promoters.

There are three ways by which an organization can make its CSR sustainable even though its CEOs come and go. In all these instances the business link must be clearly demonstrable. CSR can either be, (i) competence-driven, or (ii) community-driven, or finally, (iii) consumer-driven. As in each case CSR is not just philanthropy, it would require the company's A team to be in the forefront. Further, CSR should not be driven by advertising, but in order to enhance the standards of an organization's performance on multiple axes, or what is nowadays called the triple bottom line. Besides, there is no single off-the-shelf model that would suit every company. Each enterprise must judge for itself which form would best suit it.

When CSR is *competence driven* then the enterprise seeks to leverage its known and tested skill-set advantages to reach out to those who have hitherto been outside its reach. This is done to increase its area of operation and as a result learn more. Examples of this are Tata Hotels. They went out to help the management of destitute and old peoples' homes with their skills in hospitality management and returned with a fund of knowledge that soon became central to their main line of work. Likewise, many IT companies, such as NIIT, WIPRO, and Infosys, have initiated computer literacy programmes, and indeed educational packages in general. These not only help to generate a larger market, but also to provide insights into the kind of services that would be required by future generations.

Community-driven CSR is of the kind that IKEA launched in the carpet belt of east Uttar Pradesh. IKEA wanted to ensure that children do not work in factories from which it outsources goods. Bearing this in mind they set up educational and women empowerment projects in areas where they have a business presence in east Uttar Pradesh so that child labour would be an unattractive option for parents. Another example is afforded by

Lipton in Etah, where the company set up veterinary hospitals so that the cows in the region would be healthier as also would the financial position of the farmers who deliver the milk to them. The initiatives of cooperative sugar factories in Maharashtra can also be mentioned. They constructed small dams to help the farmers who are their shareholders, and also set up educational institutes in the vicinity so that the children of these shareholders could later find skilled jobs in the cooperatives.

Consumer-driven CSR is when an enterprise raises its standards of delivery to its customers and thereby benefits the community as a whole. Sanmar Group no longer uses certain chemicals though these have not been banned but are only under a general suspicion of being harmful to one's health. Many purchasers of cotton are in a conjoint effort to establish cotton cultivation under 'best management practices'. One day these efforts might actually lead to the large-scale production of green cotton. Likewise, many purchasers encourage supplies and input materials being bought from units set up by marginal communities and deprived groups. This again spreads the reach of these business organizations to areas that were not tapped in the past and satisfies a set of consumer preferences.

Apollo Tyres India has initiated an interesting CSR scheme by branching out to HIV/AIDS awareness and control. Most of its consumers are truck-drivers who live for long periods away from home, are susceptible to unsafe sex, and could well become victims of HIV/AIDS. Apollo Tyres has set up health clinics and detection centres in many of its transport hubs that not only help prevent HIV infection, but also assist victims and their families who have contracted HIV and may have developed AIDS. In this way, the management of Apollo Tyres believes that it is not only helping a larger social cause but also drawing closer to consumers and potential consumers.

CSR is still a far cry for the majority of merchant capitalists, but should this practice entrench itself among the big players and listed companies, the demonstration effect across the economy might be significant. In short, we must seek ways of re-tooling the merchant capitalist if India is to move from mere sectoral growth to all-round development and to sustain it over the long term. Needless to say, unless workers are continually upskilled and their health and educational facilities brought up to par, merchant producers will continue to exploit poverty and will hold out, at least for the foreseeable future. This is too long for a liberal democratic society to wait.

5

THE MIDDLE-CLASS MYTH
WHO BUYS WHAT IN INDIA?

The buzz after liberalization is that India is teeming with a
high-consuming 'middle class' that would make any consumer
industry salivate. Many estimate the number of middle class
Indians to be somewhere between 200 to 300 million. That is
an impressive figure, but what kind of middle class are we really
talking about?

If it is IT professionals, then the best of them have formed
a long brain line that would hopefully transport them to Silicon
Valley. Besides, even in India, as we discovered, there are only
three million professionals in the ITeS sector. This should give
us reason to pause and take fresh stock of the middle-class
stories that abound around us. Is the middle class really that
large? What exactly are the defining features of this middle
class? In doing this should we not also include within our ambit
merchant producers and sweatshops, and the ever-growing
number of marginal workers?

Recently, in the autumn of 2007, the Indian government
launched a huge tourism promotion drive in New York under
the rubric 'Incredible !ndia'. This found a large and sympathetic
audience primarily comprised of non-resident Indians (or NRIs).
Many of these expatriates have convinced themselves that India

is now a giant economy and world class. Why shouldn't they? As leading Western economies are handing out these encomiums the credibility factor is obviously very high. After being subjected to humiliation for years because of their origins from a near-basket-case country, this new tone of high praise clearly holds a therapeutic value for them.

The NRIs have also responded generously, but they would definitely not have been impressed by India's foreign reserves. NRI remittances topped US$24 billion in 2005-06. Till 1980 most NRI remittances came from the Middle East and it is only in recent years that the contribution from North America is catching up with this.[1] Let us not therefore make little of the contribution of those outside the IT sector to our foreign exchange reserves. Even so, when all this is added together, to what extent has this led to a vibrant middle-class and a developed consumer economy?

If we now go below the grey-matter mark, then is our consumption standard at least indicative of a strong middle-class? As a taste of things to come, it is worthwhile mulling over the fact that only 3 per cent of Indian households own cars. Does our boast not sound ridiculous, especially when over 4.5 million American households below the poverty line own cars, with 290,000 of these actually owning three cars?

It has often been commented that the administration artfully dodges bare-knuckled poverty figures by readjusting survey methodologies and definitions. What we have now is a reverse tendency of inflating figures by statistical manipulation. Definitions of what constitutes the middle and upper classes are pegged at such low levels that almost anybody can make the grade.

If India's economic growth is limited to a few favoured areas such as in the services and IT sectors, of which a lot is made, and in the merchant producers' sweatshops, about which many prefer to remain silent, then one wonders where and how this expansion of consumerism is going to occur. Where are these super-consumers coming from? The numbers just do not add up.

Although figures for abject poverty may be falling, about 30 per cent of Indians still live on US$1 a day. That is why the move from village to sweatshop means exchanging one form of poverty for another. Abject poverty continues and may have worsened in the decade ending 2004–05. Poverty estimates are again highly notional and difficult to quantify, but the number of people who are poor and marginally poor has risen from 51.2 to 55 per cent in the past decade. Those who belong to this category spend between US$0.30 to US$0.50 for their daily consumption needs—the 'abysmally poor by any standard'.[2] What needs to be underlined is that Scheduled Castes (ex-Untouchables) and Muslims are over-represented amongst the poor. Social grimness overlays the economic grime and this can scarcely be overlooked.

Even so, the government only qualifies those who are below the levels of 'abysmally poor' to be Below the Poverty Line (BPL). This would naturally give the impression that there is growing prosperity and a nationwide reduction of poverty.[3] This study by Professor Sengupta embarrassed the government hugely, and predictably finds no mention in the 'Incredible India' fantasy in New York. The sense of discomfort in ruling circles was enhanced by the fact that he is an economist of considerable reputation and a member of Parliament nominated by the dominant party in this government. What is more disturbing is that 'faster post-"reform" GDP growth has not been accompanied by more rapid poverty reduction. It has, in fact, been accompanied by an increase in inequality'.[4]

The Human Resources Crunch

The ideological hustle on India's huge consumer market has been so convincing that even though there is blood in the water, the sharks have yet to smell it. The FDI trickle, such as it is, keeps flowing in volumes (but largely to privileged sectors) sufficient to keep the optimism afloat. When the starting point is low, and when the standards set are hardly exacting, it is easy to be satisfied. When wise people say that economic booms and busts are all in the mind, there could not be a better example than India. There are various highly inflated estimates of the middle class. This ranges all the way from the number of skilled human resources, and ends with our burgeoning consumer market. Both, in my view, are highly exaggerated. One could say that the exaggeration of one demands the escalation of the other.

In a 2006 CEO Round Table conference hosted by the IMA in Goa, top executives in India had to accept the uncomfortable truth that there was a shortage of skilled manpower in the country. It is true that we have a large number of highly skilled workers, but if we were to put them in perspective in terms of our total population then a different picture emerges. It is not just that our literacy rate is at best 61 per cent, but only 5 per cent of our own workforce has had vocational training compared to 70 per cent in Germany, 80 per cent in Japan and 95 per cent in South Korea. Further, India's total stock of suitable young engineers (with seven years or less of work experience was just 130,000 individuals in 2003 ... while the United States had over half a million suitable engineers'.[5] As if this statistic is not staggering enough, take a look at this: the number of degree holding engineers on a per million basis in India is exceedingly low when compared to other countries. For example, the 'US had close to fifteen times as many, Germany ten times, and even the Philippines six times as many' qualified engineers.[6]

We can deflate the 'great Indian engineering myth' by looking at the total numbers too.[7] There are not as many Indian engineers as is often made out because holders of sub-baccalaureate technical degrees are also counted among the engineers. India undoubtedly produces more sub-baccalaureates of this kind than the US does. However, if one takes into account graduates of four-year engineering programmes from reputable institutes then in 2004 India produced only 112,000 such graduates as compared to 137,000 in the US.[8] Only one-third of those in the IT sector have proper engineering degrees. The remaining two-thirds have sub-baccalaureate and diploma qualifications.[9] Can such figures justify the descriptions of India as a flourishing knowledge-producing society? Couple this with the factoid that was underlined earlier that the ITES in India employs only 3 million people.

We tend to believe that India is at the forefront of technology because a large number of international companies (primarily in IT and the service sector) are outsourcing their work to India in fields that require low-level skills. Add to that cheap labour, which is a major consideration in the technical manpower sector too. These jobs may be white-collar but are not quite starched. Business Process Outsourcing Units dominate the ITES sector, and this demands at best an average knowledge of English and some computer technology applications. The ITES sector is not interested yet in expanding its verticals and going beyond low-end services in banking, financial, and telecom services.[10] Our delusion regarding our human resource base is also bolstered by the fact that a large number of our homegrown, highly trained engineers find their way to the US and do exceedingly well there. This flight from India does not however necessarily raise the country's brainpower, though it may lead to higher foreign exchange remittances. However, it has also been estimated that nearly 160,000 students leave India for overseas universities draining our foreign exchange by US$10 billion per year. This is enough to set up forty Indian Institutes of Management (IIM) or twenty Indian Institutes of Technology (IIT) every year.[11]

Removing Poverty through Statistics

Such inflated figures of skilled personnel support the belief that India constitutes a huge consumer market. It is true that the number of consumer items have increased significantly over the past decade or so. In terms of percentage there has been an impressive growth in the production of a large number of consumer items, from cars to TVs. However, do such figures justify the big picture of a booming middle-class economy?

It is not clear how one can estimate that there are 250 to 300 million middle-class consumers in India. One reason why the numbers are so impressive is because we have depressed the standards of what constitutes the middle and upper classes in India, just as we did when we examined the poverty figures. Sometimes, all it takes to be middle class in India is to afford the equivalent of $0.87 purchasing capacity per day. We must bear in mind that there are only 30 million tax-payers in the country, and tax is deducted at source for only a third of this number.[12] Likewise, in India , one need only have the spending capacity of US$2.30 per day to be considered upper class.

Obviously, when standards are so low, almost anybody can be middle class,[13] and a great number upper class to boot. Such standards would be laughed out of the room in the West, and yet in India we self-consciously scale down expectations to consider the purchasing of hair oil or soap, or even buying a mobile phone, as the markers of middle-class status. Our standards are so different. What is good for India is not good enough for the Western world, not even for China, and yet we use terms like 'middle class' without appropriate caveats and conditions. This is why all manner of wild numbers are bandied around regarding the depth and range of our middle and consuming classes. In many cases, I think, this illusion is also propped up because these statisticians and purveyors of numbers are looking at the elite sections around them and then generalizing for the rest of the society.

The Consumer Market Illusion

Let us take a few instances of the areas in which we are told to believe that India's consumer market has soared to unbelievable heights, and that the middle class must have gone up too.

Cellphones

In 2005 there were 90,000,000 cellphones in India.[14] In 2006 the figure was upward of 130 million and it has probably crossed the 200 million mark in 2007. Incidentally, China has 449 million cellphone subscribers.[15] Does this signify a burgeoning and fast-growing middle class? Not yet. In India it is not uncommon to find migrant workers with a mobile phone. These are the same people whose daily diet is no better than the humblest gruel, who shuffle barefoot from job to job, whose children have swollen bellies and running noses. Surely, the use of a cellphone by such people does not automatically elevate them to middle-class status.

It would be instructive for all those who are struck by this apparent paradox to ask these poor people why they own cellphones at all. I did a spot study of three labour teams in Delhi who were working for private contractors. I also talked to many casual job seekers who gather at designated market places and at truck and tempo stands in different parts of the city, and here is what I found. Many of them carry cellphones though they are wearing torn pyjamas and have probably not eaten a full meal in days. They don't even have a clear plan of what they will do tomorrow, but the cellphone is an essential aspect of their survival kit.

Why cellphones, I asked them? As it turned out, cellphones make a lot of sense to the wandering poor. This is the cheapest and most economical way to stay in touch with their families in faraway villages. The alternative for them would be to use private kiosks for trunk calls, which are more expensive and not as reliable. In any event, if there is crisis at home they cannot be reached. Against this background, the purchase of a mobile phone is not a luxury but a cost-saving necessity. Now that they are accessible they are assured they can be immediately contacted should there by any crisis at home This spares them the expense of a weekly or fortnightly call to some uncertain, and unreliable, village booth to get news of their families.

What is more, should all be well on the home front they need not be compelled in the same way to make their periodic biannual trudge to their villages. Domestic decisions too, that had earlier to wait for them to turn up before they could be sorted out, can now be handled long distance with the help of a cellphone. All these factors save money, which is scarce among this class. Buying a mobile is thus hugely cost saving and emotionally comforting in a way that well-to-do urban

Indians will rarely understand. Cellphones cut across classes, and that is why they are not a clear marker of middle-class prosperity.

What makes such communications even more economical is that when they buy cellphones the poor buy the cheap varieties and use them only to receive calls and rarely to make them. In India, fortunately, there is no charge for receiving a call; the caller pays for it. Today, people who make as little as US$2 a day can purchase a cellphone.[16]

This also explains why the vegetable vendor who sells his wares from a pushcart, the washerman who operates out of a shack in a back alley with no electricity, the plumber and electrician who hang around shopping centres for years, (and with whom we have developed a rapport that shows every sign of spilling over to the next generation), all have cellphones. Does that make them rich? No.

They all have cellphones for they have shrewdly realized that it helps them in their meagre business. I can now call them up to deliver at my doorstep and they can receive my instructions at absolutely no cost. This makes it worth their while, and more, to keep cellphones near at hand. In this way they can respond almost instantly to their consumers' demands. A washerman without a cellphone is obviously at a disadvantage, and so are the street vendor and the petty technician. The possession of a cellphone does not automatically spell wealth or define consumer status. It is however a lesson on how there are consumers in millions out there for accessibly priced products.

As income estimates and projections are based on conjectural databases, it is best to proceed in this exercise by paying attention to who buys what. In this way we have direct information on how many real 'middle-class' consumers there are in India.

Cars

Perhaps the cellphone argument may not be a good illustration of prosperity, but what about cars? We see cars snarling up traffic, not just in large metropolitan centres like Delhi or

Mumbai, but also in towns so small that they might not even show up on the map. This presents us with a comforting impression of continuing prosperity, untidy, but nevertheless striking. It is important then to begin with the most egregious example of India's supposedly huge and expanding prosperity, and see how deep this middle class really is in contemporary India.

Only six million households own cars and jeeps.[17] This constitutes just 3.5 per cent of 177 million households in India. Predictably, the distribution is 5:1 between urban and rural India. Other research broadly supports this finding. Only 8.2 million own cars or jeeps in a population of over 1 billion.[18] If each household consists of about five people then we can say about 4.55 per cent households belong to this category.[19] In the US, just for the record, there are 237.24 million registered cars.[20] In fact, in the US, 4.7 million households own cars but are officially Below the Poverty Line. As mentioned earlier, as many as 290,000 of these own three cars or more.[21] Our notion of the middle class in India needs drastic revision because even the best-heeled of our so-called affluent citizens find it difficult to afford more than a single car.

Our tendency to magnify our capacity to consume is because we play with percentages and do not contend with actual figures. For example, although the production of passenger cars has risen by 80 per cent we should note the low base-line figure. Between 2001–02 and 2004–05 the number of cars produced climbed from a meagre 513,000 to a still meagre 961,000. In percentage terms the rise in impressive, at about 80 per cent, but we are still dealing with low figures.[22]

Let us cross check the number of cars sold by examining the production figures of such vehicles to ensure that we are not misreading the big picture. Though there is a leap in percentage terms of passenger cars,[23] let us pay attention to the abysmal numbers produced in comparison to elsewhere in the developed world with much lower populations. In the US 11.2 million cars were manufactured in 2005–06. Japan actually tops this number as it produced 11.48 million cars that year. The corresponding figure for India is only 1.9 million, which would probably not even figure on the radar of any major car-manufacturing company as the sign of a likely competitor. In 2005-06, tiny South Korea manufactured 3.8 million and not-so-developed Brazil approximately 2.6 million cars. China during the same period produced 7.1 million cars. These figures should give us some pause when we pronounce 'Incredible India' in glowing terms. Many smaller countries outshine India by far when it comes to consumer demands and prosperity.

Consider now the production of cars by some major companies. Against such major international companies, what our car manufacturers are rolling out is akin to jingling small change.

Production of Cars (millions) in 2006

Manufacturer	Millions of Cars Produced
GM	5.7
Toyota	6.8
Volkswagen	5.4
Ford	3.8
Tata	0.190468
Mahindra and Mahindra	0.136199
Maruti[24]	0.744000

India has just 7 cars per 1000 compared to 500 per 1000 in Germany. However, even when we compare ourselves to other developing countries we are way behind. In Thailand there are 27 cars per 1000, in Mexico 130 per 1000, and in Malaysia 147 per 1000.[25] Has India such a big consumer market after all? We are, after all, way behind not just in percentage terms but even in real numbers.

Motorcycles and scooters do a lot better than cars. Even so, in 2003 the number of registered two-wheelers was 45.3 million.[26] The price of a motorcycle is about one-fifth of what it takes to

buy a basic car. Add this number to the owners of four-wheelers
and even then we can hardly approach the vaunted middle-class
figures.

Sundry Consumption Goods

The sale of durables in India when segregated by class draws us
to the conclusion that when it comes to low- and medium-
priced categories there is a proportionately larger market than
when we come to commodities that truly define the middle
class. The low-income groups figure impressively when it comes
to bicycles, table-fans and transistors, but fall behind when we
take into account colour television sets, and more so with
refrigerators and washing machines.[27]

The growth of consumer goods has come principally from
low-priced commodities. Cheap cosmetics, for example, have
registered a huge growth of 15 to 20 per cent over the past few
years. In this segment the preference is for small pack sizes,
which is in line with the general tendency of looking for less
expensive products.[28] Double-digit growth notwithstanding,
the impact of cosmetics and toiletry is very low in India.
Currently the per capita expenditure on cosmetics in India is
around US$0.68 compared to US$36.5 in other Asian countries.
The size of India's cosmetic market is only about US$950
million. The presence of international brands is very low in this
sector as only a small section can afford to buy them.[29]

Once again a quick comparison with China. In 2005, sales
in China of high-end fashion products and accessories and other
luxury goods topped US$2 billion. This makes for as much as
12 per cent of the global market.[30]

What is worrying is that the percentage spent on non-food
items is growing. Given the low levels of consumption power
the proportionate rise in non-food income signals that less and
less is being spent on food.[31] Normally, the fall in the proportion
of food to non-food signals, according to Engel's law, prosperity,
but in a situation of abject poverty this has a totally different
meaning.

In fact, as recently as between 2001 to 2002 even the actual money spent on food in rural India fell by about Rs 2 per month,[32] notwithstanding steadily rising prices. Unfortunately, the government's supply of food to the Public Distribution System, which is specifically meant for the very poor, has also fallen over the years. On account of a paucity of funds the budget estimate for this purpose was revised downward, in spite of rising prices, from Rs 256 million to Rs 242 million.[33]

Once we let these figures sink in, the image of a buoyant, prosperous middle-class India takes a beating. Now we can fully appreciate the optical illusion of prosperity that a small, but highly visible, number of the rich in ITES, telecommunication, and high-end service have created, both nationally and worldwide. This is primarily because these are the classes of people with whom the well-to-do associate. It is their cars that we see on the streets around us; it is their homes that we look at with envy.

Reconceptualizing the Middle-class

Who are the members of this prosperous middle-class? Nowhere in the world is the middle class actually in the middle. The middle class came into its own in Britain only in the mid-nineteenth century. It was a very commodious class but excluded landowners, members of the liberal professions, and weekly wage earners. All those in between, from the humblest clerk to the wealthiest money magnate, were middle class.[34] In other words, middle class was an attitude to life and did not necessarily connote wealth and convenience. The middle-class in contemporary Western societies constitutes virtually the entire population apart from a minuscule part of the very rich and a small number of the very poor. It signifies a way of life and not the possession of consumer items, which is taken for granted!

When we project the picture of a glowing and incredible India which places do we visit? We traverse the Indian versions of the Silicon Valley, or the upmarket areas of Delhi and Mumbai. Who visits the slums? Who has gone to a sweatshop?

In short, who really cares so long as the packaging is right? The truth is that the image of a triumphant India about to conquer the world market is nurtured by the fact that scholars, journalists, capitalists (large and small), and foreign traders never stray too far away from 'people like us'.

The constituents of the Indian middle-class actually belong to elite sections of the country. Amidst the grinding poverty of millions, they can afford a lifestyle that somewhat resembles those of the European and American middle-classes. The distance between this section of society and the rest is so vast that they have no empathy for the millions who live and toil underfoot. Among other things, this also delays the realization of substantial citizenship, which is much more than merely observing the letter of the law.

Contrast India today with Europe of the mid-nineteenth century. Approximately 150 years ago, France and Germany were thinking of social welfare and workers' health insurance. In Britain too around that time, Whig aristocrats, and a fair number of Tories too, along with the growing middle-classes, devised policies to protect the poor and elevate their conditions of work and living. Sadly, unlike Europe, India did not have a Bismarck who, impressed by Napoleon III, thought of a welfare state. Though India had kings, pretenders, and potentates, not one of them could be likened to the 'socialist' Napoleon III[35] who created parks and built hospitals for the poor. Our consumption-obsessed rich and prosperous 'middle-class' have never reached out to improve the conditions of the poor, leaving it all to the long run.

In Britain, even Whig aristocrats went out of their way to institute State measures that contributed to broad-based social welfare on a long-term basis. Their policies led to the growth of a broad-based middle class and the gradual marginalization of poverty. There was, therefore, a strong project element in the making of a middle class in the West. It was not left to long-term trickle-down effects, nor was it determined in terms of gross consumption figures. That was there, but only as an index of how an improvement of economic standards can actually change social relations between people and classes. In India we do not have a middle-class project and that is why we talk of this category purely in terms of consumption. Should we not attempt instead to create a middle-class society where consumption is just a by-product?

By contrast, in India, the prosperous sections of society behave as if nobody of any significance exists outside their circle. Now that socialism, or what passed for it, is no longer a threat, there is little point in talking about the poor who have slithered into the shadows as 'those others'. Relieved of this burden, politicians recommend laughable measures to alleviate the conditions of the poor, as if their living conditions are akin to those of Western Europe.

Let me cite just two instances from recent times to drive home this point. In order to curb the rising tide of suicide in 2007 among desperately poor farmers, the chief minister in Maharashtra suggested wide-ranging psychiatric care and counselling to enable the village poor to more manfully bear their domestic tribulations. It is as if the chief minister was talking about habitual gamblers and those in drug de-addiction centres and not about debt-ridden farmers who see suicide as the only way out for themselves and their families. Instead of attending to the problems of indebtedness and low infrastructural facilities under which cotton farmers in Vidharbha labour, the ministers are advocating breathing lessons by Sri Sri Ravishankar and religious discourses by other assorted swamis.

Again, when the conditions of rag pickers suddenly, and whimsically attracts the notice of certain decision-makers and pricks their conscience, a great show of concern is made in a completely inappropriate fashion. Instead of providing alternative gainful employment, the government recently handed out 6000 pairs of rubber gloves to help the poor rag-pickers to continue their drudgery. Not only is the number inadequate but also the measure itself is not attuned to redressing poverty. As one rag-picker said with disdain: 'They are providing us with gloves and boots just so we don't get sick and stop working.'[36]

It is as if the politicians in India live in a world far removed from those over whom they rule. Unmoved, even in their imagination, by social concerns, the Indian ruling elite often think of patently outlandish measures when confronted with the plight of the poor. Their heart is certainly not in poverty removal but, to borrow Oscar Wilde's phrase, to keep the poor alive.

The true picture of a rising middle-class India is a blatant exaggeration when we look at actual numbers and are not seduced by percentage points. There are lies, damned lies, and statistics, but even so we should exercise some caution in the way figures are produced and interpreted. For instance, neither the increase in non-rural employment in merchant producers' sweatshops nor the swelling number of cellphone owners actually signifies an emerging middle-class. How then are the rich able to do so well, live so lavishly, and convey an appearance of well-grounded prosperity? A middle-level manager in an IT firm can have servants, chauffeurs, and a live-in maid and need not worry about the kitchen, picking up children from school, groceries and washing, as their counterparts must do in the West. Also, a rapacious merchant producer, not too overly well-endowed with either entrepreneurial or managerial skills, has no problem hiring the least-expensive labour in order to exploit the growing export market. How is all this possible?

The Middle-class Project

Clearly, the term 'middle-class' does not sit well in India; it finds barely any standing space. When we refer to the Indian middle-class we are unconsciously thinking of those who can approximate the lifestyles of the common person in the West. What we forget is that while such people are few and far between, and indeed occupy superior status in India, in Europe and the US, on the contrary, almost the entire society is middle class. There are a few at the top who lead a kind of underground life. They are so affluent and out of sight that we don't even know where their landing strips and clubs are hidden. Then there are the poor who often compare with the worst in India or Bangladesh. Everyone else is however in the middle to a lesser or greater degree.

Till the 1960s it was not uncommon to find American sociologists distinguishing between lower upper middle-class and upper lower middle-class, and middle upper middle-class, and so on, because they wanted to emphasize rapid social mobility in their societies. However, as consumption patterns were very similar between these classes they had to rely heavily on cultural attributes, learning, and tastes to make such distinctions work. In India we are not really bothered about what goes on in the head so long we can display our acquisitions on our sleeve. Even so, we compare very poorly against the truly Western middle-class.

However, the most important reason why the term middle class looks sickly in India is because there is no project attached to it. As we saw, the making of the middle class was a project on a national scale throughout Western Europe from the latter half of the nineteenth century. This meant providing quality health and education for all, and, in some instances, also workers' compensation against accidents. The aim was to create a middle class to bridge the gap between the privileged and the rest of society. In the West the idea of the middle class started out as a project although it may have later become a statistic. In India we are besotted by consumption statistics and have forgotten about the 'middle-class' project. What we need to realize is that without this project that seeks equalization, statistics about the middle class will always appear dismal and mean very little. Even a frayed white-collar worker has somebody in the kitchen to kick around till suddenly the gap widens and there is nobody to kick but oneself. Instead of looking in vain for the middle class, let us ask ourselves what impedes the coming of the middle class in India. Then, perhaps, we will start getting meaningful answers and, who knows, the middle-class project too might begin.

Where however will this task begin? Can we hang around our urban homes and hope that it will grow spontaneously around us, or should we pro-actively, and self-consciously, reach out and draw rural India into this project?

6

THE HOLLOWED VILLAGE
HOW RURAL IS RURAL INDIA?

By late 1980s it was clear to me that the recommended literature on village India would just not suffice. I began scouring other sources of information and found some worthwhile data produced by agronomists and other economists of that genre. They wrote about the stagnation in agriculture, the pressure on land, and the frequent out-migration from the village. I found all this very fascinating, but at the same time when I sought a new perspective on villages at the conceptual level it was either missing in their works or very timidly and timorously hinted at. Such was the persuasive power of the old scholarship on rural India.

There were of course those who did mention that the village was changing, but they assumed generally that these transformations were outcomes of urban influences on the rural world,[1] or peripheral to the agrarian structure.[2] What they missed out was that the rural economy was being hollowed from within. This compels people to reach out for alternatives, many within the village and many outside it. Neither the sporadic acquisition of commodities by a few villagers, nor the grafting of certain urban technologies (such as those that are IT-based) signals either rural revival or a happy arcadia. Instead

84

we find apprehensions and aspirations mingling freely as most villagers reach out to a somewhat unfamiliar world. It is not as if they are shrinking from that world, but their skills do not really match the qualifications essential to enter it.The agrarian policies spelt out by the government and by other observers of village India advocate land reforms and a more aggressive support policy for farmers. However, as I see it, old-fashioned methods will not work even in thought. The fields are no longer the ground under the feet of most villagers. All this should compel us to rethink our prevailing understanding of rural India and how its inhabitants can find reasonable alternatives outside agriculture. That is the sign of the times and there is little point in turning our attention away from it. Agricultural policies need to be thought out in the context of such changes, and based on the assumption that nothing has really happened except the deepening of the same old misery.

When I began studying villages I was struck by the emptying out of rural India, emotionally, economically, and, obviously, also in terms of numbers. This did not sit well with the roseate picture of a happily urbanizing village or even with the old-fashioned notion that the village was standing still with large landlords whipping everybody else into submission. It was indeed the absence of this last feature that first impressed me when I began my forays into village studies in the mid-1980s. It took a while for this reality to congeal, alongside the other characteristics of rural life, and only then did the phenomenon of the hollowed village begin to make sense. Now I could conceptually link one to another: urban sweatshops, rise in small-scale informal industries, and the impossibility of agriculture providing a reasonable future for those in the village. However, once I grasped this reality I realized that it was time for me to stop teaching students outdated material and to go around and research this aspect for myself and see where exactly traditional village India still lingers.

It is often assumed that the better-off areas are more susceptible to urban influences than the poorer ones, so I travelled extensively in Punjab, west and east UP, parts of north and north-east Bihar, and chunks of Jharkhand. These trips were to disparate economic zones of India. While the northern parts are relatively prosperous, Bihar and Jharkhand are among the most backward states in India. If the former is the abundant agricultural breadbasket, the latter is an empty rice-bowl.

Similarities and Differences Amongst Indian Villages

I was in for a surprise. East UP and further eastwards resembled north-west India in ways I was not conceptually prepared to accept. Rather than plot the distance between the two regions, I was now more impressed by the similarities. In east UP, in Bihar, and in Jharkhand too, people were uprooting themselves and heading out to seek jobs elsewhere. In these poorer districts there was as great a dissatisfaction with agriculture, even as a way of life, as there was in the richer north-western states. As much as in Punjab and west UP, the hitherto downtrodden

Humble home of a 'rich' Jat farmer

Scheduled Castes here were pushing their way up. How was all this possible? Were these not places where large landlords held sway and where poor peasants cowered at their very presence?

To begin with, there were few large landowners in sight. In fact, over the three years I kept visiting east UP villages, I encountered only one person who claimed that his family actually owned over fifty acres of land, although I think he was bluffing. He was more prosperous than the rest, but while everybody admitted that he was well off, the figure of fifty-acres-plus raised eyebrows in disbelief. Whenever I tell my colleagues of my inability to find large landowners they roundly criticize me for not searching assiduously enough. Therefore, each time I go to a village I try to seek out these village magnates by asking more and more complicated questions, but at the end it is just a waste of time.

I admit that there are parts of India, notably in Punjab, where operational holdings are expanding and therefore the number of such units is going down.[3] But the impact of this is virtually negligible at the all-India level. Even in instances such as in Punjab, it is not as if the large landlords are returning. An increase in size of operational holdings is because an emerging class of enterprising farmers is leasing in land from those who want to leave agriculture for more lucrative prospects in other fields.

However, when we consider India as a whole, there is a sharp rise in the number of small holdings ranging up to two hectares, but a clear decrease in the numbers of holdings above this size, i.e. from middle farmers upwards.[4] In other words, large and medium operational land-holdings are finding it hard to hold on and the ranks of small farmers are continually growing.[5] One gets an indication of this from the fact that the total amount of land operated as large farms has fallen by roughly 38 per cent, accompanied by a very impressive increase in the area under small and very small operational holdings.[6]

The percentage distribution of large farmers is, however, not uniformly spread through India's villages. This is probably why those from one region tend to disbelieve findings from another. Even in Punjab the picture is variable. In Talhan village (Jalandhar district) many prosperous farmers have operational holdings (not outright ownership) exceeding thirty acres. Yet, in Punjab there are also villages like Khara in Tarn Taran district where only two families owned over twenty acres of land. In Behirchi village in Saharanpur district of west UP, again, only two had around twenty acres of land and about six owned over ten acres. These constituted the rural rich in that village. The remaining had less than five acres, and about seventeen families may technically have been landowners but were utterly marginal farmers. About 253 families in the village were landless, and this constituted the majority population. Again, in Baijalpur in the east UP district of Ballia, only five had holdings above five acres (nobody touched ten acres), about 117 of them held less than two acres, and the remaining 163 had holdings somewhere in between.

In short, it is unwise to generalize on the basis of one or two villages. That is why the old style single-village monographs do not quite answer the questions that are arising today at the all-India level. I will return to these villages again to provide a flavour of the variations in Rural Non-Farm Employment (RNFE) in them, but in the meantime, on to broader issues.

From the brief presentation of a few villages what becomes immediately apparent is that the prevailing picture in one village is quickly undone in the next from the same region. That is why it is necessary to change gear and adopt the *macro-empirical method* advocated. We must let our empirical nose lead the way in both conducting surveys of our own and in looking at those undertaken by others. According to figures available in the years 2000-01 Rajasthan, Punjab and Haryana had the highest percentage of large operational holdings in the country. Among the states with the lowest number of large landowners, Bengal leads the pack followed by Bihar. The contrast is really quite remarkable.

Percentage of Lage Operational Land Holdings[7]

Area	Total number of holdings	% designated as large
Rajasthan	5.8m	8.24%
Punjab	9.9m	7.2%
Bihar	11.5m	0.07%
Bengal	6.79m	0.01%

To some degree the low proportion of large operational holdings in West Bengal is an outcome of Left Front rule in the state for over three decades. In the 1970s the left government in West Bengal put in place the Operation Barga scheme, which aggressively implemented the 'land to the tiller' programme by giving ownership rights to '*bargas*' or sharecroppers. Even though agriculture is doing relatively better in some north-western states of India, the decline in growth is marked across the country. That is why there is large-scale frustration and migration from these regions too. The movement away from agriculture is probably stronger in Punjab than in many other states, but the trend is noticeable across India. This is the kind of similarity that impressed me when I went to east UP. Agrarian India, whether relatively rich or poor, holds little attraction for the villager.

Farm Facts

It is not surprising that this should be the case. When the number of operational holdings rises but the total area that is cultivated falls, there is only one interpretation for it: farmers are becoming smaller and poorer in quick time.

This fact is reflected in two sets of statistics, both conducted by the National Sample Survey. In spite of population growth, the total area operated registered a steady decline of about 25 per cent between 1960-01 and 2002-03, whilst the number of operational holdings doubled during this period. The average area too fell by half during these forty years or so, as did the area leased in as a percentage share of total area operated. According to the fifty-ninth round estimates, only about 6.5 per cent of the area operated constitutes leased-in land.[8] This indicates a shift from tenant cultivation to self-cultivation. As landholdings are getting smaller, the role of tenants is decreasing, and in the past fifty years, family farms are becoming more conspicuous in villages. This squares up with my empirical observations on rural India.

Poor, rich farmers of western Uttar Pradesh. Both of them belong to the proud Jat caste.

In terms of total land cultivated for food crops there has been a fall between 1990-01 to 2005-06.[9] Given that so many work in agriculture, the investment in agriculture as a percentage of GDP has fallen between these years.[10] In terms of real investment in the agrarian sector, there has been a clear fall of about 20 per cent.[11]

Do Indian politicians really put their money where their mouth is when it comes to the agrarian sector? Regardless of what the WTO might say, subsidies for agriculture in India are much lower in comparison with those in the US, OECD, and Japan. If we add up the figures for India from the Central Statistical Organisation and for the rest of the world from the OECD *Monitoring and Evaluation Report of 2000*, an interesting picture emerges.

Agricultural Subsidies Per Farmer

Country	Subsidy per farmer US$	Subsidy per hectare[12]
India	66	53
Japan	26,000	11,792
US	21,000	129
OECD countries	11,000	218

Quite indisputably, all Western developed societies spend more State money (in real and in percentage terms) for agriculturists than India does. In terms of total domestic support and aggregate measure of support as a share of the total value of agricultural production, we find that the US spends three times as much as India does.[13] The data clearly show that Indian politicians perhaps protest too much when they loudly claim that their sympathies lie with the farmer.

Rural Non-farm Employment

As agriculture is on the downswing, most villagers see non-farm employment as their only escape route. This means that villagers are not only migrating elsewhere for jobs, but also that more and more of them are seeking non-farming jobs while in the village. This phenomenon is captured by the somewhat tedious term, rural non-farm employment, or RNFE. It can no longer be taken as read that a villager in India must almost always be a farmer. Indeed, in most cases nearly half the village economy is non-farm (or non-agricultural) today. What are the compulsions behind this trend? Statistics ambiguously point to falling rates of growth in agriculture, and to the increasing exodus from country to town. Naturally, there is a tremendous increase over the years in rural non-farm employment and this decisively destroys the Indian village of our imagination.

The most recent estimates show that between about 29–32.5 per cent of villagers are engaged in non-agricultural occupations.[14] This is not a small number, and, in all likelihood, this too may well be a conservative estimate as the percentage of main workers in RNFE in Punjab, Haryana, and Rajasthan are about 40 per cent or more.[15] If we take out Rajasthan then RNFE in Haryana and Punjab is over 45 per cent.[16] Now that is really something!

The service sector attracts a majority of those who are engaged in RNFE. According to Chadha, in twelve of the seventeen states, the service sector plays a much 'weightier' role than manufacturing when it comes to RNFE.[17] At any rate, the rural non-farm sector contributes as much 45.59 per cent of net rural domestic product.[18] What then accounts for the growing incidence of RNFE? True, as we mentioned earlier, the scope for agricultural employment has fallen rapidly, but alongside this rural aspirations have been refocused. Chadha argues that the growth in agricultural production creates many types of post-harvesting activities that relate to trade, and this is where a high degree of non-farm employment occurs.[19] Though this argument can be sustained up to a point by looking at the quality and extent of RNFE in Punjab and Haryana, it is difficult to explain how the figure for this is so low in Maharashtra and quite high in Assam.[20]

It has also been suggested that RNFE is an instance of 'distress employment'. Unlike many other historical instances when the fall in rural employment is accompanied by a high rate of agricultural growth, RNFE has continually increased in India in spite of stagnant rates of agricultural growth. This is yet another similarity across regions in India. Thus, the rural unemployed venture out in search for jobs and are willing to do whatever comes their way.[21] An inverse relationship between land-ownership and RNFE[22] has been found where 88 per cent of a sample engaged in RNFE had less than 10 acres of land suggesting that RNFE has a distress aspect[23] as there is little doubt that the poorer the individual, the greater the pressure to seek off-farm employment. It must however also be mentioned that owning around 10 acres of land in India does not really signify a poor distressed farmer. The availability of off-farm employment also drives local villagers to seek jobs outside the village.[24]

This exodus of local people obviously draws in a sizable number of migrants who are willing to work for less. Even so, because wages outside agriculture are better, those who live in the vicinity can take advantage of any work first. However, the degree of urbanization in a district has little impact on RNFE.[25] Certainly, had agricultural income been plentiful, perhaps such labouring jobs in urban areas would have been less attractive. However, the jury is still out on whether or not it is distress employment, pure and simple, that drives up the figures of RNFE.[26]

The availability of jobs outside agriculture is, almost axiomatically, a very important factor for RNFE.[27] What one would really like to know is the nature of these jobs and their provenance. Men are the principal takers of jobs that arise from investments in public utilities and construction.[28] Villages with gas, electricity, and water show a greater incidence of RNFE.[29] Statistically, where land productivity is high, RNFE is also high,[30] but this cannot be posited as a general condition either. In some cases, we observe distress RNFE. In others, the incidence of RNFE is driven up by better wages,[31] which increases the bargaining power of farm labourers. What however remains indubitable is that there is a growing increase in the number of those who work in non-agricultural operations in the village.

Finally, not all non-farm employment occurs in the villages. Indeed, we must not ignore the number of people working in off-farm jobs outside the village. The census enumerators have not quite grasped this factor and hence the census figures are probably not very reliable. A large number of landless villagers work in towns and cities during the day, but return at night, or even during the weekend.[32] This obviously implies that transport facilities also encourage RNFE.

The story is therefore mixed and worth elaborating with field notes, without positing, however, that only one factor is responsible for RNFE. I think it would be best to suggest that RNFE is a supra-local phenomenon whose specifics are encouraged by local factors. Besides, RNFE is also an indicator of other changes that are occurring in the culture of the village. It is probably an index of greater political competitiveness as well as changes in the family structure consequent upon occupational transformations.

Some Field Data on RNFE

A few live examples from the field might help to fill out the picture on the nature of rural non-farm employment. What do farmers do when they are not actually farming? In substantiating this aspect of rural life, I will present material from four villages in north India: two from Punjab, and two from Uttar Pradesh. These are the so-called prosperous regions of India, but in terms of economic prosperity the villages themselves are quite varied. In Punjab, Tarn Taran district is poorer than Jalandhar, just as in UP, Ballia is more backward than Saharanpur. Let us examine the RNFE picture in these parts. It should be noted that we are not talking here of people who have left the village in search of jobs but of those who have stayed behind and work in non-farm operations in the village. The findings in this section are based on my field study to these villages in 2003-04.

Village Talhan (Jalandhar District, Punjab)

We will begin with Talhan village, which is in the prosperous Doaba (or deltaic) region of Punjab. Watered by two rivers, its soil conditions are congenial to growing a range of crops, such as wheat, rice, vegetables and oil seeds. As one enters the village there is no mistaking the presence of rich farmers, so imposing, even by urban standards, are some of the houses. According to the 1991 census, the total population of the village is around 2,442 and Scheduled Castes constitute over half the population. These SCs call themselves Adi-Dharmis, but were once known as Chamar, a pejorative appellation.

Grand homes in the village are overwhelmingly owned by Jats. These houses are not only plush from the outside but are also outfitted with all amenities. Even so, many of these farmers complain that agriculture is not a paying proposition if one were to bear in mind the kind of investments required in terms of land, labour, and capital. It is also quite clear that much of the overt prosperity is financed by remittances from abroad. The lure of migrating from the country is very strong in this village, and perhaps also in the rest of Punjab. In Talhan, it is difficult to find a Jat family without a close family member abroad. Besides, in my estimate, one out of three Adi-Dharmis has a family member living outside India.

Even though the villagers are obviously quite well off, they advance many reasons for the relative unattractiveness of agriculture. The irregularity and insufficiency of water and electricity rank very high in their list of complaints. The water table is now as low as 90 feet in some fields. Also, they believe that the soil has been overworked and has lost much of its nutrients. As one Jat land owner put it: 'Just as excessive use of antibiotics makes the body resistant to drugs, likewise the excessive use of chemical fertilizers has damaged the productivity of the fields.' The villagers also widely believed that multiple cropping had robbed the soil of its 'strength'. The high-powered committee set up by the Fertilizer Association of India had published a report some years back stating the nature of nutrient depletion from the soil due to over-tillage.[33] Leaching, de-nitrification, and the volatilization of nitrates are the major reasons for the loss of soil fertility caused by the erosion of the topsoil and flooding of land for paddy. The use of organic fertilizers would help matters as it releases nitrogen at a slower rate than industrial fertilizer. However farmers increasingly depend on industrial fertilizers to cope with the pressure of multiple cropping.

Farmers in Talhan were of the general impression that in the past not all the land would be cultivated every year. This would allow the soil time to regenerate its nutrients. Consequently, they believe, the wheat and vegetables grown under those circumstances were much tastier than they are now. Some earlier practices, like not sowing on certain days of the month, are also no longer observed in the village.

As the soil is losing its nutrients, several farmers believe that sowing should be delayed and not begun immediately after harvesting. It is, however, not feasible for individual farmers to do this by themselves without some form of collective endorsement. If most farmers start cultivating immediately after harvesting, then the farmer who has held back will suffer as the pests, driven off the mature crop by insecticides, would then attack the younger crop which is still too weak to fight back, though it may be helped by a hefty dose of chemicals.

Besides, even when the farmers ready their crops for sale after harvest they do not know where to market them and for how much. They would prefer a fixed price to a fluctuating price, even if the market price is higher on certain occasions as this would at least enable them to avoid one major uncertainty. Sugarcane was once grown in this village, but over the past decade its cultivation has been largely discontinued. This is not only because the quality of cane has dipped, in terms of its sucrose content, but also because sugar mills always delay, and even default on, payment. Therefore, farmers of all categories, even prosperous ones, are uncertain about their agricultural future which explains, to a large degree, why so many of them leave the village and even migrate to foreign lands. This is certainly not on account of pure distress, but rather because of a lack of hope for the future.

A large number of Jat landowners also engage in RNFE. Non-farm employment is, at least in this case, not the preserve of the poor, and hence the distress thesis does not quite work in areas like Talhan. Jats from well-to-do rural families can be found running telephone booths, trucks and taxis, grocery stores, tailoring shops, and gymnasiums. Occasionally they are even driven to work as factory labourers. A decade ago Jats would never descend to running a grocery store or a tailoring shop, but today many of them are compelled to take to these professions. In Talhan, for instance, Jats run at least three grocery stores.

The Adi-Dharmis have virtually left farming and can be found in all kinds of other occupations in the village. Exporters often engage women from this caste to stitch footballs for some international company. In fact, the Adi-Dharmi temple where this activity takes place is like a community centre with as many as forty-eight Adi-Dharmis engaged in this occupation. What is however very interesting, and perhaps reveals most graphically the changing nature of rural culture, is that an Adi Dharmi runs the sole beauty salon in the village (see photograph below). Local Adi-Dharmis also run three sweetshops which I found to be quite busy with a fair number of customers. Interestingly, even members of the powerful Jat community

Beauty school in Scheduled Caste hamlet, village Talhan

buy from these shops, regardless of the fact that their Adi-
Dharmi owners were once of untouchable status.

Village Khara (Tarn Taran, Punjab)

Wheat and paddy are the principal crops of this village, but
sugarcane and maize are also cultivated quite extensively. Unlike
in Talhan, potatoes are not grown here as the soil is not as
sandy as in the Doaba region. Once again, farmers complain
about high input prices. Moreover, the water scarcity in this
village compels farmers to bore deep wells that cost around Rs
80,000. An owner–cultivator said that the water table was quite
high till very recently, but now one must dig as far down as 70
to 90 feet to draw water. The term *pani ka akaal* (water famine)
is widely used to describe this phenomenon. The belief that they
have fallen from the good old days also finds much resonance
here. In the words of an elderly villager, once gold would
flourish easily in the fields and now the land has become
infertile.

By all accounts, young people are leaving the village in
large numbers and their elders are not always standing in their
way. They all admit that agriculture does not really provide an
alternative for any of them. Even Satnam Singh, a substantial
landowner with about forty acres of land, could not keep his
sons in the village and two of them have gone abroad. One of
his sons, who works in Hong Kong, has invested in a market
complex not far from the village on the road to Amritsar.
Satnam Singh has been able to purchase tractors from his sons'
earnings abroad. In this way some of the foreign remittances
are also finding their way in to agriculture.

Some of the largest landholders we came across in Talhan,
like Son Singh, Manjit Singh, and Nirmal Singh, leased in
significant amounts of land. Manjit Singh, in fact, owns just
eight acres of land, but by leasing in fifty-two acres he operates
one of the largest farms in the village. In Khara, by contrast,
hardly any land is taken on lease. The reason probably is that
in Talhan the incidence of overseas migration is much higher

than in Khara and a family member who earns in dollars or pounds abroad helps make agriculture a working proposition at home.

Once again we find that many Jats and Scheduled Castes in Khara have taken to RNFE. Jat Sikhs, like Baljeet Singh who owns 5 acres of land, or Balwant Singh with only 3 acres, say there is no alternative but to seek RNFE. The number of SCs in dairy farming is quite large and both Jats and SCs have become industrial workers in sizeable numbers. They travel outside the village to Amritsar on a routine basis. It is not as if only the poorer farmers take to RNFE, Kartar Singh, who owns 22 acres of land, has set up a health club, managed by his son, on the Amritsar road.

In this village too castes are entering occupations that militate against the traditional views and prejudices of the region. Jats and SCs are almost equally represented in running grocery stores, tailoring, and embroidery shops. Two SCs and two Jats also own sweet shops. Interestingly, as many as nine Jats work as tailors, a profession that they would have unhesitatingly rejected even a few decades ago as being below their status. Once again, over thirty Jats in the village work as factory labourers.

Let us now move on to west UP.

Behirchi village (Saharanpur, western UP)

By now the lament about agriculture is all too familiar. Even the Tyagis, a prosperous agrarian community in west UP, complain that agricultural occupation is no longer what it used to be. As a Tyagi remarked: 'There was a time when the words of the Urdu poet, Ghagh, rang true when he said: '*Uttam kheti, madhyam baan; nishidh chakri, bhikh nida.*' Translated, it means that agriculture is the best, followed by business, salaried jobs, and beggary, in that order. They now however feel that priorities have changed as salaried jobs today pay much more, and one can be very prosperous in business. Indeed, the latest take on the poet Ghagh is as follows: '*Uttam chakri, madhyam baan,*

nikrisht krishi, bhik mahan.' Without losing too much of the
flavour these lines could be translated as: Regular employment
is the best, being a merchant is in the middle, farming
impoverishing, but begging for votes is the best of all. This is
not just a reversal of the earlier adage that privileges the farmer
on the occupational hierarchy, but it has an added sting in the
tail. The politician, who begs (*bhik*) for votes, is now on top of
the heap.

Soil erosion and the over-use of land are again listed as
some of the principal reasons for the decline in agricultural
prosperity. There is just no time for the land to 'relax', as a
Tyagi put it, echoing the complaint from Punjab farmers. The
ex-untouchable communities who are now Constitutionally
designated as Scheduled Castes resent the fact that they do not
get any water and have to, on occasions, purchase it from
Tyagis who are very reluctant to execute this transaction. The
Tyagis, on the other hand, complain that the SCs have received
huge handouts from the government, particularly during the
days when the SC leader, Mayawati, was chief minister of UP.
Instead of leveraging on such largesse, the Tyagis allege, the
SCs in their vicinity squandered their money in worthless
expenditure and marriages. They cite the case of Judda Singh,
a Harijan, who gave a motorcycle as dowry to his son-in-law.

Tyagis were quite quick to take advantage of the Green
Revolution. They invested in electric tube-wells, tractors,
improved varieties of sugarcane and wheat, as well as in fertilizers
and pesticides. They are still committed to agriculture, though
they realize that there are lucrative opportunities in other
sectors of the economy. As Tyagis have a near monopoly in the
ownership of agricultural machinery, they also rent out such
equipment to poorer farmers, even to SCs, but only after first
using them in their own fields.

Interestingly, a large number of Harijans work in a stud
farm that breeds horses. Once again, RNFE has little to do with
traditional occupations. The striking feature in the RNFE
picture of Behirchi is that quite unlike Punjab, where Jat
farmers are well represented in a wide variety of RNFE, Tyagis

are rarely found outside agriculture. This is an index of the resilience of traditional prejudices in Behirchi. Unlike the Jat Sikhs of Punjab, Tyagis do not want to muddy their hands in trifling non-farm jobs that might adversely affect their status. Sikhs are obviously not that conscious of occupations that are beneath their station. One finds a wide variety of castes, but not the Tyagis, working in brick-kilns and construction sites, pulling rickshaws, breeding horses, embroidering and tailoring, and running grocery stores and barbershops. Apart from two Tyagis in dairy farming, the Tyagis are loath to take up any village-based non-farm occupation.

In cities, Tyagis of course hold a variety of jobs, and some are even successful entrepreneurs. But none of that is to be found in Behirchi village. A Tyagi nurse-cum-maid looked after my late mother during her last years. This lady often resented the kind of work that her job compelled her to perform. She told me:

'I have not kept up with my family and friends in my village for I am ashamed of telling them what I do for a living. I would never work as a *dai* (a maid) if I had not become a widow. I had *dais* working for me when my husband was alive.'

Today her social circle and network is almost entirely limited to the contacts she has with the nursing agency that periodically finds her work for a commission.

Baijalpur village (Ballia district, east UP)

This village, with a population of about 3,500 people, is even more multi-caste than Behirichi. The Thakurs are the most prosperous caste in this village, but even the Yadavas are economically quite strong, and much more numerous than the Thakurs. Other poorer castes, ranging from the Harijans to the Rajbhars to the Dhobi and Nai, together constitute over two-thirds of the population. The SCs feel discriminated against in the village and are never invited by the upper castes to any of their ceremonies. As in Behirichi, the upper castes claim that the SCs have been spoilt and made indolent by government handouts.

The upper caste Thakurs are hardly to be found among those who seek off-farm occupations. Thakurs are in salaried jobs and in transportation. Yadavs, Rajbhars, and also Harijans are well represented in different non-farm jobs, but rarely in the salaried class. Brick-kilns as well as coolie jobs in sugar mills attract a lot of Rajbhars and Harijans. One does not however find local villagers in occupations such as running beauty parlours, or gymnasiums, or cable-television services, as one does in Punjab villages. In that sense, this village wears a much more traditional garb than the rural areas of Punjab. The aspirations of people too seem to be much more limited.

Comparing Punjab with UP

The differences between Punjab villages and Behirichi and Baijalpur are quite clear. The rich Jat peasants are in the main much more enterprising than their counterparts outside Punjab.[34] It, nevertheless, needs to be said that Jats are not in the main happy entrepreneurs. They believe that agriculture is their forte, and as that is a dying occupation, they are forced to branch out into other economic avenues. In Talhan, there was a strongly expressed view that the best thing to do was to somehow get enough money and go abroad, even if that meant selling their land. These Jat farmers argued that they would at least get money for the work they put in when they went abroad, unlike the situation in India. Many of them said that even if the famous entertainer Daler Mehndi was involved (as it was once alleged) in illegally smuggling people out of India to destinations in the West, he was doing the youth in Punjab a great service. One man in his late 30s said: 'Daler Mehndi is helping us to get out and the laws are stopping him. He is doing us a good turn.'

In addition, there was also a clear awareness that environmental degradation, particularly the depletion of soil nutrients, was a very imminent danger to agriculture. This aspect was widely recognized in the villages we visited both in Punjab and Uttar Pradesh. Water tables are going down, nitrogen is being leeched from the soil and, consequently, greater amounts of agricultural inputs have to be purchased. Some farmers even complained that the soil was being flogged too often with multiple crops but were unable to pull back any longer because of the constraints of circumstances. In every village we were told that the food tasted much better before the Green Revolution. That the Green Revolution brought greater agricultural production in comparison to earlier times seems to have been forgotten.

Non-farm employment, or RNFE, is very impressive both in numbers as well as in terms of scope. Once again it is not as if it is always a case of distress diversification. Some well-to-do people, particularly in Punjab, are in off-farm jobs as well as in enterprises that have little to do with farming. In the case of poorer villagers too, many of them find better-paid jobs outside agriculture.

In addition, there have been some instances of ex-Untouchables showing a great deal of enterprise. For example, we found SCs running sweetshops in Punjab with even Jats among their clientele. In villages outside Punjab, and particularly in Baijalpur, when SCs went outside agriculture for jobs they usually ended up performing various kinds of manual labour.

Unlike in UP, untouchability is not practised in stark terms, though Jats thoroughly despise castes such as the Adi Dharmis and Mazhabis. Thus, while there are indications that villages in the eastern regions of India are less dynamic than those in the north-west in shedding some of their values and prejudices, what is common in all instances is the general disenchantment with rural life. The ambition to leave the village for better prospects outside, or to stay on in the village but not to work on the land is too pronounced to overlook. It is also true that while RNFE attracts people from diverse castes, their location in the structure of employment outside the farm depends a great deal upon where they come from, and to the kinds of household to which they belong. What is also common is that the SCs are not without ambition, and in terms of RNFE they show a great degree of aggressiveness. In every village the SCs resent the treatment of the hitherto dominant castes, and have in most instances given up performing the menial tasks that were traditionally their lot, and which they believed, and rightly so, to be humiliating in character.

The Hollowed Village Economy

What I have so far said about RNFE from survey data and census statistics, as well as from my own empirical observations, leaves little doubt that agriculture is no longer quite the mainstay of the agrarian economy. Besides, the lessening importance of agriculture is accompanied by a general undermining of traditional values and practices that have origins in farming and in the closed village economy. The rural ethos that was once supposed to imbrue village life is not nearly as prominent today. There was a time, not very long ago, when a Jat farmer in Uttar Pradesh or Punjab would proudly proclaim that he would *not* trade his status as a tiller of the soil for anything else as this was the noblest of all occupations. However, even a quick look today would clearly reveal that this pride in being agriculturists has been considerably diminished.

Today the once proud agrarian castes seem to have lost their old swagger. Now they want an urban foothold, and would even condescend to taking up occupations in towns and cities that they would not deign to perform in their own villages.

The degree of rural transformation, particularly a deep sense of alienation, is not fully reflected in census figures, or in statistical surveys, though they provide us with useful indications that should encourage serious contemplation of the nature of the rural economy. However, in order to comprehend the depth of disenchantment that prevails in the villages, there is nothing like spending time in rural India collecting qualitative information. It is not that the traditional cultivator did not face problems in a variety of areas, having always lurched from crisis to crisis. Good monsoons brought floods, and bad monsoons brought droughts. A bumper crop of mangoes meant a glut on the market and falling prices. The failure of the onion crops too would bring tears. The artisanal nature of agriculture has always kept farmers, not knowing quite how to manage their economy, on tenterhooks.

This was however the only occupation they knew, and there was always the hope that should the elements work in their favour then nothing could be better. Today, even in green revolution areas, where there has been a spectacular increase in mechanization and chemical inputs, the despondency in rural homes is so thick that one could run a plough through it. In addition, the vagaries of the weather still afflict the farmer, and that is why the irregularity of electrical supply and the paucity of other infrastructural inputs can throw the best agricultural calculations out of gear. It is not surprising then that whenever the occasion arises, villagers are more than willing to up and leave for a future outside the mud walls of their homes, and in fields as distant from agriculture as industrial labour.

The village is shrinking as a sociological reality, though it still exists as a space. Nowhere else does one encounter this sense of despondency as one does in the rural regions of India. In urban slums there is squalor, there is filth and crime, but there is hope and the excitement that tomorrow might be quite different from today. It would be very hard to find a slum-dweller eager to trade in his crooked shanty for his old mud hut in the village.

Alongside the transformation in the village economy, the joint family is disappearing, the rural caste hierarchy is losing its tenacity, and the much-romanticized harmony of village life is now exposed for the sham it perhaps always was. If anything, perhaps Dr B.R. Ambedkar's analysis of the Indian village rings the truest of all when he said that the village was a cesspool of degradation, corruption, and worse. If village India was able to carry on in spite of all this in the past, it was because there was little option for most people, rich or poor, outside the confines of the rural space. That another world has opened up outside the village clearly threatens rural culture, but one must place that in the context of the hollowed-out rural economy.

The nature of intervention of modern democratic politics and economics in rural India has contributed to the complete loss of charisma of the rural way of life. With the abolition of landlordism and the introduction of adult franchise (the two necessarily go hand in hand), old social relations that dominated the countryside are today moribund, if not actually dead. The beginning of the downfall of rural institutions began with the degradation of agriculture and the subdivision of holdings. In a situation where roughly 85 per cent of landholdings are below five acres and about 63 per cent are below even three acres, villages can hold out little hope to their populace. What land reforms and land redistribution could not accomplish, demography and the subdivision of holdings have done to landownership.

Where are the big landlords? There are some, but they are few and far between. Does this however make the village an egalitarian utopia? Far from it! Medium-sized owner–cultivators contend against landless labourers, both economically and socially. While the rigidities of the caste systems no longer operate in their pristine form, caste prejudices and identities die hard. The stigma of tradition sits incubus-like on social relations even if the prescriptions of tradition cannot be followed today with equal facility. Other than the lack of economic opportunities, the nature of social relations in rural India drives many poorer castes and classes out of the village. Clearly, the poorer one is, the greater the temptation to up and leave the village before time runs out.Where landholdings are so fragmented there is little scope for agricultural regeneration. Planners would be happy if agricultural production could be sustained year after year, and elated if there is a modest increase of even two per cent. In 2003, there was in fact a negative growth-rate. In small plots there is always a preponderance of family labour and the Chayanovian logic of balancing drudgery and needs usually operates in such cases. However, for that to happen without emotional philippics, the needs horizon must curve within the village perimeter. Only then is the family farm a precious gift to be harvested in perpetuity. Needs now have however escalated and the family farm is no longer what it was earlier cut out to be.

The Fragile Economy of the Owner–Cultivator

Just because a majority of Indians live in villages, it would be hasty to conclude from this that the village determines India's national culture. Most of the political debates in India do not have a rural character at all. This is quite surprising given the fact that a large number of politicians in Parliament and the legislatures have rural origins. Occasionally a Mahender Singh Tikait or a Nanjudaswamy will stir things up in the villages, but in the main, the political ideologies that inform most of the national parties do not have a strong rural component. The usual concessions are made in terms of subsidies or minimum price for agricultural produce, but the kernel of political ideologies do not reflect any major preoccupation with the village. Even Laloo Yadav and Mulayam Singh Yadav hardly evince rural concerns. Playing the arithmetic of caste does not necessarily mean committing oneself to the chemistry of the village.

Yet, because it is also a question of arithmetic, politicians often vie against one another in projecting themselves as champions of the beleaguered owner–cultivators. Today in political discourses nationwide, very little concern is shown to agricultural labourers. Even here however there is a strong element of political gamesmanship at work. In the name of protecting the poor farmer, political parties have in general opposed the institution of tax on agricultural incomes. The small owner–cultivator has not been taken in by these political moves. As many of them have repeatedly told me, this tax concession makes no difference to them as their incomes would be below the taxable amount anyway. According to them, the exemption on agricultural tax is to help the rich entrepreneurial farmers and those in cities who want to escape the burden of taxation by diversifying in a limited sense into agricultural production, or in animal husbandry, or poultry farming, and the like.

At the same time, politicians are alive to the fact that the opening up of agricultural imports would ruin the owner–cultivators who comprise substantial numbers. As this would lead to political and economic instability, they are obviously cautious about it. Even so, rural activists like Sharad Joshi of Shetkari Sangathan welcomes an open market. Joshi believes that the peasants in Maharashtra would do very well if they could take their produce abroad. Sharad Joshi's calculations should be closely examined, for his bookkeeping is obviously less than careful. It is difficult to imagine that the Indian farmer could compete with the West, where agriculture is industry. Indeed, this is precisely why India constantly opposes moves in international forums to let transnational market dynamics control Indian agriculture.

While the owner–cultivators are politically protected, their futures are left unplanned. In 2000, the National Agricultural Policy formally recognized that agriculture has become 'a relatively unrewarding profession', and that efforts to revive it have to be multi-pronged. They have identified some alternatives to straight agriculture, such as horticulture, floriculture, and the cultivation of aromatic and medicinal plants, apart from animal husbandry and fisheries. While these recommendations look good on paper, vast infrastructural deficits have to be first overcome. Narayanamoorthy points out that even after the government invested Rs 35 million (at current prices) in the so-called Accelerated Irrigation Benefit Programme, the area under irrigation remained unchanged between 1995-96 and 2003-04. Also, fixed-capital expenditure by the public sector in agriculture has been declining since the liberalization of the economy began in 1990.[35]

Institutional credit to agriculture has also declined from the 1980s onwards leading to greater reliance on informal sources of credit with their usurious interest rates.[36] To begin with, the conditions of owner–cultivators do not in general encourage them to make heavy investments in chancy cash crops. Tens of thousand of farmers, particularly in Maharashtra, Andhra Pradesh, and Punjab (all prosperous regions of India) have committed suicide to escape their debt burdens. There is no clear, unambiguous statistic on this but the scale of suicides in rural India has sent shock waves across India. Those farmers little realized that they would have to pay with their lives for seeking a better economic future. Predictably, and quite logically, farmers who commit suicide, roughly 2,000 in 2007, are the ones who are ambitious agriculturists and risk takers, which is why they are almost invariably cotton farmers.[37] These farmers are frequently unable to realize their aspiration because agricultural prices rise and fall for a number of unpredictable factors. Cotton is probably the most susceptible as its needs are very tightly calibrated. Too much water will damage the crop, too little pesticides will ruin it in no time and, besides, it is also susceptible to international price fluctuations. What adds to the farmers' woes is the lack of basic facilities, such as transportation systems, cold storages, modern silos, and a sound marketing framework. As the structures within which farmers operate are unrelenting, once things begin to wrong for them matters only keep getting worse.

But most of all villages lack a sound economic base from which to launch into more enterprising brands of agriculture. Small holdings tempt high risks, but the hope of making it over the debt curve is far too tempting for those who had seen better lives as agriculturists. As a Punjab agriculturist said to me: 'When Basmati rice was at Rs 1000 per quintal we thought we should get into it. By the time we did it had plummeted to Rs 600, and now it is much lower, and we have been economically finished.' Therefore, if value has to be added to agricultural production, either by luring farmers into producing high-priced cash crops, or into agro-industry, vast infrastructural deficits must be overcome. Small farmers may have the aspirations to participate in these ventures but are so far too feeble to realize many of their dreams.

Without infrastructural backup, which only the State can provide, the hope that the production of non-food crops will revive the village is not very realistic. Regardless of how feasible this strategy will eventually be, there is no gainsaying the fact that agricultural production of food can, on current form, hardly be romanticized or valorized for its own sake any longer. Though the majority of Indians live in villages, the village leaves little impress upon the national culture today.

If anything, the most vivid picture of contemporary rural distress emerges from figures on rural indebtedness. We find here a most alarming situation. According to the fifty-ninth round of the National Sample Survey, 48.6 per cent of farmers across the country are in debt. As if this were not bad enough, in Andhra Pradesh three out of four farmers are in debt.[38] It is all the more tragic that under these circumstances, instead of reaching out to help, many leading politicians are labelling suicide victims as 'mad'.[39]

As much as 64 per cent of the debt that farmers incur is from non-institutional sources, of which the bulk is from moneylenders.[40] Most of these loans are either to meet marriage expenses or to cope with medical emergencies. Formal sources account for 27 per cent of the loan, and is usually used to augment land or for house repairs. A paltry 7 per cent comes from NGO-sponsored saving schemes and others.[41] As informal sources of credit are so vital for the poor, they are very often in some form of debt as the rates of interest for such loans go up to 120 per cent per annum. Andhra Pradesh and Tamil Nadu top the list of the states where farmers borrow the most from these moneylenders.[42] Indebtedness of this magnitude propels desperate farmers to desperate measures, which is why so many commit suicide.

The waiver of loans by the State happen from time to time to win votes, but such a measure only addresses formal bank loans. The farmer's indebtedness to moneylenders and sundry input agents still remain to be paid at high interest rates. When bank loans are written off by the government, the interest cycle starts again. Agriculturists go to banks for loans which, in due course of time, they find difficult to pay back. So they return to informal sources to succour themselves, and soon they are in the same unenviable situation all over again.

7

THE CHANGING OF AGRICULTURE
WHAT FARMERS REALLY WANT

The belief that India is an overwhelmingly agricultural society must be examined and revised. The sectoral distribution of Rural Net Domestic Product for agriculture is down nearly 18 per cent since 1970-71[1] as workforce changes in India do not match the production structure of its economy.[2] The NSS points out that the number of rural people working in urban India has doubled between 1987-88 and 1993-94. Also, the annual GDP growth in agriculture in value-added terms has declined alarmingly from 3.5 per cent in the 1980s, to an unbelievable negative growth-rate in 2000-01.[3] Trends also show that urban households earn more than their counterparts in villages, and that this disparity is growing. In a 1975-76 survey, urban households earned on an average 1.82 times more than rural households and today the figure is closer to 2.1 per cent.[4] Though there is a noticeable increase in inequality in urban India, poverty levels are on the whole much lower there than in the countryside.[5]

We cannot easily account for all the factors that have led to the process of cultural alienation from the village; nevertheless we can maintain that the relative stagnation of the rural economy has significantly contributed to this process. This can be gauged not only from the growth-rates between industry and agriculture, but also from the remarkable on-going shift in the number of agricultural workers of all descriptions.

Clearly, the village economy is no longer able to support farmers, and this is what makes the city so alluring. Villagers want to be where the bright lights are as futures can no longer be planned on agricultural earnings. Gross morphological figures can also confirm the draw of the town. Agriculture forms approximately 20 per cent of GDP and it is bound to get even less. The number of hospitals in urban areas is double that of rural India though about 70 per cent of the population lives in villages. Predictably also, facilities at the household level for drinking water and electricity are much higher in urban areas. Over 75 per cent of urban households are electrified as against only 30 per cent for rural India. Add to this the fact that urban incomes are on an average nearly double of rural earnings and the case for leaving the village becomes very strong.

Of course, the few remaining wealthy landed people often have considerable political leverage in villages and form a vested interest group. However, unlike in the past, they are neither significant in numbers, nor, barring a few exceptions, with holdings large enough to employ landless labourers over the better part of the year. Some of them live in cities most of the year, while others, financed by foreign remittances and non-farm enterprises, recreate an affluent urban ambience in their rural setting. In stark contrast to the poorer villagers with urban aspirations, when the rural rich engage with the outside world they do so from a position of relative strength. Yet, they too see their future outside the village, or in interacting with the town in enterprises that require both rural and urban inputs.

The culture surrounding agriculture must be understood against this background. It is not a stable culture. History has not left behind a consistent legacy, nor does rural culture have a temporal overhang that is safely cantilevered on present commitments. Agriculture is an economic residue that generously accommodates non-achievers resigned to a life of sad satisfaction.

The villager is as bloodless as the rural economy is lifeless. From rich to poor, the trend is to leave the village and, if that entails going abroad, then so be it. The proportionate decline in the number of small and marginal farming households is most striking, and this is also because they comprise the majority in rural India. Against such a background, the spate of suicides among farmers in India is cause for grief but not surprise.[6]

Re-conceptualizing the Indian Village

The village has often been essentialized as an idyllic locale where community ties bind the population together. These villages were supposedly little republics, timeless and unchanging, engagingly obdurate in their unchanging equilibrium. Such conceptions counterpose the supposed primal innocence of the Indian village to the harsh and immoral life of the cities. The essential being 'authentically' lives in the village. Charles Metcalfe and James Mill were among the early proponents of this view. Even Marx, despite his insistence on dialectical movement, accepted this 'village republic' idea of rural India. Dynasties may come and go, ambitious monarchs and potentates may fight great wars, but the steady hum of village life is scarcely ever disturbed.[7] Colonial administrators saw the village as the atom of Indian civilization, no less[8] and much of this can be found in Gandhi's exhortation that the Indian village be revived to its earlier authentic existence. He, of course, recognized many of the shortcomings of rural life, but nursed the political goal of returning the village to its pristine ways.

Gandhi's ideas on the village did not pass unchallenged in the years leading up to the national movement. Peasant leaders, like Swami Sahajanand Saraswati, underlined the harshness of village life and saw villages as places where the landlords plundered poor peasants and lived off the fat of the land.[9] The much-written-about *jajmani* system, of labour exchange in kind along lines of caste hierarchy, was clearly a romanticized vision but 'the power wielded by the dominant caste was real'.[10] They were the kingpin patron of the village,[11] with village life, politics, economics, and rituals included, pivoting around them. The gradual de-escalation of the role of the patron[12] was seen with the breakdown of patron-client relationships which may have been initiated by the patron with the introduction of cash crops and newer forms of cultivation.

One of the earlier efforts in taking agrarian change seriously from a sociological perspective was in the renowned volume *Village India*.[13] A select group of distinguished anthropologists dismissed the idea of Indian villages as being so many self-contained republics and went on to point out how the great culture of Hinduism interacts with the little cultures of the villages, a process in which both are transformed. During a forty-year study on two villages, a growing relationship was found between town and country. Even till the late 1960s and early 1970s, the importance of farming, accompanied by the incidence of hired labour, even though mechanization had made some inroads into agriculture,[14] could be seen. There was not that much evidence of non-farm occupations, apart from the number of tea stalls that had sprung up in the villages studied.[15] The poor suffered a definite fall in their standards of living,[16] though the rich peasants had certainly grown richer with the opening up of the jaggery market.[17] Otherwise, however, the villages were not greatly influenced by the world outside. Their merchants bought from outside but sold wholly within. Even their university graduates were not expected to 'exert much influence over village affairs'.[18] In spite of these changes, it appears that the villages examined over this longitudinal time study still looked up to agriculture as their economic mainstay. This is despite the worsening of the conditions of a large number of poorer farmers in the fifteen-year interim between the first and second studies.

Tensions between agrarian classes soon became the topic of many academic writings, somewhat eroding the earlier partiality towards detailing rural quiescence.[19] Thus, for some time academic writings have refrained from describing village India as a quiet, idyllic haven. However, they saw all tensions as endogenously generated by contradictory economic interests. Therefore, they believed that the resolutions of these tensions and conflicts were also endogenous and to be sought within the village. Such a slant would no longer be convincing in an examination of rural India. Agrarian exploitation and the near complete dependence on agriculture no longer characterize the countryside. Besides, unlike what was said to prevail in tradition, we do not find a close relationship between caste and occupation. Traditionally, caste and village were in synergy. If the village was said to be tranquil, it was argued that the caste ideology was responsible for it. True or false, such a division of labour no longer prevails in rural India.[20]

The Imagined Village

Rural life was portrayed in a variety of ways in the past. For example, Bimal Roy's *Do Bigha Zameen*, a 1950s classic, is a moving account of a poor peasant struggling as a rickshaw-puller in the harsh environs of a metropolis to enable his family in his village to survive. The film begins with a song in praise of the rain gods, but when the monsoon fails, the protagonist of the film has no choice but to seek work in the city in order to pay off his debt to the moneylender. Later, Shyam Benegal, ideologically committed to a radical revision of a placid village commune, brought to the fore the colours of rural violence, largely perpetrated in his films by landlords or their henchmen. If films such as *Mirch Masala* or *Nishant* vividly portray exploitation in rural India, other films such as Manoj Kumar's *Upkaar* glorify the village, the agriculturalists, and the rural way of life in general. In these visions of arcadia, the village is a homogeneous community with a thriving moral economy. The agriculturalist is the salt of the earth in more ways than one, and Mother India inexhaustibly yields food in her villages for her millions. The hit song, *Is desh ki dharti, sona ugle, ugle herey moti* (this land from which sprouts gold, diamonds and pearls) exemplifies this sentiment.

The city is where the undesirables live with their crass and immoral ways; it is the home of the black marketer and the swindler. Villagers do not drink, smoke or play the fool in nightclubs as city people do. *Khottey Sikke* and *Adalat* are two other films that advanced a similar message. *Lagaan*, the mega-hit of 2002, also depicted the village as a community, where everybody pulled as one against the extortionate demands of British administrators in colonial times. The departure from the earlier 'rural' films was that it presented the indigenous upper crust with sympathy and did not demonize urban life. A clear signal of changing tastes!

The opposition between town and country, or between India and Bharat (Manoj Kumar was called Bharat in at least one of his movies), was a fairly recurrent theme when Indian cinema dealt with the village in the past. In Bimal Roy's other great classic *Devdas*, the hero Devdas lives in idyllic enchantment with his lover in his village. When Devdas is forbidden from marrying the woman he loves he takes off for the city of Calcutta, and there, with dogged determination, he succumbs to alcohol. In Mehboob Khan's *Mother India*, the heroine searches for her husband who has run off to the city and consequently can hardly keep track of his disintegrated character.[21] Today, the myth of a bucolic India no longer attracts viewers. It is difficult to recall a film made after the late 1990s that extols the Indian village, or glorifies it at the expense of the city. Such counter positions no longer seem to resonate among rural or urban cinema-goers.

Indeed, even the little cultures of the previous generation are lost today. In earlier decades the importance of agriculture was profoundly felt by villagers. This was reflected in their songs, in their tales, and in their many proverbs that encapsulated popular wisdom regarding ways to forecast rain or drought or to pick the time to sow crops. For example, the following ditty tells a farmer how to read the monsoon cloud:

Pacchura badal purab ko jaye,
Moti pakave patari khaye

(If the cloud is moving from west to east then it is not going to rain, and so one should have thin and not thick bread.)

Or take the following verse:

> *Sawan maas bahe purwai,*
> *Bargha bechi bisaho gaai*

(If in the month of Sawan [a monsoon month] the wind is blowing easterly then a farmer should sell his bulls to purchase cows as there will be no rain and little need to plough the fields.)

Then there are also straight pieces of advice:

> *Jau genhu boven paanch paser*
> *Matar kai bigha theesri ser*
> *Boven chana paseri teen*
> *Teen ser bigha jaunhari keen.*

(A farmer should sow twenty-five seers [one seer is roughly one pound] of seeds of wheat and barley, thirty seers of pea-seed, fifteen seers of gram and three seers of jowar seeds.)

These and many other aphorisms were widely known in the villages of Uttar Pradesh in the past. We had to go to elderly people, those above sixty years of age, to collect some of these sayings and verses as the younger villagers were not particularly conversant with this tradition, though some of them knew snatches of these ditties. This is probably because agriculture has changed considerably with the Green Revolution and with the introduction of chemical and mechanical inputs, which make these words of wisdom somewhat redundant. In the past, an elderly farmer in Baijalpur (UP) said: 'Nobody would start ploughing on a Sunday, but today this is not an important consideration. As many of us have to rent a tractor it all depends on when our turn comes up. So these restrictions do not apply any longer.'

The New Rural Politics

Agrarian politics also tells us that the imagined village of the well-to-do urban Indian is quite far from its ground reality. The villager is understood as being rooted to the soil, not very rational, given to superstition, and devoted to upholding the traditions of the joint family. In politics, the villager is also considered to be pre-political and pre-ideological, even if the reality of rural power struggles periodically makes it to the front pages of newspapers.[22] For these reasons the farmer is said to be backward, and his methods equally dated. At the same time, they believe that the village ought to be made attractive to live in, probably figuring in their mind's eye the European villages that they see in films or in their snapshot vacations across the Western hemisphere.

Much is being written today about peasant power in India. It is true that since the days of zamindari abolition there has been a growing assertion of owner–cultivators. Even so, for over two decades after Independence, agrarian politics was largely centred on agitations of agricultural labour demanding higher wages and better social conditions. In struggles of this kind many political parties with a national presence played a significant role through their mass fronts. These demands of agricultural labourers took many forms: from land to the tiller, to a full-scale attack on the skewed structure of landownership.

Those were the days when there were still a few substantial landowners in India. That movie however ended long ago, and anyway the script was overdue for a major makeover. By the 1980s it was clear that landless labourers had no viable future in the economy of the village. The increasing incidence of family farms made hired labour less critical for agricultural production than earlier. Where there was substantial agricultural prosperity in the years following the Green Revolution, such as Punjab and Haryana, labour could be hired from among migrants who came from east India and who were ready to work for pitiable wages. Today, many of these migrants have settled in Punjab and have raised families in this state. Their children often do not know the mother tongue of their parents nor have they ever visited their homes. Their adoption of the overt symbols of the Punjabi way of life is so complete that unless one engages with them in long conversations, their Bihari or

Jharkhandi origins would never surface. They have grown their beards, wear turbans, speak Punjabi fluently and unselfconsciously, and have the same kind of body language as the local Sikh. This is not unlike the second generation NRI who has little familiarity, or even desire, to strike up a relationship with the home of his forebears.

In this context it needs also to be borne in mind that in many parts of India, particularly in Punjab and west UP, those who worked earlier as agrestic labour are no longer willing to work in the same capacity. The Harijans and the Adi Dharmis of UP and Punjab respectively, have more or less set their minds against labouring on others' fields. In a significant way the large-scale emergence of family farms also crystallized this preference as the need for hired field labour dried up. Cumulatively, this led to the diminution of the agricultural labourer's presence in rural India. By the time the 1980s came around, agricultural labourer movements that involved huge rural unions and supra-local organizers became more or less a thing of the past.

Now it was the turn of Mahendra Singh Tikait and Nanjudaswamy to strike out for the owner–cultivators. This happened in the mid-1980s, by when it was clear that large farms were on their way out, and with them full-time agricultural labourers were also becoming extinct. It was now the age of the small farmer, the owner–cultivator who toiled largely with the assistance of family labour.

In these agrarian mobilizations it was clearly stated that anyone who did not own land was not really a farmer. The farmers' movement led by the Bharatiya Kisan Union in Uttar Pradesh, Haryana, and Punjab made this point very clear. Their list of demands did not include agricultural wages. The paramount issues for them were the cost of electricity, the level of subsidies and the floor price for agricultural produce. As far as these farmers were concerned, agricultural labourers did not exist at all. This is not surprising as their interaction with hired labour lasted at best for a fortnight during each harvesting season. Outside of this short period their family labour more than sufficed.

Even as the owner–cultivators were becoming restive, a new configuration was taking place in rural politics. In the past, when agricultural labourers mattered most in rural uprisings the target was always the local landlord, *jotedar*, or *thanedar*. With the shift to the owner–cultivator brand of agitation the enemy was no longer local, but supra-local, even the government of India. Not surprisingly, the BKU and Kshetkari Sangathan were continually moving into the cities to impress the validity of their demands upon the public and recalcitrant politicians. Thus, while the interests of these movements were still agricultural in the main, the nature of their activism established

Bharatiya Kisan Union leader Mahendra Singh Tikat addressing small owner cultivators behind the Red Fort in Delhi.

a strong link between town and country.[23] Concurrently, the same category of owner–cultivators demanded reservations in urban jobs and educational institutions. The Mandal Recommendations of 1990 were perfectly timed to coincide with the urban aspirations of cultivating castes, such as the Yadavas, Gujars, and Jats, by providing them with reservations in government jobs and educational institutions. An urban job was clearly a prize catch for communities that had prided themselves for generations in being farmers first and last.

What Farmers Really Want

If one were to ask agriculturists what policies would most benefit them then the answers would vary significantly. Many in Punjab, especially the Jat Sikhs, would like to emigrate and want the procedure for leaving the country simplified as much as possible. When I asked them why they did not choose to move to some city in India they said that in India, no matter how hard one works, there is little money to be made.

Generally, owner–cultivators seek a good floor price for their crops, but increasingly they advocate some form of insurance that will act as a security buffer against the vicissitudes of market prices for cash crops. They want electricity on time, and even said that if they were assured of adequate and regular electricity then they would not mind paying for it. They argue that the input prices are far too high, in spite of government subsidies, and that is why they see no future for themselves and for their children in the village. It was indeed very curious to hear Jat Sikhs in Punjab complaining insistently that their condition in the village was miserable. I am contrasting this to the optimism and boisterousness with which I had associated them with barely fifteen years earlier.

The landless villager has few demands regarding the village other than improved living facilities: more water, electricity, and schools. They are however keenest that the government encourage the setting up of factories near their villages in order to enable their children to earn a decent and regular income. Any mention of setting up industry in the vicinity of their homes always elicits the enthusiastic approval of villagers, whether or not they are owner–cultivators. Most villagers aspire to send their children outside the village even though some of them may admit that it is perhaps too late for them to personally make the transition. I was impressed by the fact that the poorer villagers, especially the Dalits, were very keen to leave the village to earn non-agricultural incomes. They said that their eagerness to break free from agriculture and find jobs in other sectors stems from the fact that in cities and towns they will at least be assured some money at the end of the day. As one Mazhabi Dalit Sikh said: 'I am a poor rickshaw-puller, but I come back every night with my earnings in my pocket.' To work for an owner–cultivator (or *jameedar*) is not very reliable as they do not pay up on time, and when they do, it is often not the full wage.

It is also quite clear that the Adi Dharmis and Harijans are much more optimistic and enthusiastic about their future in non-rural settings than the Valmikis and Mazahabi Sikhs (the so-called scavenger castes). Harijans and Adi Dharmis are economically better off than the scavenger castes and they also have a fair degree of understanding of the provisions of the Constitution and of the political and economic opportunities that are now available to them. They seem to have a clear edge in terms of non-rural connections and income. This makes them more aggressive in their general demeanour towards the established and better-off farmers. This is reflected not only in the way they bargain with them during harvesting time, but culturally too they are distancing themselves from either mainstream Sikhism or Hinduism, as the case may be. Also, when it comes to searching for non-farm jobs they are easily much more successful than those Dalits who are economically and socially below them.

Therefore, in terms of the many diacritics of village life, much seems to be changing in rural culture. Old taboos against holding certain kinds of jobs are disappearing; the caste system does not operate the way it did in tradition, though there is a strong assertion of caste pride and caste identity. Untouchability is not widely practised although there are pockets of upper caste intransigence. On the economic front, even prosperous landowners seek a future outside the village or in non-farm enterprises. We did not find many instances of satisfied farmers. Most have grievances against the government for not providing them with better amenities. The most striking feature of all is the growing incidence of RNFE across the board. Without the mediation of tea leaves and crystal balls it is easy to predict the deepening of this trend in the days to come.

Whither Agricultural Policy

In the years following Independence, India launched the anti-zamindari (or anti-feudal) campaign, which for all its faults paid rich dividends by taking the democratic impetus deep into the countryside. This drive was accompanied in many parts of India by land-to-the-tiller campaigns, which were most successful in West Bengal's much acknowledged 'Operation Barga' programme. In the late 1960s, the Green Revolution was launched in India, and this initiative was backed by setting up a number of agricultural universities in India where basic crop research would be conducted. By all accounts, the Green Revolution has run its course today. This can be clearly seen in the falling rates of growth in agriculture. In such a scenario no agricultural policy is in place to give a clear vision to the future of rural India. Regardless of party affiliations, there is a curious absence of any serious considerations anywhere on this subject. Yes, there are fire-fighting missions that cancel electricity dues or provide greater subsidies, but where is the policy?

The absence of a clearly formulated agricultural programme is evident when one talks to members of the so-called social élite and opinion-makers.[24] When asked how rural India should be developed, they are most frequently without answer. Sometimes they say that land-ceilings should be raised, or that the farmers should be encouraged not just to produce crops but to add value to them. When asked how this value should be added the answers vary, with suggestions ranging from producing cash crops more intensively to connecting farmers to agro-industry. As one respondent said: 'Farmers should not just grow wheat but produce wheat flakes too.' How this is to be accomplished, and what form of infrastructural deficits must be surmounted to do this are not at all clear.

There are also those among the social elite and opinion-makers who believe that genetically modified crops would provide the answer, but they admit that India is not ready for that yet as we do not know the consequences of such innovations. Some of them, however, add that if India could gain so much by the Green Revolution then the Gene Revolution could also be of much positive value. When I asked senior members of the ruling BJP and of the Congress how they could make the Gene Revolution a reality they did not seem to have a worked out policy for this. A senior Congress leader said quite ruefully: 'We really have nothing to give to the agriculturists. What we say therefore is 'Congress *ke haath, garib ke saath*'.[25] I know it is unsatisfactory, but unfortunately we have nothing substantial to offer.'

The social elite and opinion-makers, including political personalities, instinctively reach out to globalization and industry as the pacesetters of India's development. They rarely think of the village, and if they do it is without any comprehensive framework. To summarize, we can place their views in the following categories:

- raise land ceiling
- encourage cash crops
- integrate agriculture with agro-industry

As all this reflects, there is no sustained formulation of an agricultural policy. Much of these views are off-the-cuff, popular conceptions of what agriculturists want. Most of them are convinced that a villager in India today is dearly tied to the countryside. When they are forced to think of rural India they imagine that if somehow villagers could be made to stay in the village that would not just solve economic problems but also bring the villager a great deal of happiness. That is why they imagine agriculture as industry, when the facts on the ground hardly warrant such an assumption. Only four members of the social elite that I interviewed admitted that villagers would prefer to live in cities today. One of them however hastily added that this would not be the correct thing for them to do.

The issue of raising the land ceiling is not a viable option, either politically or in resolving the pressure on agrarian holdings. Neither can cash crops be encouraged as small farmers primarily depend on what they produce on their minuscule plots to feed themselves. Cash crops are also notorious for fluctuations and pest attacks, which are clear disincentives for poor cultivators. Under such conditions, integrating agriculture with industry and linking small and marginal agriculturists to the supply chain are not feasible either.

The major problem afflicting villages today is the minuscule size of landholdings that dominate the countryside. These holdings are not economical, but small and marginal farmers continue to operate them. This is because these holdings are all they own and they do not want to risk losing them by leasing them out. The 'land to the tiller' policy, which was so useful to them in the past, might now help to dispossess them of what little they own.

Ironically, when the 'land to the tiller' law was promulgated soon after Independence it was meant to protect the small farmer and sharecropper. Partly owing to the success of this drive, the holdings have become smaller and more numerous. In West Bengal, where 'Operation *Barga*' (or, sharecropper) was a major success the average landholding size is among the smallest. This policy was needed at that time to clip the wings of erstwhile landlords, and to that extent it has been a success. Landlords of the kind we read of in history books right up to the mid-1950s no longer exist in significant numbers to make a difference. Over the years the area leased in as a ratio of the total operated area has fallen dramatically from 10.70 per cent during 1960-61 to only 6.5 per cent in 1992.[26] To a large measure, therefore, sharecropping is history.

However, as we encounter the possibility of its modern reincarnation in the shape of contract farming and as the boot is now on the other foot, it pinches. Will the 'land to the tiller' law rob cultivators of the little they own and transfer it to large operators, some of whom may have bases outside the village, or as in the case of the multinational, even outside the country? In some cases, as several farmers told me, they would rather leave the land fallow than lease it out for fear they may not get it back.

The issue of security for the poor cultivator when contracting their land to large-scale operators has, by and large, remained unaddressed, but it will not go away. In the meanwhile, already some major companies such as Syngenta, Cargill, Hindustan Lever, ITC, Pepsi/Fritolay, and A.M. Todd have entered the agricultural sector and have had modest success in contract farming. Predictably, however almost all such contractual relations have been with the larger farmers.[27] Unlike the small owner–cultivator, the bigger farmers are powerful enough to secure themselves against the threat of losing the land they have contracted out. Data clearly indicates that output is much greater in contract farming, even so only about 15 per cent of the land is devoted to it, highlighting that even the better-off landowners are afraid of risking it all in contract farming by betting entirely on the market.[28]

That leads to the question of what has been done in terms of policy? The Ministry of Agriculture in its *Annual Report of 2006-07* has provided a 'model' law, and not a real one, to provide institutional structures that will support and develop contract farming. Opportunities for such projects are mentioned in fairly optimistic terms, but there is no actual legal framework on the ground. The government has recently formulated the Agricultural Produce Marketing Committee (APMC) Act, which was circulated to all the states for their suggestions. However, as agriculture is a state subject this model Act is only suggestive in nature. The Act hopes to bring under its ambit regulations that will not make small farmers vulnerable to the big players. Crop insurance has also been suggested in this context[29] but there is still no established State policy regarding contract farming.

An effort to bring small farmers within the ambit of contract farming would entail large numbers of contracts in order to make such an operation meaningful. That is why it is so urgent to help marginal and small landholders with legal safeguards so that they can turn in their land for contract farming without fear of wholly alienating that asset.

Further, there are no established norms regarding the obligations on either side when they enter into a contractual relationship in agriculture. According to an official of a large local subsidiary of a multinational:

'When the market price is higher than the price we agreed upon at the time of the contract, the farmer will calmly sell his produce elsewhere. We have no legal recourse under such circumstances. It could also be the case that only a part of the produce will be given to us and the rest is concealed for sale in the open market on the plea that the crop was poor this season for a whole set of reasons.'

The small farmer has a contradictory complaint:

'If the market price falls, then the contractors do not take our produce by condemning it as substandard. We can do nothing about it. Further, they do not pay in time and we have to keep running to their offices to get our bills passed. There are forms to be filled, and receipts to be attached, and a whole set of formalities to go through before we can see our money. Sometimes, these offices are far away so we have to spend money and time to get to those places.'

It is fairly clear that if contract farming were made a viable option for small farmers, it would help them in a number of ways. To begin with, they can, as is done in Europe, lease out their holdings to big operators, use the income as a backup and move to urban centres. Second, once contract farming becomes a safe proposition, land that has remained fallow for want of cultivation can be put back into use. Third, as operations will now be at a much higher level, crop yields too will be greater and over time the small landowner can hope to earn higher returns from leasing out his land. Finally, if land records were to be maintained properly then that too would lend security to small farmers and aid the cause of large-scale contract farming.

Today records are often non-specific and are not all kept up-to-date and small farmers are afraid to leave their land for extended periods of time without leaving a relative or parent at home. This fear not only hinders mobility but also adds to the burden of maintaining uneconomic holdings.

The National Agricultural Policy as it stands today is largely a document full of good intentions but with no practical import. The policy document of 2000, after accepting that agriculture has become an 'unrewarding occupation' only lists a number of things that the government would like to do and should do, but not what it has done. It recognizes the need to reclaim fallow land, rationally utilize water resources (there is no nation-level scheme yet for water-harvesting), sensitize farmers to integrated nutrients and pest management systems, raise the productivity of rain-fed and irrigated crops, encourage horticulture and animal husbandry, and so on. The National Seeds Policy (2002) also hopes to establish a Plants Varieties and Farmers' Rights Protection Authority (PVP), a National Gene Fund, incentives to farmers for contributing to exciting new seeds, a 'Seed Village Scheme', and lots more.[30]

The imagination of State planners has been exercised to the full and nothing is omitted from the wish list. However, while all this might sound promising to credulous ears, they make little sense to the villagers. They are, therefore, left with stark alternatives: either stay home in perpetual misery or take a chance and head for the cities.

8

FROM VILLAGE TO VICINAGE

A RURAL LOOK AT URBAN INDIA

When an Indian farmer sets out on most mornings with his lunch pail he is not heading to his handkerchief-sized plot. He bends his knees instead towards the bus stop or in the direction of the crossroads just outside his village. He is out looking for a job and hopes against hope that there is a labour contractor somewhere who is also looking for him. These non-farm uncertainties are the everyday stuff in the life of a so-called NSS 'farmer'. If in the past this farmer relied on the caprices of the rain gods, today he looks to the jobber who might pick him up for the day, or just as randomly, the man next to him. Tomorrow may be his day, but maybe not. Who can predict the rain?

Who is a Farmer?

Voltaire famously remarked that our definitions should be accurate before we enter into a discussion. An important reason why State interventions in agriculture lurch from one band-aid solution to another is because definitional lapses of key terms go unnoticed even at the highest administrative levels. Consequently, State initiatives on important national issues lead even the most ardent policy maker astray.

The National Sample Survey, for instance, defines a farmer 'as a person who possessed some land and was engaged in agricultural activities on any part of that land during the 365 days preceding the date of the survey'. The problem is with the phrase 'during the past 365 days'. This is a very generous definition of a farmer because even if an individual works for one day or a few hours in a day in the past 365 days he is listed as a farmer.[1]

All too often such minor details are either overlooked or artfully inserted to make life easy for the data-gatherers. If the question had been more specific then the survey official would have to pause to obtain the information that is relevant instead of just whipping out the questions one after another.

The figure that over 60 per cent of villagers engage in agriculture would have to undergo serious downsizing if the word 'for' were inserted instead of 'during'. This too is not a good definition as it would then exclude perhaps all those who live in rural India. Clearly, getting a measure of who is a farmer is not such an easy task after all.

Agriculture is just not the mainstay of the rural economy in large swathes of village India. This is not so much because urban India has attracted the simple folks away to a life of dissolution and worse, but because the scope of agriculture has been hollowed from within. When I ask a villager what his occupation is then in all likelihood he may say that he is a farmer. He may have also worked on his land at some time during the past 365 days. When however I return to him in the evening I discover that he has done all manner of things other than farming in the intervening hours. This indeed is the picture day after day, with a few breaks in between. Even so, this individual would be classified as a 'farmer' in the NSS.

Was this man lying when I asked him about his occupation? Was he purposely misleading us crusaders so that he could go on living among the heathens? The problem actually lies with my question and not with his answer. When this villager said he was a farmer he was not telling us what he actually does, but of the job he actually knows. He has grown up on a family farm and he is aware of what the winds and the clouds have to tell him, and of how much water and chemicals are required; but he spends just a fraction of his time on the fields.

The downgrading of agriculture in the rural economy has forced villagers to seek alternative sources of employment wherever they can find them. So not only has the contribution of agriculture to GDP fallen over the years but even the total land under cultivation across all classes of rural households steadily declined. This clearly signals acute pressure on villagers and so they naturally seek alternatives in non-farm employment in villages or, better still, in an urban job even if that is in a sweatshop. That is why they head *en masse* every morning to bus-stands and market squares looking for jobs. If they are lucky they are spotted by some contractor and hired for a day or a week, and if fortune really smiles on them, they head off for a long-term employment, even if that is in the service of merchant producers. What happens to the village when this occurs?

From Village to Vicinage

According to the official Indian definition, an area is considered rural when at least 75 per cent of the male workforce is engaged in agriculture, and where the population density is less than 400 per sq. km. Of the two, only the population density criterion is faithful to the reality of the Indian village; the other defining feature has, in the meantime, fallen by the wayside. It is only in very exceptional circumstances that 75 per cent of the male workforce in a 'village' is engaged in agricultural operations. If one takes into account cases where agriculture is a subsidiary occupation then the number of full-time farmers tumbles further.

Is the village then to be understood largely in terms of its housing conditions, its poor civic amenities, its low levels of health care, and population density? If that is the case then perhaps we might say that about 68 per cent of India lives in villages. This should not however be taken to mean that 68 per cent of rural households pursue agriculture as their principal occupation. It is the character of the neighbourhood that now constitutes a village as the emphasis is no longer on a specific source of livelihood for the male workers. Does the village then become a kind of vicinage without a definable central theme?

It would be unprofitable to search for hyphenated terms such as part town-part village, or admixtures such as rurban, or urban village, and so forth. These terms are conceptual palliatives that do not really address the main issues. It is not as if these villages are becoming more urbanized. It is not as if there is a spurt of schools, quality hospitals, better civic amenities, and so forth. True, the number of villages with electricity has more than doubled over the past three decades, but not every house has electricity, as we found earlier. Indeed, current figures indicate that about 53.2 per cent of rural households do not have proper shelter and about the same percentage have no electricity either. The much commented-about movement from country to town is, therefore, barely noticeable in village India. That is why it is always necessary to supplement macro-data from other sources with field observations of one's own— hence, macro-empiricism once again!

One way of viewing this change in rural India is to see it in terms of the urban world drawing in the villagers to their cities and their industries because of attractive returns from non-agricultural incomes. True, an average urban Indian earns twice as much as an average villager does, but there are so many more who have not found jobs in cities and continue to live in these 'villages' and work in non-farm activities and not everybody can get a factory job, even in a sweatshop.

To understand this trend that is converting the village into a vicinage of a certain description, it is important to first accept 'the hollowing out' of the agricultural sector. There is a kind of rural implosion that is sucking out the air from even the most basic ambitions of an ordinary cultivator. Rather than viewing the emergence of RNFE or rural to urban migration primarily in terms of the pull from the cities, the push from the village also needs to be factored in as a major variable. In other words, had the village really remained agricultural as it once was, then perhaps urban India would have been less compelling.

Urban migration is not a negative trend by itself. If one were to look at the history of economic development worldwide, there is no doubt that this transition would have had to take place. The issue really is: what are the forces that are making for such change in villages and how is the urban world responding to them. If rural migration is largely an outcome of economic distress then the presence of cheap labour enhances the prospects of sweatshops in both cities and small towns. This aspect of India's economic growth is rarely mentioned because it looks sleazy. It also demands a new mindset that views the poor as rational beings and appreciates what compels the villager to prefer a life in the cities to that of the country. This is the issue to which we should now turn.

Naukri or Mazdoori

I lost several months of field data simply because I was using the wrong terms when talking to my village respondents. When I asked them if they had any source of income outside of agriculture a large number of them said they had no such jobs. In the early years of my acquaintanceship with the village I took that as a clear response that did not require further interpretation. I too believed that villagers should till the land, for what else should they do?

As time went by I began to notice the regularity with which a large number of villagers, primarily men, went off looking for non-agricultural jobs virtually every morning. I still did not quite realize that something was amiss. However, those were still early days so far as my awareness of village life was concerned. I put this anomaly out of my mind assuming, as others did, that villagers were villagers after all and agriculture was their principal, if not sole, source of bread, but perhaps not butter.

Then later, months later, it occurred to me that I had been using the wrong term all this time. I was asking them if they had a *'naukri'* outside agriculture, and most of the villagers to whom I addressed this question honestly said 'No'. It is not as if they misunderstood my question, perhaps understood it only too well. In villages the term *'naukri'* means a regular job for which one is paid by the month, or at least by the week. For jobs where the person is paid by the day or even by the hour, the term is *'mazdoori'*, or pure labour. For city people like me, *naukri* generically stood for employment or being hired out. The villagers were much more specific. If I said *'naukri'* then it meant regular employment but *'mazdoori'* was something else and it was the latter that most of them periodically managed to secure. For them, securing a *'naukri'*, even in a sweatshop, would have been a dream come true. Sadly, I was not wise to this distinction till much later, which is why I had to forfeit some very valuable information.

When the villagers lucks out with a *'naukri'* what is the best-case scenario? It does not take very long to obtain information from villagers as to where they find, or hope to find *'naukri'* of one kind or another. It is also worth one's while to check the same problem from the other end, and that is by interviewing migrant labourers in *'naukri'* in urban and rural establishments. Indeed, this investigation should be taken a step further to include those who work in village-based cottage manufactories but have a sustained relationship with urban buyers. After all, 71 per cent of the unorganized sector is reportedly located in rural India.[2] In these rural manufactories payment for one's work is almost always based on the 'piece-rate' wage system. Within a loosely defined time frame, a certain job has to be accomplished for an urban buyer with whom the villagers have contracted, howsoever informally.

We now get a little more perspective on how villagers relocate themselves from one kind of poverty to another. If rural jobs kept them barely above subsistence levels for all these years, these urban jobs in sweatshops are not that much better, but at least they are available. Therefore incentives to leave house and home for *'naukri'* of this kind would only be meaningful when rural opportunities become scarcer by the day. Piecemeal job contracts at the cottage level, or working as hired labour in sweatshops of various descriptions can only be attractive when placed against the hopelessness of the rural world.

Why are these establishments where the rural migrants find jobs no better than sweatshops? Merchant producers, as discussed, profit by buying cheap and selling dear. Sweatshops are not only characterized by poor physical working conditions and pay, but also by the fact that work in them is a dead-end game with little scope for mobility for the labouring class. This is an additional feature of sweatshops: apart from low wages in the present, they offer little opportunity for better wages in the future. We should recognize that much of our urban prosperity depends on these rural migrants and on their substandard lifestyles.

Carpet Weaving in Manufactories

Rural manufactories tell us a lot about villagers who are looking for ways to augment their agricultural income or, as in most cases, about those who have no agricultural income at all. In the latter situation, jobs in these manufactories become the sole source of their earnings.

Carpet weaving is one such activity. It is widely prevalent in rural manufactories, particularly in east UP. These manufactories can even be a single-family homestead, in which case the dwelling space doubles up as working area too. As India is the largest international supplier of carpets (touching 11 per cent of the world's exports of this commodity), examining the conditions of production in this industry can be quite illustrative. Carpet weaving is mostly done in Sant Ravidas Nagar, Jaunpur, and Mirzapur districts of east UP. It has also spilt over from there to contiguous areas of Bihar and Jharkhand. Carpet weaving is a fairly established practice and has been around for decades. It has received a fresh boost in recent times as many foreign buying agencies have discovered a market in their respective countries for not overly fancy carpets, which Indian villagers can produce at very low price. Carpet weaving thus gains an international dimension as well. Is it surprising then that the carpet belt of India, such as it is, should also comprise the poorest regions of India? A quick tour of them will help us understand the social factors that accompany carpet weaving, and also the social characteristics of the workers in this industry.

An engagement took me to parts of east Uttar Pradesh (UP), near Varanasi, to audit some of the carpet-producing units there. Spread out over a period of over three years or so I must have travelled there on at least a dozen occasions, if not more. I was perpetually taking off to places around Varanasi that would hardly feature in any tourist brochure. Just a few miles away there are villages mired in poverty and strung together by the numerous carpet-weaving looms on which poor, part-time cultivators, part-time masons, part-time labourers, part-time anything, toil. The looms are situated largely in dugout pits, and they are all uniformly dark and hot with trapped air. A full day's work yields a meagre Rs 50. I later extended the area of my research to Bihar and Jharkhand too for in these states there were villages which had a tie with east UP carpet manufacturers.

As the carpet districts of UP are of such great significance to weavers in Bihar and Jharkhand, it is time we turned our attention to this region. The major districts covered here are proximate to Varanasi and have become synonymous with carpet weaving and agrarian distress. In villages such as Khyokhar, Chak Sundarpur, and Amilahara in Sant Ravidas Nagar, or in Newada and Ghanipur in Jaunpur district, the migration of men to cities as far away as Mumbai, Surat, or Vapi is just too massive to be ignored. Initially, carpet weaving was an option for most of them, but as the demand for carpets could not keep pace with the supply of prospective carpet-weavers, and also because wages for carpet weaving are very low, alternatives were sought elsewhere. Perhaps the most dramatic instance is from Ashapaur village in Sant Ravidas Nagar where all Scheduled Caste families had at least one member who had migrated elsewhere.

Though the trend for men to migrate from the village to distant areas is prevalent all over this region. For example, in Newada village in Jaunpur, over 60 per cent adult males are away, primarily in Mumbai, Surat, or Kolkata. I was struck by the looming despondency among carpet weavers who are left behind. Most families do not entirely depend on carpet weaving, but this constitutes the major chunk of their monthly earnings. Some of them have agricultural land, but it is too small to make ends meet. At best, the average size of their holdings, as I found from my own investigations, was less than a third of an acre. Children of carpet weavers did not think much of their parents lifestyle and would idealize relations and friends who had migrated and would return periodically with money in their pockets and stories in their heads.

Although Sant Ravidas Nagar has many villages from where a large number of men have left, this picture does not hold in all the villages. In Amilahara, for example, most men remained in the village and wove carpets there. As the men were around, the women were nearly always veiled in public. Interestingly, in those villages with fewer men around the women are much less housebound and less veiled outside their home.

I expect it stands to reason: when the men are away from the villages, women walk into the empty spaces and fill them out, in a form of gender empowerment by default. In large tracts of Uttar Pradesh and Bihar, there is a high incidence of households with *de facto* female heads. It is not as if these women are single parents as a Western reader might quickly assume. In five villages I visited in Jaunpur and Bhadohi districts. a little over 18 per cent of households were, in real terms, headed by women. The male members are far away in some city or township striving to make a living while the women and children are in the village doing the best they can. I found many NGOs waxing eloquently about how the gender balance had changed in villages because these women were now very conscious of their rights and stepped out of their homes to go to the bank, to argue with errant school-teachers, and take on government officials.

To a large extent the euphoria of the NGOs was because they were bred on a Western notion of rights. But they missed the point; these women in poor rural households were taking the lead simply because the men were away. Their new role was because of the gender gap and not a gender revolution. As the *pater familias* is away, the mother has to take decisions regarding crops, health, and education, and a hundred sundry matters. She has to balance her budget, meet other women to work out some strategy for survival, and keep her old in-laws happy to boot. This is the fate of most contemporary village women. They do not just sit at home heavily veiled but participate in the outside world quite readily, without the ideology of self-conscious feminism. As a village woman in East Uttar Pradesh told me:

'I want my husband to spend more time here but we need the money he earns. I have learnt to do a lot now that he is not here, but I wish I could share the burden a bit. He comes when he gets time off, and to tell you the truth he doesn't do much, and I continue to work the same way. But I am glad he goes back for we need his money. I have to send my children to school, get their uniforms and books.'

As time goes by I think there will be fewer men even in those villages that have not yet seen significant migration. I was initially taken aback when I saw so many adult men in Amilahara which was quite different from the other villages in the region. Elsewhere I had hardly found one able-bodied man who lived round the year in these villages. Here in Amilahara, however, there were so many men, poor, dirtily clad, and usually unshaven, hanging around in the evening as they usually stop weaving when the sun sets; but there were some who continued working in the light of flickering kerosene lamps.

What struck me in Amilahara was that migrating for jobs away from the village is not just a question of individual initiative. People don't just buy a railway ticket and head out for Mumbai as they do in the movies. There has to be a network in place which villagers can access to escape their rural confines. I got a feel of this when I was looking at migration and contract labour in small-scale industries, but now I had come to a village which made the importance of network so visible. For some reason, Amilahara had escaped the sweep of extant networks that embraced other villages. In fact, there were just four families here who had jobs in neighbouring areas not far from the village. For reasons not apparent, Amilahara families did not have access to networks such as those in Chak Sundarpur or Khyokha.

I believe there is really no pattern to explain why one village is blessed with contacts and the other is not. Networks that link villagers to jobs outside probably begin randomly with some enterprising people who make the first move. Then, if they are able to establish themselves, they become important points of contact for others to move out as well. This is probably true of all migration, whether in land or overseas, but one needs to see the effects of this in real life to vividly appreciate this phenomenon. Amilahara was both cursed and sustained by carpet weaving and had little contact with paying jobs in distant places.

There are several other places like Amilahara, such as Aghauli and Gangaut in Mirzapur district, where again most of the men are home. They, however, are all waiting at the threshold, hoping that one day the road will open up and lead them to a railway station and then beyond to Mumbai or Panipat. Some of the grown men in Amilahara are now more or less resigned to their lot, but they hope their children will have a better life.

This is the second important lesson I learnt, first in Amilahara and then confirmed in other villages such as Aghauli and Gangoot. When I first met these carpet weavers I asked them when they had learnt to weave carpets. These were men old enough to have teenage, or near-teenage, children. The answer usually was that their fathers had taught them this craft. How old were they when they were first introduced to the looms? Apparently they started quite young—when they were between 11–13 years old. It was just as well they began early for it takes about a year or more to be really proficient in the task and to get used to the rigours of weaving in a pit. What were their fathers thinking of when they trained them as weavers? Obviously, to augment their meagre and uncertain earnings from agriculture and add a second string, as it were, to their bow.

Then I asked them the most natural follow-up question, and was I in for a surprise? When these carpet weavers told me in some detail when, how, and, most importantly, why, their parents introduced them to carpet weaving, I naturally turned to them to find out whether they had had in turn taught their own children this skill. When I first posed this question I hardly expected the answer I received. All the carpet weavers of Amilahara, one at a time, separately told me that they had *not* taught their sons to weave, nor did they plan to do so. In their view their children would be better off if they left the village and found some other occupation. Carpet weaving would take them nowhere just as it had taken them nowhere. No matter how many weavers I asked the answers were always the same: even their words were similar.

Pressing on with a 'second string to the bow' logic I asked whether they were not being unfair to their children. Would they not be seriously disadvantaged and more vulnerable because they had not been taught to weave? The answer I invariably received went something to this effect: 'We don't want them to end up us like us, and neither do they? We want our boys to have a future and they should just leave at the first opportunity and not seek temporary solutions. That is what we sought and look where we are today.'

That is all very well, but what measures had they really taken to prepare their children to take that step and move away from weaving? To this they replied that though their parents were generally illiterate they had studied up to third or fourth grade but their children had completed middle school and beyond and were qualified to take up a better paying profession if only they could find someone to sponsor them somewhere. In the meantime, while their fathers were labouring over carpets, these teenage boys were just loitering around, whistling to themselves, and kicking loose gravel with their bare feet. Here therefore were dozens of young adolescents who, along with their parents, were searching the horizons every day to pick up signals that would take them to jobs and better futures in distant places.

Far from being miserable strands in a shabby carpet weave, here were people who were risk-taking and forward-looking. They urged their children to seek a future outside rural confines even if that meant breaking up the joint family. They were not concerned about tradition and family values, in any old-fashioned sense. The one value they treasured above all else was to see their children in circumstances that would not be a repeat of their own.

The only route they know to a possible better future is to migrate to a *naukri* in a distant city. When a migrant leaves the village and finds work in a factory, either as a regular salaried worker (which does not happen immediately) or as a day-labourer (which is most often the case), he usually goes alone. He might fetch his family one day, but that happens much later, unless they are working in brick-kilns or in construction gangs. Their networks serve well in getting them to a job or near a job, but they are of little use thereafter, and are of no consequence when it comes to sorting out issues of payment, wages or overtime compensation.

The other significant fact about the calibre of the workforce is that it is not only poorly qualified in terms of education but, in general, not particularly skilled either. There are exceptions to this general rule: master-weavers in Panipat in Haryana, or Tirupur in Tamil Nadu, as well as glass-blowers of Moradabad and Khurja in UP require special skills and are well paid. If however one were to take in the profile of the vast numbers of migrants who find jobs in the cotton-textile, hosiery, carpet-weaving, or metal-work factories, then a large majority of them would require only very rudimentary skills. These skills are of the kind that could be learnt in about a month or six weeks. In fact, they could be put to work straight away and they would gain the needed proficiency on the job.

Tailoring, which otherwise demands a fair degree of skill, can be performed without much training in most garment units. The garment factories that employ these workers have machines that are usually purchased from Europe or America. They are very specialized and capable of hemming, saddle-stitching, or making curtain pleats almost on their own with very little assistance from those manning them just by changing the adjustments in the sewing machine itself. All the tailor must know is how to keep the hand steady and not waver in line. Likewise, metal welding does not take much time to master either. This is both a good and bad thing, depending on how one looks at it.

The Network at Work

As these jobs require little training, workers are hired and fired summarily. Further, a migrant worker is not overly worried about this as he also knows that a break for a month or more at home is not catastrophic as there is usually a job at that level that they can take up when they return, perhaps not immediately but soon enough. These low-level, semi-skilled jobs are available if one has the network and is aware where one should look for employment. Even factory owners prefer to keep a hand who has worked and trained with them rather than look for new hands all the time.

The network does not always find a job for the migrant worker but it provides him with initial hospitality, the first contacts, and a few smart tips about how to go about looking for a job. This includes not just keeping up with job contractors but also to pay attention to news circulating by word of mouth and keeping regular track of vacancies at the factory gates. These are important aspects of accumulating social skills which only the network can nurture in a migrant. It is the network again that also helps the migrant worker to find a contractor.

This is very important as most of the labourers engaged in such factories are, of course, contract workers.

Coming Home on Leave

Where do the dispossessed and impoverished farmers go when they are forced out of the village? They find work in these small-scale units, if indeed they are fortunate. Even with the conditions in these establishments, they would prefer such work for they are now paid by the month and not by the hour; it is not *mazduri*, but *naukri* time now. Even when they are paid on a piece-rate basis the period of employment is not less than a month. This is a sight better than being a day-labourer and not knowing where tomorrow's job will come from. It is this aspect of somehow surviving *in extremis* that makes a low-paid job in the small-scale, unorganized and often unregistered sector, so desirable.

When the migrant returns home after several consecutive months, often as many as ten, his family and friends greet him with great fanfare. He is the successful villager and has some money jingling in his pockets. Presents are bought, sweets are passed around, but it is also harvest time so there is work to be done. If the labourer has his own field then that is where he bends his back during this short season.

If, however, he is either a marginal or landless farmer he can hire himself out to a landed person, for it is only in these few weeks of harvesting that the demand for labour is high and a worker enjoys a certain bargaining power. The crops cannot be left standing in the fields for very long. In this way, it is rather like a paid holiday for most of these migrant workers when they return home.

Besides, after months of leading a solitary life and being kicked around by contractors and employers he feels good to be regarded as a kind of role model at home. People now come to him for advice on how best to secure a future for their children, what they should do now to get a foothold in the cities, and can they recommend a 'contact'? The network is thus renewed.

Clearly, it is a rare piece of good fortune to find a job as a labourer, casual, contracted, or permanent, in these small-scale establishments. Not everybody gets them. The carpet weaver who has not taught his children the skills that his father taught him is hoping that some day his son will gain an entry and a *naukri* in one such small-scale unit. In his eyes then, and in the eyes of many others around him, his son would be something of a success.

For a Future beyond Sweatshops

Let us now revisit the slums. These are associated, rightly so, with filth, squalor, violence, and non-existent civic amenities. Yet they are not dumps of hopelessness and refuse. In these quarters, ambitions are born and nurtured, and often come within grasping distance. Sometimes, one comes face to face with a dream only to see it slither away; but then there is the hope that tomorrow will be better than today.

Like the urban slum-dweller, the villager too now recognizes the value of education if they want their children to do better than just work as day-labourers. The only way the carpet-weaver can get his son out of the village is by educating him to at least the middle school, if not high school, level. Between 1983 and 1999 the fraction of the average household expenditure spent on education rose from 1.23 per cent to 2.82 per cent in absolute terms, while per capita private expenditure on education rose from Rs 1.51 per month to Rs 16.35 per month.[3]

It is not uncommon to see a three-wheeler scooter-rickshaw turn up in a village at about 2 p.m. In spite of its severely constrained space, it disgorges sometimes up to ten children who are returning after school. These children (both boys and girls), returning from a private school, wear ratty ties, limp skirts, rubber sandals (some are even barefoot). Some villages have a number of such private schools in the vicinity charging fees ranging from Rs 40 a month upwards to Rs 150 a month.

What is striking in this scene is not that scooter-rickshaws can be so capacious, but that the children emerging from it are from poor families. Their clothes, their nutritional status, and general bearing amply testify to this. Private schooling should not automatically semaphore rich kids, as it tends to. A large number of impoverished families are tightening their belts an extra notch to be able to send their children to school. I have met children from these schools, one whose father was a casual labourer in Varanasi, another whose mother was a widow but who earned some extra income by rolling *bidis*, and yet another whose elder brother has a job as a cleaner in a transportation company, and of course, there were several who were children of carpet weavers. There were children from all kinds of families, but they were all poor.

In an east UP village, in Jaunpur district, I came across a boy of eight in an Alternative Learning Centre (ALC) that was being run by UNICEF with IKEA support. This child was from a Below Poverty Line family and nobody in his home had ever been to school. He was the first to do so, and that too at an ALC which is run somewhat informally and where education is playfully communicated, and often, as I found, with great effect.

Poor children attending a private school

The charter of ALCs is to pick up children who had either never been to school or had missed out on schooling, and then train them so that they can enter the regular education system at their respective levels. It is generally hoped that such ALC-trained students would then enter government schools and stay there for a considerable period of time and hopefully until they complete their schooling. The report on this is not firm yet, but there are strong suggestions that such ALC children tend to stay as long as the others who joined directly.

The important point is that the kind of education these children receive in ALCs is really quite innovative and a great deal of information and skills are actually passed on by teachers specially trained for this purpose. I have seen little children talk about photosynthesis, about volcanoes, about how a chrysalis becomes a butterfly, about different continents, and about longitude and latitude. Besides, they also learn to read, write, and count. What more could one ask for?

True, all the ALCs were not of the same standard, but those

An Alternative Learning Centre in east Uttar Pradesh. The children are from the poorest families of different castes in the village. The teacher is very popular for his enthusiasm but is paid only Rs 800 per month—lower than the legal minimum wage.

that had enthusiastic teachers certainly did a great job. Parents could clearly see the impact that education was having on their children, and that encouraged them to support their children through higher levels of education in mainstream schools. The ALCs were often conducted in the village beneath the shade of a clump of trees, and sufficiently near home so as not to engender in the child any sense of estrangement. Mothers, neighbours, and relations were always around carrying on with their daily chores not far from where classes were being held.

Well, to return to our child of eight introduced earlier. He was an enthusiastic learner and his parents recognized this trait in him sufficiently early. When they saw how quickly their child picked up information from his ALC teacher they began to become ambitious parents. Abysmally poor though they were, they somehow managed to send him to a private school. This story is over three years old and the last time I heard from them the child was still at school and progressing well. He had entered science competitions and had written a short letter in English to his parents, who could not decipher a word of it, but laughed with endless pride when they received it. What comes through quite transparently is the determination with which

There is a dog too in the Alternative Centre

poor rural households gather their meagre resources in order to educate their children. Will the future live up to their expectations, or will they be disappointed yet again? Will the stringy school-tie bind the young as firmly as the traditional old-school tie does for the better-off children in posh private schools? I hope, along with countless others, that the answers to both these questions will be positive in the fullness of time.

School teacher, at government school, with no pupils

Schools engender hope in families, but the sheer ineptitude and unconcern of government schools inspire cynicism more than accomplishment. Where private schools score over government schools is that their teachers turn up regularly and the children are actually engaged during school hours. I was moved by a mother who said that it would take ten years of her life to see her son educated, but that she would see many happy years after that.

I was also moved by a contrary sentiment when I came

across a school in north-central Bihar which had no children, not a single one, but where the schoolteacher was drawing his salary while basking in the winter sun. He begged me not to expose him, or to bring his happy condition to the notice of authorities, but he could not stop me from taking a picture of him with folded hands and in a posture of entreaty. That was my way of hitting back, but it only satisfied my ego and little else. The picture is on the preceding page.

9

NORMALIZING 'CASTE'

FROM SYSTEM TO IDENTITY

In mid-February 2004, when EU Commissioner Chris Patten visited India, I asked him why Hong Kong and Singapore, which are no bigger than Delhi or Mumbai, were beneficiaries of much greater amounts of FDI than we receive in this huge subcontinent of over a billion people. Earlier that evening, at a not-so-small working dinner, he had said how the world was gratified with our democracy and with our free and open press. This is what I found intriguing. If the world was so pleased with us, why then does international FDI tend to fly further eastwards leaving us with a few droppings as it journeys overhead? Surely a country of our size should fare much better?

According to the UNCTAD, *World Investment Report* (2007), the FDI flow to India was approximately US$17,000 million in 2006, while it was nearly US$42,000 million for Hong Kong and a little over US$24,000 million for Singapore. More importantly, while India attracted FDI stocks in 2006 worth US$50,680 million, which was a huge jump from earlier years, it was still well below that of Hong Kong and Singapore which received US$769,029 million and US$210,089 million respectively.

On the positive side, we outstripped Pakistan in this

department from 2000 onwards.[1] As we in India derive quite lot of satisfaction by comparing ourselves to Pakistan and not to other fast-growing economies we don't quite digest the point of how far behind we still are in terms of attracting large-scale foreign capital. This question also makes sense in another context. Our export figures, as I mentioned in an earlier chapter, are not up to the standards of other East Asian countries with a smaller population, uncertain democracies, and fewer trained human resources.[2]

Comparisons of the growth of India with that of China can be profoundly embarrassing, to India anyway. Shankar Acharya argues against attempts at too facile a comparison between these two countries. Not only is India way behind China in terms of human development indicators but also in economic terms. Against China's FDI inflow in 2004 of US$60 billion, India could manage only US$5.5 billion in 2004.[3]

When Chris Patten had visited India in 2002 he blamed bureaucratic red tape and overstretched public budgets for India's poor infrastructural facilities. In a discussion held in CATO Institute in Washington on 22 April 2002, Swaminathan Aiyar, quoting a CII study, said that an Indian entrepreneur spends 15 per cent of working time with government officials whereas in other developing countries this proportion is only 5–8 per cent. True, the report itself may be biased in favour of the entrepreneurs: it was after all the CII that sponsored the research. Nevertheless, this underlines the corporate view on red tape and government inefficiency. Chris Patten's position is entirely in consonance with it, and it may well be right. Everybody in India, from the lowest to the highest, has had to face the government apparatus and very few have anything positive to say about it. However, in 2004, Patten was somewhat cautious. In his answer to my question, he was inclined instead to present a more sympathetic portrayal of India and the economic strides it has made in recent years to become a substantial market force.

That still did not however answer my question.

Primordial Passions as a Price for Democracy

As I pressed on with it other business people in the gathering stepped in. Many of them said that though India's democracy was certainly remarkable, it was also responsible for weaknesses in the implementation of policy. As democracies have to play footsie with public sentiment, no political party in India can afford to ignore deeply held loyalties towards caste and religion. Naturally, policies never get implemented while corruption and patronage reign. The majority opinion around the table was that too much democracy is not a good thing, especially in a backward, culturally and communally divided country such as India. As one of them said, 'After all, ours is not a dictatorship and inefficiency is the price we have to pay for democracy.'

From what I could tell, this was the majority opinion around the table. Nobody would dare say this in print, for it is not good business to offend politicians. There are contracts to be had, payments to be received, and water and electricity connections that need to be in good repair. Hitting out at power-wielders can be potentially hurtful.

How valid then is the charge that we have a poor record of public policy and probity as our political system is held to ransom by passions of caste and creed?[4] Mark Tully puts this view across more forcefully when he writes:

> 'Perhaps it would be taking this theory too far to suggest that politicians have deliberately opened up other fronts to take Indians' minds off good governance, but it is certainly true that caste and communalism, as religion-based politics are known in India, have crowded that issue out.'[5]

There is obviously a lot of support for such a point of view particularly as it raises certain issues which seem, on the face of it, quite incontrovertible. Caste kills initiative because it ordains a status hierarchy based on birth. It also creates a deep sense of alienation across society as castes are so deeply marked off from each other that it would be impossible to reach a social consensus on anything at all. As if this were not enough, we are held back because so many languages and creeds are boxed into a one nation-state. This basic incompatibility between diets, customs, and idols often makes for frequent political eruptions. India is seen as something of a marvel, sitting as it does on a powder keg of diverse cultural pressures.

There is just no excuse for the bigotries that caste and religion can unleash. India has seen many rounds of such clashes and paid for it with huge losses in both public and private property, over and above hundreds of innocent lives. Even so, is there something wrong with the explanation that primordial patriotism to caste and religion play a significant role in downgrading the performance of Indian state? Let us first acknowledge a significant inconsistency at work. When discussing India's economic miracle there is scarcely a word about the hindrances posed by caste. However, when it comes to explaining why we are still not top-drawer as a country we are quick to blame caste and primordial identities, our cultural baggage, for our backwardness. This is yet another reason why India is considered to be so exotic, strange, and paradoxical.

Consciousness of caste and religious difference are not necessarily responsible for the huge delivery failures of successive Indian governments. There is a fundamental error in the proposition that a democracy can succeed only if people are culturally unencumbered and can shake off all traces of prior primordial associations. There are religious assemblies in the West, and also elements of racism and political bigotry, but that does not mean that these democracies do not deliver. Why then do caste and religious differences hold up the implementation of public policy in our democracy? Is then democracy intrinsically at fault? Or the way we practise it?

This chapter and the one to follow on the nation-state and ethnicity provide us with yet another opportunity to revive our earlier discussion against exoticization. By encouraging a dialogue between superficial observations and allowing diverse voices to speak up, we can demonstrate how scientific enquiry can humble and take the shine off purely cultural explanations.

To 'normalize' does not mean to wipe the slate clean of differences. Rather, by seeking parallels and by placing them in comparative contexts, the mystical aura disappears and now we are ready for a more detailed 'grass-roots' analysis. Culture will not be banished, but it will play a major supporting role. In particular, the malleability of culture will be highlighted in terms of how it adjusts to changing scenarios whose contents need to be empirically filled out every time. As we have been arguing all along, only a distrust of the cultural explanation will bring empirical facts, which would have otherwise remained unsung, to our notice. That is how we effect the move from being 'cultu-real' to 'mate-real'. Contrary to the popular impression, a cultural explanation is in fact neither full-bodied nor richly flavoured. In truth, it is an unknowing victim of intellectual bulimia as it compulsively expels serious empirical nutrients from its system. As it is limiting to be either only 'cultu-real' or 'mate-real' we need to reconcile several contradictory facts that are at the surface level and in your face.

First, the caste story, because we must exonerate caste from the charge of holding up development with its myriad customs, taboos, and intolerant beliefs.

The Caste Conundrum

More than any other institution, it is caste that is thought to set India apart from other societies in the world, and this is the motherboard that excites and justifies all manner of exoticization of India from a variety of quarters. If an institution as strange as caste can govern the lives of a billion people, goes the cliché, then surely there must be something very strange about this lot. That is why caste is convincingly cited as one of the primary reasons why we cannot go all guns blazing down the development route.

What is it that is so strange about caste that defeats an application of both universal categories and hence a sensible, everyday attitude towards India and Indians? Why is it that the moment caste is mentioned we suspend our usual sense of judgement and are willing to entertain the most incredulous possibilities?

The reason why caste appears so puzzling is the belief that large sections of the population are so thoroughly socialized into the hierarchy of purity and pollution that they willingly participate in their own subjugation.[6] Thus, 'low caste' Hindus, who are considered to be untouchables by the 'higher castes' do not object to their degraded status and, in fact, further this ideology by their willing submission to it. That is what is so strange about caste.

There are other unequal and hierarchical societies but nowhere do the dominated classes believe that they are inherently unworthy and that is why they are at the bottom of the social order. In the case of caste, the argument goes, the situation is completely different. One would expect that those who are positioned at the bottom would strongly object to an ideology that separates communities at birth in terms of the principle of purity and pollution. Instead, the argument runs, the lowest orders accept their humiliation willingly and by their acquiescence to this order acknowledge that they are fundamentally polluting and constituted of the basest bodily substances. Where else can one find such uniform ideological acquiescence to a fundamentally hierarchical ideology? No wonder universal analytical categories cannot decipher the inner logic of caste.

This is what is at the surface when we discuss caste. People are indeed discriminated against on grounds of birth through condemnation to an unclean status. It is also true that millions of subaltern castes even today cannot realistically expect to escape poverty and a life of degradation. However, as this is the surface reality presented to us, one that is most accessible, we must start our discussion from here even while we contest the notion that caste is responsible for India's backwardness today.

It is difficult to controvert textual exegeses when they argue that castes are sanctioned in mainline Hindu sacred texts. This is because in no other traditional religious literature of equal magnitude is such a proposition about fundamental inequality so clearly justified.[6] I agree with this statement for, to the best of my knowledge, I cannot think of another world religion that divides its believers in such obsessive detail that it becomes a ritual obligation on everyone's part to ensure that these walls stand. To this extent the culturologist is right. The Vedas, the Smritis and the Puranas are the most significant sources of Hinduism, and the hierarchy figures in all these with greater or lesser intensity. Even so, something is missing. What is absent is that we are hearing just a single voice.

Two Voices of Caste

First, the traditional point of view. Propertied castes that have enjoyed dominance for generations argue that if they are born high it is because they have better substances in them than the lower castes. A Bhumihar (a landed caste that claims to be Brahman) labour contractor in Varanasi was complaining to me about the audacity of the lower castes, and how they have forgotten their true station in life. When I reminded him that we are all made of blood and flesh, he argued back that our essential substances are different. When I retorted that where one is born is a matter of chance, and how would he feel if he were of a low caste, he indignantly replied that this was not possible. Why not, I asked. 'Very simple,' he replied, 'if I am high caste today it is because of my karma and the karma of my ancestors. Those Untouchables deserve to be where they are because of bad karma. *They only have themselves to blame.'* There was now a fundamental epistemological divide between us, making further conversation along this theme impossible. Had Michel Foucault been listening in to this chat he would have said that the taxi driver and I had incommensurable thresholds of discourse.

What I did not tell this arrogant Bhumihar/Brahman is that karma is handy to justify upper-caste privileges but I have not met a single member of the so-called lower orders who explains traditional subordination in terms of it. If they did, then of course, Moffat and Dumont would be right to say that

Hindus at the bottom of the sacred hierarchy do actually participate in their own subjugation. What did the so-called lower castes have to say about this?

This is a story I have often related but it could easily suffer one more round of narration. I was researching in some villages in south Gujarat, and on one occasion we hired a lady to help with some basic cooking. She was introduced to us quite baldly, and dismissively, as a member of the supposedly low 'Dubla' community. We were asked if we had any objections on this ground, and of course, we said 'None at all.'

In a few days our relationship with this Dubla lady became more informal and she began to speak up more about her life, her shattered dreams, and her fresh hopes. This was in the 1970s and I, like many others, believed in that '70s thing to which we radicals, and even educated liberals, subscribed. It was widely believed at that time, particularly in left-wing circles, that knowledge had to be freed from past prejudice and taken post-haste to humbler quarters where they were hungrily awaiting intellectual rations. Naturally we opposed caste and we thought it was necessary for us to explain to the so-called low castes that they had been fooled into accepting the ideology of the ritual hierarchy which only harmed them. People were all born equal and it was untrue that some possessed better substances than others, and so forth. We all thought that once this doctrine went home the subordinated communities would throw caste out of their windows and high above the muddy barricades of their lives. Fed by the dominant scholarship on caste the way out was simply an ideological one. It was false consciousness versus the real thing: the struggle would be long but eventually truth would supervene!

Quite predictably, I set out to cure my Dubla friend of the belief that she was a 'low-caste' person and to instill in her a sense of pride in who she was. I did not realize then how her answer would change my entire understanding of caste, and indeed, my life as an academic. She said that obviously she knew that she was neither polluting nor low and that nobody from her community really feels that way either. This is because, she claimed, they were all descendants of a proud caste of warrior Rajputs that ruled this very region where we were now based. She went on to say that her ancestor, several centuries ago, had ruled this land but committed the cardinal error of providing shelter to a low-caste man. This man ingratiated himself with the ruler, won his confidence, and one day literally stabbed him in the back, usurped his throne, and drove his descendants to poverty and worse. She however added that a day would come when they would reclaim their rightful place as proud Rajput warriors.

My initial reaction was of disbelief and I thought that our friend had concocted this elaborate story and that she was certainly an odd case. Later I met members of her family and found that they too held the same view regarding their caste background. That set me thinking, and since then I have read and collected numerous origin tales of a number of castes (or *jatis*) and have found that in none of them is there an admission of being lowly born, or of possessing base and polluting bodily substances. In all the *jati*-origin tales that I have seen and heard, and they must be over a hundred, not once have I found anywhere that those who we consider low caste actually ever accept their degrading status. My conception of the problem obviously changed after this realization. Castes, high and low, were proud of their origins, of their customs and beliefs, and there was a contestation across the board regarding which hierarchy was intrinsically most truthful.

Thus, far from participating in their own subjugation, *pace* Dumont and other textual exegeses, people of low castes dispute their subjugation on grounds of being impure. They indeed argue that they are as good, if not better than, the so-called 'upper castes'. Once we accept this, the mystery that surrounds caste is suddenly resolved and the heavy ornate veil is lifted.

Contextualizing Caste

The cultural baggage becomes lighter now, and this enlivens in our minds certain questions that would not have struck us so long as we believed that the lower castes participate in their own subjugation. We now need to know, for example, why it is possible for the progress that we have had so far to defy dogmas of caste, and why, indeed, do these dogmas come into effect only when we discuss our many failures to excel as a nation-state. Besides, why do people hold on to caste, or any cultural phenomenon even when it hurts their worldly aspirations? Why have poorer castes accepted their position for generations but are mobilizing today? Why are Brahman priests often mocked although they are supposedly at the top of the ritual hierarchy? Why do the Kurrichans of Malabar believe that if they see a Brahman the first thing in the morning their day will be off to a very inauspicious start? Why do Jats of UP bristle at the suggestion that Brahmans are superior to them? Why does the once much elaborated relationship between caste and occupation appear so distant today? Why are caste identities so powerful if the agrarian economy is collapsing and the move to urban areas so clearly visible? Why is it that we often find people of different castes eating together, especially in urban India, and yet holding on to their caste identities?

The only way to resolve these and other questions is not to return to texts but to the field for more data, some of which can be surprisingly commonsensical. Observations from the everyday world of how people actually live in villages and cities, in factories, sweatshops, and farmlands will provide much more reliable answers to these issues than texts can as the latter preach to the converted and do not address the sociologist. A more 'normalized' view of caste can be presented from garden variety facts that can be collected from these mundane sources, although that might not satisfy the culturologists' appetite for the strange and the unfamiliar.

There is no doubt that members of certain castes will not take up occupations that they see as degrading even if they have no other option. This is indeed remarkable. When however we look closer we find that they are quite happy to perform these occupations when they go abroad or, at least, far away from home. When it comes to social and marital alliances there is a marked preference for staying within one's own caste, and yet when it comes to political agitations internal caste rivalries are selectively forgotten and enduring political alliances are formed. This is in spite of the fact that every caste has a lively lore that ridicules and belittles other castes. On the one hand, again, why do castes often dispute their status as being backward and polluting though they fight to claim government privileges that are offered to people from these backgrounds? Once we juxtapose these many apparently irreconcilable realities even a diehard culturologist will find it difficult to propose an exoticized one-dimensional answer.

How often have we come across Indians of the so-called 'high castes' washing toilets at international airports far away from their native villages? How often we have come across Indians of the so-called 'high castes' energetically selling water bottles and roses to tourists in Europe while they would shudder at the suggestion that they do the same jobs at home? Many of these Indians avert their eyes when they see me, or others like me, in these faraway places as the embarrassment of being caught out and exposed by members from their own village and vicinage always looms in their minds.

This is surely quite a common reaction and there is really no need to factor in caste in this case as the all-important variable. Nobody would wish to lose face, which is why when pressed by economic necessity they would rather leave for distant shores where their engagement with lowly jobs is anonymous and nobody from the village would be any wiser. Is that so difficult to understand? Losing status in a situation where one's position had once been enviable would be difficult under any circumstance, in India as much as in the West. Why, even in the West successful professionals are embarrassed when their children can do no better than master manual skills.

Therefore, to make the break from one-dimensional exotic renditions of caste (or any other social phenomenon) let us bring in the comparative details from the bleachers and put them into play. It is only then that we realize that ideologies, even the dearest ones, are always waiting to be craftily moulded by the context in which they are placed. The most appealing configurations are always those that give the appearance of being pristine while reaching out to something that is entirely new. Humankind always seeks to bond and belong, which is why we are always susceptible to community ties that are capable of breeding hostility. I would consider this to be our most significant anthropological failing and it has plagued us from the beginning of time.

The Many Hierarchies of Caste

To return to our original caste conundrum, even in tradition, lower castes never participated in their own subjugation. The Mauryan Empire was founded by a lowly Moreya, the Rajputs came to the fore in medieval India and slaughtered their way to the throne, the Jats slowly lumbered into dominance in the fourteenth and fifteenth centuries after the Persian wheel was harnessed to agriculture, the Ezhavas of Kerala shook off their untouchability status as recently as the closing years of the nineteeenth century. So really it is a matter of the historical depth of our enquiry. Besides, how much lower-class revolt did we see in feudal Europe? In the closed natural economy of the village the principal role of armed retainers everywhere was to keep the liegemen in their rude cottages and rooted to their lord's demesne.

Now that the sanctity of who is high or low has lost its rationale, there are no longer universally accepted or pure 'high castes' or 'low castes'. Status claims would, therefore, have to depend on who can most effectively make their caste hierarchy work on the ground. However, as all claims are of logically equal status, the successful enforcement of a particular ideology must depend on factors outside caste. It is then a question of wealth and power, and should the so-called low caste come into positions of dominance they would impose their ordering upon the communities to which they have hitherto been subordinate. Out goes 'lower caste' romanticism, but we gain much in its stead. Now there is no need to request special lenses to study

India as, like other oppressed all over the world, the so-called low caste Hindus too do not accept that they are inherently base and polluting.

The earlier assumption that I, and many like me, entertained about the so-called lower castes was completely untrue. The poor Dubla I had met in a south Gujarat setting opened my eyes to the fact that those we called lower castes were not intrinsically ashamed of their bodily substances. This is because they nurtured their own standards of esteem all along and did not in any way believe in the views of the privileged castes. They were not like cattle herded willingly into different groups so that the upper castes could thrive.

I did not realize then as profoundly as I do now, that pride in one's caste automatically implies a strong aversion to bowing to somebody else's notion of hierarchy. Perhaps my naïveté was because 1970s caste politics was confined largely to village-level brutalities and had not found expression at the upper reaches of politics, nor was the mobilizing power of the subordinated communities as impressive as it is today. We had just begun to experience caste coalitions during elections, but this was still not a sufficiently rampant phenomenon to demand a re-examination of our precious verities, or a reordering of our priorities.

Although this meant I had to radically revise my earlier views, it also gladdened me as I could now view caste in an enlightened de-exoticized way. This hoary institution had been normalized in my eyes and the origin tales of scores of so-called 'low caste' *jatis* helped me through the long night. From that time on, as you may have noticed here, I either use the term 'high caste' and 'low caste' in quotation marks or I prefix them with the phrase 'so called'.

Now the surcharged units of caste politics began to make sense. At last I could figure out why Edmund Leach was wrong when he said that the moment competition enters the picture, castes must disintegrate.[7] As castes have diverse symbolic wells of energy, as each caste has its own much valorized origin tale, and as no caste ever accepts that they are beneath others but in fact superior to them, there is no reason for caste identities to disappear. Yes, caste as a system has certainly taken a beating, for the vertical arrangement of whichever kind is constantly contested on the ground. Indeed, the more the system is undermined, the greater is the vibrancy of caste-based identity. We are now better positioned to understand the truth about caste politics and how competition and strife and order and reorder are its alliances in complete violation of the sacred hierarchy.

Why the Caste Calculus Fails in Politics

In 1990, when I was working on the farmers' mobilization in west UP, I took a detour to a village dominated by the Gujar caste because I had been told that an election meeting was being held there. My trip was made easier when I met a Gujar taxi-driver from the same village. It so happened that the candidate belonged to a neighbouring vicinage and was doing the rounds shoring up his support base at home. On the way back I started chatting with the driver about my experience in the village that afternoon. Matter of factly I told him: 'You will of course be voting for this Gujar candidate.' He first slowed his car, and then took it to the side, turned to me, and asked in true puzzlement, 'Why, sir?' That was my first lesson then and thereafter not to take caste membership and politics for granted.

If we begin to question this relationship, it is not very difficult to realize that caste cannot be held responsible for our political inefficiency just as it cannot explain victory or defeat in elections. Pressured by this realization, I undertook a study of parliamentary elections in the 1990s of three major states, namely UP, Bihar and Maharashtra. I will not detail the particulars here but the result of this exercise showed that caste and political performance just did not tally. The strength of the Yadavs or the Jats in this area or that one did not automatically ensure their victory or of their party in those areas.[8] More recently I undertook a study of the 2007 elections in the UP legislative elections when Mayawati and the BSP (Bahujan

Samaj Party) swept into power with an absolute majority[9] and found to my surprise that there is no such thing as a Scheduled Caste political stronghold (see Appendix 1). In many of the areas in which the BSP won in 2002 it lost in 2007, and in many regions where the SCs are in greater numbers and also where their literacy rate is high, BSP victory could not be taken for granted[10].

The electoral outcome of the 2007 election in UP is extremely significant. Mayawati began her career as a radical as can be champion of the Dalits, but had never won an absolute majority in previous elections. This time around in 2007 she appealed to the poor of all castes, without taking her eyes off the Scheduled Castes, and won an unprecedented victory. As I mentioned earlier, this victory cannot be explained in terms of Scheduled Caste presence or absence (see electoral map in Appendix 1), but rather in terms of appealing to the poor in general. Mayawati had Brahmans as her advisors and close party confidantes. This could never have been imagined of the early Mayawati who had then recommended a thorough hiding of Brahmans (along with merchant and ex-landlord castes) with shoes and slippers as the ultimate humiliation. However, this time around, one of her prinicipal slogans in the 2007 elections was that even poor Brahmans deserve affirmative-action-style reservations of seats and job opportunities, just as Scheduled Castes and Scheduled Tribes do (more on caste-based reservations a little later). This took the sting out of caste politics in the name of caste politics. Such a long journey, but the end was worth it, at least for Mayawati.

In fact, all too often we take the glib stories of caste dominating politics straight from the popular media and from politicians without subjecting this assertion to the simplest of tests. KHAM and AJGAR acronyms, used for caste alliances, are often cited but what is overlooked is that in the case of the former, Harijans and Muslims (the 'H' and 'A' of the first acronym) are important constituents and in the latter there are contending and competitive peasant castes, such as the Gujar, Jat, and Rajput (the 'J', 'G' and 'R' of the second acronym) within the same combine. Clearly, caste logic cannot dictate such alliances. A Gujar and Rajput or Jat view each other with hostility, and how can Harijans and Muslims form part of the same caste alliance?

Once this aspect is dilated upon, the shortcomings of the popular version of caste alliances falls apart. It must now be clearly acknowledged that it is not caste so much as actually existing secular interests that bring people together though they belong, as is to be expected, to different castes. In many such cases, the combines make sense at a political level even though they defy textual caste logic. Leaders want to distribute seats and privileges among themselves, and the only way they can keep rivals out is by forming caste alliances at the top. However, as these caste blocs come into being to cope with singular contingencies they never really last very long. A new set of pressing issues, a new political rival, and the old bonhomie falls apart. The ordinary voter has nothing to do with all of this.

That caste never stood in the way of political mobilization and the secular demand for economic betterment is a story that most of the popular media and exotica-tuned academics are loath to entertain. This phenomenon is not something that is very recent. It has been recorded and amplified by historians with material going as far back as medieval India. The best examples are in fact from the struggle for Independence when people from diverse backgrounds and communities joined the movement under a multi-caste and a multi-religious leadership. The movement of the sharecroppers and indigent farmers during the 1930s and 1940s give adequate body to this point of view as also do trade union movements. Peasant leaders came from different castes. Some like Swami Sahajanand Saraswati, the once unassailable peasant leader from Bihar, came from a so-called upper-caste community, but then there was also a Madari Pasi, who was from a subaltern and impoverished caste, but nevertheless led the peasant revolt in Uttar Pradesh in the 1920s.[11]

There are three reasons why caste cannot explain political outcome, no matter how hard culturologists and professional pundits may try. First, there is no caste that is large enough to form a political majority in either a legislative or parliamentary constituency. In the best possible scenario the Yadavs constitute no more than 20 per cent of the population, and that too, very rarely. Usually they constitute around 10 per cent where, according to the popular press, they are supposed to be politically powerful. The Jats have never gone beyond 8 per cent of the population even in the much talked about Jat bastions. The Marathas fare better as they comprise approximately 32 per cent of the population of Maharashtra, but are internally fractionated along political lines from the Shiv Sena to the Communist parties.

The second reason why caste and politics cannot be easily correlated is because most voters are not professional casteists and have other things to worry about besides their primordial ties when they go to vote. If no single caste can swing the election in its favour by its numerical presence, it is obvious that when people go to the polling booth caste calculations will not help.

The third reason why caste calculations fail to determine election outcomes is because no caste, as a caste, thinks well of any other caste. It is often incorrectly assumed that peasant castes naturally call out to each other, or Scheduled Castes are always in perfect amity and agreement within their ranks. This is far from true. Gujars hate Jats and vice versa, and there is also the widely noted phenomenon of untouchability among untouchables.[12] So much for caste loyalty, both internally and horizontally.

It might however still be argued that even if caste loyalties are of no use, why can it not be said that caste voting blocs are still around? After all, there is the vertical hierarchy, and those at the top could easily mobilize those at the bottom to do their bidding. This however does not work either because the dominant castes of yore no longer control the village economy. I pointed to this aspect in earlier chapters when discussing the vanishing village. The gradual slide from power of these erstwhile landed families began in the 1960s, and today there is no such thing as a ruling caste in any significant way in rural India.

From Caste System to Caste Identity

The plight of rural agriculture explains why the caste system has collapsed, or is at least in a highly dilapidated condition. This does not however mean that caste identities have also waned: on the contrary, they are thriving. Now this would appear contradictory, even incomprehensible to some. How can the caste system collapse and yet caste identities remain strong, and in fact, become stronger? I believe I have an answer to this because of my fateful encounter in south Gujarat with my Dubla friend.

What is the significance of separating system from identity? When the caste system rules then politics and economics are not a major concern and they enter into the picture only surreptitiously at the interstitial levels[13]. As Dumont argued, all castes acquiesce to the hierarchy of purity and pollution, from the Brahmans at the top to the Untouchables way down at the bottom. As this hierarchy embraces all castes, each caste must ideologically subscribe to the maintenance of the system as a whole.[14] In that case democracy is just a sham, for only that much will be allowed to enter the political process that does not offend the hierarchy and system. Also, as this supposed all-pervasive hierarchy even orders occupational divisions,[15] economic compulsions are naturally banished from active consideration.

In this scheme of things there is no room for multiple hierarchies or for caste pride to be manifested down the line. However, because the village economy held and the members of the local dominant caste could exercise the hierarchy that was most precious to them a contrary reality of proud, submerged identities and contested hierarchies did not seriously engage the academic.

The fact of multiple hierarchies which the Dubla lady brought to my attention is really the key. If there are indeed multiple hierarchies embedded in the caste order then this implies that all origin tales are equally valid or invalid, true or untrue; take your pick. It cannot however be said that the

Brahman tale of origin that is appended to the *Rig Veda* (the most ancient Hindu sacerdotal text) is superior to all others, some of which exist only in an oral form. According to this *Rig Vedic* myth, Brahmans come from the head of the primeval being, the warriors from the arms, the commoners from the stomach, and the low castes of helots, slaves and worse, from the heel. Looked at closely in comparison with other origin tales, this too is fantastic and equally unbelievable to the rational mind, but all too often we gloss over this as it is a part of the *Rig Veda*, no less.

Some origin tales relate that even so-called low castes claim their origins in Lord Shiva. Members of such castes believe that they are Shiva's children and originate from Shiva's seed, but that in subsequent periods they fell victims to deceit and chicanery, and sometimes they were even cheated by idiosyncratic Hindu gods, of which there are many. In some instances, Brahmans of one kind got together to deny the more legitimate Brahmans their rightful status, in other cases, the gods were jealous, and there were times when the gods were embarrassed by their fecundity and hid their offspring in dubious quarters. Over and above this, there are many tales of once noble warriors defeated by traitors (like the Dubla story), or evil kings undermining upright subjects.[16]

These origin tales indicate that the caste system, as a system, worked primarily because it was enforced by power, and not by ideological acquiescence. It is only when we are armed with this perspective that we are conceptually prepared to study the relationship between caste and politics. If in the past it appeared as though there were few obvious disagreements over the hierarchy, then this was primarily for two reasons. First, the relationships between castes were played out within the confines of the closed natural economy of the village. This left no room for manoeuvre for the subaltern communities and castes. Second, during the pre-colonial period, caste hierarchies were contested and renegotiated episodically following the upheavals arising from a major social discord, usually a war.[17] As such instances were rare, it gave rise to the illusion that castes have never competed and have been politically inactive.

The tranquillity that this vision of the 'pure hierarchy' inspired should have been shattered irreparably when certain castes began to clamour for a higher status following the census operations of the colonial regime. According to O'Malley, during the 1911 census enumeration a number of castes objected to being placed at inferior levels in the hierarchy, or wanted to be known by a term other than the traditional one assigned to them. Such petitions came fast and thick because the impression had gone around at that time that the census was not just about recording numbers but also about assigning rank and prestige.[18] Around this time caste associations, or *sabhas*, began proliferating to press for higher status both in the census records as well as in everyday interactions.[19] Some enlightened rajas, such as the ruler of Tranvancore, also helped in this initiative by elevating certain castes.[20] The Baroda prince awarded scholarships to bright students from 'low' caste families. B.R. Ambedkar, the legendary leader of the Scheduled Castes and one of the founding figures of Independent India's constitution, was one such beneficiary.

The British authorities intervened in the caste order quite significantly by giving Brahmans extraordinary precedence over other castes. Whenever the colonial authorities were in any doubt as to what was 'correct' custom they rushed to the Brahmans for advice.[21] Where would the Brahmans be without this gracious gesture by the British towards them? Another service caste, a little elevated than most, but nonetheless a service caste. They would remain, as they always were, at the bidding of the ruling landed classes. If they were fortunate and in the good books of the village oligarchy then these Brahmans would serve as their family priests. If they did not quite make that grade they would then preside over the ritual needs of the lower classes. There were thus Brahmans for the well-to-do and others for the less well off, and some of them were indeed desperately poor and yearning for patronage.

At any rate, this British intervention in favour of Brahmans, particularly in south India and Maharashtra,[22] gave these hitherto ritual specialists a large measure of supra-local influence of a kind they had never hitherto enjoyed. Resentment against this growing Brahman dominance resulted in anti-Brahman movements in south India and Maharashtra from the latter years of the nineteenth century. While the non-Brahman movement in Maharashtra has now become more or less defunct, the mobilization in Tamil Nadu has evolved over the years. There are two mainstream political parties in Tamil Nadu that can legitimately claim to be descendants of the original anti-Brahman Dravida Kazagham movement.

The Decline of the Dominant Caste

The decline of the traditional élite castes in Indian politics has been discussed quite frequently in academic literature.[23] Rudolph and Rudolph characterized the newly ascendant peasant castes who challenged the hegemony of the traditional Kshatriya castes such as the Rajputs and Bhumiyars as 'bullock capitalists'.[24] These peasant castes constitute 34 per cent of the population but control about 51 per cent of the land, more than any other agrarian class.[25] As a category they are closer to 'yeoman farmers' than to kulaks, as their economic operation is a mix of 'capitalist, pre-industrial and non capitalist features'.[26]

The political rise of the self-sufficient owner–cultivators coincides with the emergence of the backward class movement in large parts of India. To put the matter in perspective, it needs to be recalled that feudal landlordism, or zamindari, as the Indian variant was known, was abolished in India after Independence. This seriously undercut the economic and power base of the traditional rural élite, many of whose members also had an established urban foothold. Though there were attempts by this class to conceal the extent of their holdings by registering their possessions in the name of fictitious owners, the writing was up on the wall. Gradually, they lost their pre-eminence in rural India, and this was signalled by the social ascendance of the middle peasants or bullock capitalists, many of whom were tenants under zamindars, large and small.[27]

This is where we need to bring in contemporary rural

dynamics to grasp how power shifted to these assertive peasant castes. The examination of the changing village in the earlier chapter is germane to our understanding of caste and politics, for only then will we fully grasp what is meant by the breakdown of the caste system and the emergence of caste identities. It is this distinction that is important for us to appreciate, for otherwise the popular exoticized view that the caste as a system is holding up development because of the groundswell of primordial passions would easily become the regnant explanation for our institutional backwardness. The damage that this point of view does, among other things, is that it robs that element of rationality that prevails among the underprivileged and gives undue credit to the manipulations of the few.

Till the late 1960s, and perhaps in the early '70s too, landownership was 'a crucial factor in establishing dominance. Generally, the pattern of landownership in rural India is such that the bulk of the arable land is concentrated in the hands of a relatively small number of big owners as against a large number who either own very little land or no land at all'.[28] The picture has obviously changed a great deal since the 1960s. The 'bullock capitalists' of Rudolph and Rudolph are small owners of land, and yet they exercise considerable political power in contemporary India, as can be gauged from the successes of Samajwadi Party and Rashtriya Janata Dal in Uttar Pradesh and Bihar respectively.[29]

It is not as if these peasant castes have suddenly become much richer. The more crucial fact is that the patrons of the past have become poorer and can no longer wield the kind of power or influence they took for granted in the past. Naturally, the idea of vote banks in the control of dominant factions no longer effectively applies today.[30] According to Sharma, the new dominants of rural India are not necessarily those who are economically at the top. They must, of course, have a viable economic standing, but they should also have sufficient numbers as well as political connections.[31] Karanth puts this idea across rather nicely when he says that 'it is not always necessary for a caste to have all the attributes of dominance ... but one or two are enough to ensure a modicum of dominance'.[32] Indeed, 'a modicum of dominance' is more prevalent today than decisive dominance. Also, as Béteille pointed some time ago, caste inequalities are not so much cumulative as they are dispersed.[33]

The morphological features of the contemporary agrarian structure inhibit cumulative inequalities and decisive dominance. Let us recall at this stage some of the salient features of rural India discussed previously. Eighty-five per cent of landholdings in India are below five acres and 63 per cent under three acres. Given this ground-level situation, owner–cultivators can hardly be expected to behave like the oligarchs of yore. In addition, a large number of rural people are seeking rural non-farm employment. Also today, 44.5 per cent of rural net domestic product is non-agricultural,[34] and that the fiftieth round of the National Sample Survey (NSS) held in 1993-94 shows that 32.9 per cent of rural households were outside agriculture. By the fifty-seventh round of the NSS in 2002-03, the percentage has risen to 35.2 per cent. In states such as Punjab, Jammu and Kashmir, Kerala, and Haryana the number of non-agricultural households in rural India is above 50 per cent, and even in the backward state of Bihar, 40 per cent of rural households are non-agricultural.[35]

These gross statistics suggest a picture of rural stratification that cannot uphold the earlier prestige that was accorded to a non-competitive caste hierarchy. It is obvious that if the earlier hierarchy held, with all its idiosyncratic nuances, it was primarily because it was buttressed by the economic power of the landed élite. As that is no longer the dominant feature in rural India, castes compete out in the open and 'conspire in the sun'. If castes are more overtly in conflict today then it is primarily because the caste system, as we knew it to be, has by and large collapsed in most parts of India. The obverse side of this collapse is the assertion of caste identities. Earlier, some castes dared not openly avow what they had always believed in for fear of reprisal from the established rural élite. This need not worry them any longer, and that is why they can now boldly assert their caste pride and status claims.

Emergence of Dalit Politics and Reservations

It is not just the owner–cultivators, or bullock capitalists, who are aggressively using caste as a vehicle of self-assertion but also those who were earlier considered to be untouchables in the traditional Hindu caste hierarchy. This phenomenon too has an India-wide character, from Tamil Nadu in the south to northern states such as Uttar Pradesh. The Republican Party in Maharashtra and the Bahujan Samaj Party in Uttar Pradesh are the two most widely acknowledged political organizations propounding the aspirations of the ex-untouchables. The legal term for them is now Scheduled Castes as they are listed by name in the Schedule of the Indian constitution which provides special privileges for them in order to redress the persecution they endured for centuries in the course of history.

In keeping with the enabling clauses in the constitution, an act was passed in 1950 granting reservation of seats in educational institutions and government services to members of the Scheduled Castes and Scheduled Tribes (they too were listed) in proportion to their population. For the Scheduled Castes it worked out to about 15 per cent and for the Scheduled Tribes about 7 per cent. This was how the famous reservation policy came into effect. India is the first country in the world where such a provision was put in place to correct historical injustices. It has since become the ground for many caste-based agitations. There is no doubt that India's reservations policy was a novel and historical step and one that India much needed. Subsequently, it may have also inspired similar legislations, such as the affirmative action policy in US and similar initiatives in many other parts of the world.

Be that as it may, the Scheduled Castes seem to prefer the term 'Dalit' or the oppressed, for that clearly underlines their willingness to fight for their political, economic and social rights. 'Scheduled Castes' or 'Dalits' do not form a homogenous group, as many often assume. Over and above challenging the position of the traditional 'upper castes' they also contest for superiority among themselves. The famous social anthropologist

I.P. Desai wrote extensively about 'untouchability among untouchables' to draw attention to precisely this phenomenon.[36] The bulk of the political and ideological struggle of Dalits is spearheaded by their middle-class caste members who are able to give voice to their demands for cultural assertion more effectively than the rest in their respective communities. It is with the aid of these middle-class leaders that Dalits today project themselves as indigenous people, Buddhists, and the like.[37] However, the poor Dalit marginal farmers and landless labourers are more concerned about questions of economic exploitation, but these are not adequately addressed by their middle-class leaders.[38] According to Rajendra Vora, no Dalit leader after Ambedkar paid consistent attention to economic issues of their poorer caste members.[39]

It is not as if the Dalits alone are pressing for a re-evaluation of their caste status; indeed this process is widespread across the entire spectrum. To a significant degree this is the outcome of altered land relations as the inability of large landholders today to economically dominate the villages has provided room for the poorer castes to break free and strive for a favoured niche of their own. This, coupled with the provisions in the Constitution, have allowed caste associations to proliferate throughout India.[40] Today there are literally hundreds of associations of this kind, each projecting its special claims.[41] Through *gaurav gathas* (tales of pride) and *jati puranas* (origin tales of *jatis*, or castes), these associations seek to instill a sense of pride in their primordial identities without which it would be difficult to harness caste identities to political aims. This is as true of the Brahman and Baniya castes,[42] as it is of peasant castes, such as the Ahirs,[43] or the Scheduled Castes.[44]

As mentioned, while many Scheduled Caste associations are content in claiming Brahman or Kshatriya status, those that are politically active are keen to point out their alienation from established Hindu myths, beliefs, and rituals. When Ambedkar converted to Buddhism he made it clear in his vows that he did not consider Buddha to be an incarnation of the Hindu god Vishnu, as many Hindus claim, nor would he follow any of the

176 THE CAGED PHOENIX

rituals of Hinduism and would abide strictly by the Buddhist code.

B.R. Ambedkar, as leader of the depressed castes, was the chairman of the Drafting Committee of the Constituent Assembly. The Indian Constitution was written under his leadership, and his role in this position was widely commended both by his contemporaries and by generations of constitutionalists subsequently. Soon after Independence, he converted to Buddhism, at least in part, because of his frustrations with the ruling Congress party. This led him to publicly and dramatically distance himself from Hinduism, the religion into which he was born. His conversion to Buddhism was a highly symbolic political act that helped to fuse Dalit antipathy towards Hinduism, and at the same time enabled them to leverage their new identity to great political advantage.[45] In recent years, the All India Confederation of Scheduled Castes and Scheduled Tribes have held many conversion ceremonies that have attracted a great deal of public attention. In these ceremonies there has always been a pointed attack on Hindu symbolic systems.[46] The point of debate is the degree to which these overt demonstrations of identity in urban India are actually carried over to the Dalits of the rural hinterlands.[47] Dalit politics today symbolically defy Hinduism by either promoting conversions to Buddhism or by claiming that Dalits belong to the original Kshatriya orders before Vedic Hindus entered the geographical space of India.

Jotiba Phule of the Satyashodhak Samaj in Maharashtra argued that the so-called low castes of Maharashtra were the original and real Kshatriyas before the Brahmans and then the Muslims overwhelmed them.[48] Many Scheduled Caste organizations now consider themselves to be 'ad' (or the founders) of true Indian culture. In emphasizing their foundational role in Indic civilization they are able to project themselves as being on top of the status hierarchy. This condition is obviously necessary to establish confidence among Scheduled Castes in their quest for political power, and is again quite in keeping with our conceptualization of castes as being principally discrete in nature.

Such instances of symbolic defiance are not limited to Hindus alone. Surinder Jodhka incisively highlights how the Sikh leather-workers (pejoratively known as *chamars*) have also challenged the established norms of the mainstream gurudwaras and their styles of worship.[49] These Sikh leather-workers now call themselves Ad-Dharmis (etymologically linked to Phule's concept of *adi*), and refuse to bow down to the dictates of the dominant Jat Sikh community. The Ad-Dharmis have set up their own gurudwaras and refuse to go to those run by Jat Sikhs. It is true that Scheduled Caste Sikhs have often felt alienated and unwanted in local Sikh gurudwaras, though Sikhism is officially against casteism. Ad Dharmi gurudwaras give the Sikh holy book the pride of place, but also have a bust or engraving of Ravidas, the devotional medieval 'low caste' saint who challenged Brahman orthodoxy. Though Ravidas's contribution is acknowledged fulsomely in the Sikh holy book, his image is not to be found in any mainstream Jat Sikh gurudwara. Ravidas is an important figurehead among ex-untouchables, especially in north India, and by installing his image in the gurudwara the Ad-Dharmis were reaching out to other Scheduled Castes elsewhere, even those outside Sikhism.

A large number of studies dealing with primary data demonstrate that conflicts between castes are rarely resolved at the village level. In the past, the village panchayat used to mediate tensions of various kinds but, as Karanth demonstrates, the caste panchayat, or council, has today lost its salience.[50] In Bihar tensions between castes are not adjudicated at the local level. In some cases the tensions remain unresolved, in other instances the matter is taken to court where it is not always satisfactorily resolved. In one instance, Sahay recalls from his field notes:

> '... members of the *chamar* caste were beaten up by the Brahmins. The case was not settled at the village level. The *chamars* went to the police and to the court for justice. When they realized that the court was not going to punish the Brahmins immediately, they beat

some of the Brahmins up and withdrew the case from the court.'[51]

The Caste Turnaround

In the first week of April 2008, nearly coinciding with All Fool's Day, a dramatic reversal of caste order took place in rural India, in rural west Uttar Pradesh, where Jats once ruled over the rest with complete impunity due to their preponderance as a rich landowning community.

In the years 1986–93, Mahender Singh Tikait was a Jat icon and the unquestioned leader of Bharatiya Kisan Union (BKU). Today the same man stands alone. Only his clan and caste in his village stood up to barricade him briefly from Mayawati's police, but they soon gave in. When the BKU was strong no government official dare collect electricity bills from west UP farmers; indeed, they would not even enter any of the villages of Meerut and Muzzafarnagar to read the metres. However, in March 2008, after a brief show of desperate pride, Tikait was led off to jail for his alleged caste slurs against Mayawati. In the old days, abusing Scheduled Castes was as natural to Jats as breathing.

Mayawati had won an absolute majority in the Uttar Pradesh state-wide elections in 2007. She is herself from the Scheduled Caste and her BSP considers itself to be first and foremost a vehicle of the ex-untouchables. Other poorer castes would be encouraged to join the BSP, but it would not lose sight of the Scheduled Castes.

Up to the years when Tikait held sway over west UP, Jats did not hesitate to say the crudest things about Scheduled Castes. I came across many such instances on a routine basis when I was researching the BKU in the late 1980s. I remember once asking a Scheduled Caste individual whether he had any land, and a passing group of Jat boys tauntingly commented that I must be wrong in the head even to imagine that a 'Harijan' could own land. I also remember the humiliation on the face of a well-dressed Dalit youth when a senior BKU activist from a village near Meerut pounced upon him in full public view and rubbished him for his 'city clothes'. The Jat farmer then turned to me and said that this was a vivid example of how the government was pampering the Scheduled Castes to the extent that they had now forgotten their station in life. Likewise, when a Jat lost his wallet in a Muzzafarnagar village, word went around that a member of the Scheduled Castes had pinched the cash, and what else could once expect from this lot. For weeks after that Jats would routinely slight Dalits as pickpockets. I have even seen Jats abuse Scheduled Castes in the choicest slurs for something as minor as taking a short-cut across their fields.

When seasons change farmers must burn the leaves and move on. Likewise, the rural Jats too had better mend their ways. Tikait has already begun on this journey. Just before his humiliating 'surrender' he likened Mayawati to his daughter ('*beti*'). Had I not heard him say this with my own ears I would have had difficulty in believing it. When Tikait was in his prime as the BKU supremo, Mayawati was just a political ingénue. True, the BSP had made its presence felt, but Tikait kept ignoring the warning signs. Mayawati's brief stints as chief minister were not impressive enough for Tikait and his men to change their abusive attitude towards the Scheduled Castes. That is why when Mayawati's police force bearded Tikait in his own den he was hardly prepared for it. Caught off guard, he attempted desperately to roar his way out of trouble, but when he failed he finished off with a bleat: all one heard was a faint mumble in the jungle.

In the BKU's heyday Tikait was an important political figure. He not only led long marches with his followers to Delhi, Meerut, and Lucknow, and brought these cities to a standstill but was also photographed with high-profile leaders, all of them beaming from left to right. Urban visitors and political personalities were always hanging around his home in village Sisauli hoping to munch *chappati* with him.

Through all these years of living it up in political high places he kept the Jat swagger alive by regaling his home crowd with anecdotes about how the other big-wigs always had to cede ground to him. Once I heard him brag how the late member of Parliament Rajesh Pilot (a powerful west UP figure from the rival Gujar landowning caste) rushed out of his vehicle when he saw Tikait in Delhi. He then went on to elaborate on the sequence of events: first Pilot opened his car door and only then did Tikait step out of his jeep, first Pilot stuck out his hand, and only then Tikait extended his, and so on. All of this endeared him to his BKU followers who sometimes went to the extent of not just calling him a 'Chaudhry' but also revering him as a Mahatma.

Surprisingly, I found many urban commentators take Tikait's 'Mahatma' honorific quite seriously. It is true that Tikait nearly always had a Muslim, who also looked very Muslim, on the podium with him in many of his public rallies. This gave rise to the superficial impression that Tikait was a truly secular person. I must confess that I too fell for this, but only for a short while. I soon discovered that the term 'Mahatma' was wholly misplaced when I learnt more about how Tikait and his followers treated the Scheduled Castes.

Tikait had no problems at all in rallying Muslim Jats and Rajputs to his side, for they too were substantial landowners in west UP. The BKU made it very clear from the outset that landless agricultural labourers were not 'kisans' and hence could not be admitted to the organization. This effectively kept the Scheduled Castes out as they were almost entirely a landless community in that region. Therefore, even for the sake of organizational form, there was no need for west UP Jats and Gujars in the BKU to revise their opinions of the Dalits.

Today the BKU is a pale shadow of its former self, and Tikait just a gap-toothed has-been. His one time supporters are no longer starchy about being noble farmers. They were in denial for decades but have now reconciled themselves to the fact that agriculture is hardly the occupation that it was once cut out to be. Their once proud landholdings are microscopic in size through subdivisions of the family property. Consequently, Jat landowners can no longer employ Dalit labourers, or exercise any other kind of economic domination over them. This in turn has emboldened Dalits to look for jobs outside the village and also for a political voice. The rise of the BSP led by Kanshi Ram and Mayawati in UP can be timed almost exactly with this period. The Jats have clearly lost on both counts: they lost out on farming and they lost caste to Mayawati.

The world that Tikait knew so well and once dominated has slipped away from under his feet. He has no alternative now but to claim Mayawati as his '*beti*', but this has so far proved to be just a one-sided adoption.

Caste Leaders in Search of Followers

Quite clearly, castes were never outside politics, only the connection is much more transparent today. While in the past ambitious castes had to 'wade through slaughter to a throne', caste tensions today are routine affairs; a daily grind, as it were. Also, unlike the case in colonial times, castes in contemporary India are no longer concerned about official rankings. If certain castes band together it is because the members of these communities occupy an identical position in India's social and economic structure. This is what gives rise to the optical illusion that caste is everything in most contemporary political mobilizations in India. The truth however is that coalitions take place across and between castes not because caste ideology brings them together (which we clearly know is not the case), but rather because they have identical secular interests. This is what leads to peculiar alliances during election times. Ahirs, Jats, and Gujars, despite their mutual antipathy, have frequently banded together to fight elections. These caste combines often do well because they address issues that affect members of a certain strata (in this case, owner–cultivators) in common. Likewise, when there was a broad-based alliance to grant reservations in government jobs and educational institutions to the so-called 'backwards', once again these peasant castes got together because they needed urban jobs. Village life, as we know, is now no longer what it was once cut out to be.

Caste identities have evolved to a much higher level, and it is now a question of self over others, and not self in relation to others. Thus, no matter which caste is in question, its involvement in politics is primarily to stake a claim to jobs, educational opportunities, as well as to positions of power in government bodies, in direct competition against other castes. Unlike the agitations regarding the census operations in 1911 and later, caste assertions today are not just to feel good, but to make it good in a highly competitive environment. This kind of involvement in politics cannot be explained in terms of a restatement of the traditional caste system.

Can this coming together to press for secular claims be seen as a manifestation of caste loyalties or a normal outcome of democratic politics? It must be the latter because these alliances come and go and also because the partners in such coalitions are not socially on the best of terms. However, their internal hostility notwithstanding, they can still rise above their ancient prejudices to make common cause for the greater good of their class. Isn't this after all what democratic politics is all about?

If rural India can vote outside pure caste considerations, then surely caste cannot be held responsible for India's inability to come to the top, or to explain its lack of public infrastructure, or its inability to provide quality level public goods. If these inadequacies are acting as brakes to our economic development, should caste be blamed? The reason lies elsewhere, as caste, neither as a system nor as identity, can determine election victory or defeat. If they appear to be so then it is primarily intellectuals and journalists who are to blame because it is they who have popularized the notion of caste arithmetic in politics. They still fail to draw a distinction between system and identity in the caste order. Nor do they realize that voters are not professional casteists and that other issues take them to the polling booths. Besides, there are logical problems regarding caste arithmetic and inter-caste partisanship that also need to be appreciated.

In 1989 I witnessed how different parties short listed legislative assembly candidates and which reaffirmed my view that caste is an obsession of the politicians. I was fortunate to be privy to this meeting as I had an acquaintance whose cousin was chairing that particular event. He was a senior party member of the region and belonged to the Samajwadi Party which is popularly considered to be an organization of the Yadav caste. This man too was a Yadav.

The candidates were first discussed between him and two of his subordinate party workers privately. To a degree this reminded me of a Shiv Sena meeting in Mumbai in the early 1970s when again aspiring members of Mumbai Municipal Corporation came to Bal Thackeray for endorsement as candidates on the Shiv Sena ticket although on that occasion the discussions were conducted in loud and clear voices, and there was no mention of caste.

In west UP it was different. Clearly, a short-listing had been undertaken the previous day and it was being reviewed today by this three-member committee before the recommendations were sent to a higher level. Four candidates pressed their way into the room to make their claims and each of them referred to how many people he had on his side and how many he had won over from other castes. In addition, one of them also mentioned his record as a loyal party worker and the successes he had had in getting the roads to a few villages repaired and also in regularizing the bus services there. All four however made their strongest pitch in caste terms and claimed leadership of their own community and a few others to boot. Three of the four belonged to the Yadav caste and one was a Tyagi.

I was able to discern two interesting issues from my fly-on-the-wall observations of this meeting. First, candidates tend to come from the caste of the leaders of the party, in this case the Yadavs, though there are people from other castes too. Most importantly however they invariably make their case in the name of caste numbers, and that is where they believe their competitive edge lies. Journalists pick up this aspect of the political process quite easily as they are constantly hovering around politicians. They then help spread the word that elections are won or lost because of the caste background of the candidates and the caste loyalty of the voters. Such pronouncements mimic the sentiment of the politicians but not of the voters.

If one looks closely at the politics of reservations then once again it will be clear how caste virtuosos and spokesmen want to fire their rockets from the shoulders of a putative caste community. They work out their strategies around caste calculations primarily to outdo their political rivals within. This compels them to run their entire campaign relying heavily on the caste factor. If they win any support it is because the format of reservations is the best that most people know as a means of getting out of the village and securing an urban job. Secular calculations, more than caste loyalty, lead to reservation politics. Political jockeying of this kind is carried out in the name of caste, but that is not the full story. Even here, as is to be expected, it is the better-off among the rural castes who are able to effectively use the provisions of reservations to corner most of the jobs and educational opportunities. For the mass of the poor, regardless of caste, public goods are hardly public, and the fruits of reservations a faint vision many social strata away.

Barack Obama and Mayawati

Caste is perhaps the most divisive institution that humankind has ever known, which is why the fight against it must seek to unite and not fractionate citizens. Unfortunately, the way it is being handled is creating greater social fissures and constant reiterations of historical hurt. How then can we move forward when it is so tempting to constantly look back in anger for short-term political gains?

Like race in America, caste in India can neither be ducked nor dodged. If it is to be wrestled to the ground and taken out for the count, we must all be ready to jump in the mud together. A giant stride towards dismantling caste can come from Dalit visionaries who are not interested in seeking instant gratification from caste anger.

The appeal of natural justice striking back is undoubtedly

compelling, most of all because the returns are instant, but that would leave caste undisturbed. The contours of conflict would shift and place different castes in opposition, perhaps with greater ferocity, but they would all be there. It is only when Dalit leaders rise above immediate gratification that the possibility of uniting castes on the platform of citizenship becomes tenable. In this campaign there can be many footsoldiers in the ranks, and they should be encouraged to enlist so that the best among them can win the conviction for which they crave. Nehruvites, socialists, secularists, and Gandhians are all very well, but to be able to effectively commandeer them in an anti-caste operation they must be led by a Dalit general.

A post-caste society will seek mechanisms that address poverty and disease because they affect us all. Brahmans and Dalits need not be one-dimensional in their advocacy or rejection of caste. To fault reservations for our administrative lapses is the other side of the blame game that exaggerates the evil that upper castes perpetrate. To lead us from these old trenches we need exemplars from among Dalits who can see the forest *and* the trees. A post-caste society is not just about capturing power but about creating common horizons.

When Mayawati won Uttar Pradesh she conveyed the impression that she was serious about taking caste politics out of business without sacrificing the dignity of Dalits. By calling out to Brahmans and Baniyas to close ranks with Scheduled Castes she not only put Mulayam Singh in the shade but ideologically isolated the Mandalites, and reckless reservationists as well. Besides, by demanding reservations for the poor from all communities she took the sting out of the exclusivity that was for long the preserve of caste politics. If she is to stay true to this course she must constantly think beyond election skirmishes and dig in for the long battle. Who knows, she might win in the near term too, as Obama has, but this consideration should not be at the top of her agenda. Will her followers however understand this kind of reasoning? Will she see it herself? Let us admit what our genes tell us: there is a bit of every caste in all of us.

10

CASTE VIRTUOSOS STRIKE BACK

THE RESERVATIONS TURNAROUND

If caste can at all be held responsible for downgrading merit and thereby holding up developmental schemes and the genuine flowering of the equality of opportunities then one must blame the turn taken by the politics of reservations. This, and not blind caste loyalties, should be put on the dock and made answerable for the excessive intrusion of caste in our public life today. However, because we have an exoticized and mistaken assumption about caste we do not fully realize that reservation politics do not emanate spontaneously from bosoms inflamed by caste passions. They are, in fact, carefully orchestrated events across a particular interest group that includes a multiplicity of castes. Why should the reservation format be used? Well, why not? The policy of reservations for Scheduled Caste and Scheduled Tribes that have been in force for over five decades has become a bit of a holy cow. Nobody has dared to either knock it down or even calibrate it. Thus, a good measure has come a long way and is now actually becoming a retrograde policy. If reservations were good once, why are they wrong now?

The Gains of Reservations

First, it would be appropriate to draw attention to a frequently overlooked fact. When India became independent, less that one per cent of Class I civil servants were from the ranks of the Scheduled Castes. By 2002, over 12 per cent of senior level officers of the Government of India were from this background.[1] At this rate it will soon be at 15 per cent, which is roughly the proportion of Scheduled Castes in India. This in itself is a demonstration of how well reservations of jobs have worked.

In addition, on account of reservations, the increase in the number of public servants in the upper reaches of the government and the political machinery has led to a higher rate of conviction, and consequently lower proportion of acquittals, in cases of atrocities against SCs. Even in the short period between 1991 and 2000 the acquittal rate has fallen significantly from 17.03 to 9.90 per cent.[2] These are surely signal achievements in a society that for centuries discriminated against the Scheduled Castes.

To re-wind to 1950, when the Indian Constitution was adopted it was declared that the practice of untouchability would be a crime. Alongside this, the Constitution also made room to put in place a policy of reservations that would enable ex-Untouchable castes (now Scheduled Castes as they were listed in a schedule of the Constitution) and tribes (likewise Scheduled Tribes for the same reason) would be given special preference in government jobs and in State-run schools.

This was by no means an easy task. As untouchability was manifested differently in different parts of India, it was difficult to unequivocally determine who belonged to this category and who did not. It was not a simple and obvious exercise that the government undertook.[3] For example, Khatiks, Gwalas, and Suryavanshis were Untouchables in one state but not in others. Bearing in mind all these complications, the final list of Scheduled Castes was made and remains operative to this day.

Reservations of this kind cannot be likened to affirmative action simply because in the latter policy there is no mention of quotas; indeed such considerations are abhorred both at the political and judicial levels in the US. In the reservation scheme, seats are allotted on the basis of the population, which is why Scheduled Castes get 15 per cent and Scheduled Tribes about 7 per cent of jobs and educational opportunities in the government sector.

To return to the basic question: Why was it necessary to introduce reservations? No modern liberal–democratic society can allow a section of its society to be discriminated against on grounds of the accidents of birth. This part is clear enough, but there is more to be said. Democracy is a time-bound phenomenon for the living. It makes people impatient to see changes during their lifetime. It promotes a levelling of social status by creating equality of conditions in the quickest possible time without jeopardizing the basic human and civil rights. As SCs and STs were disprivileged for centuries it was not fair to expect them to get up and compete on equal terms with the rest right away. They had no assets whatsoever, neither social nor intellectual, nor political, nor, least of all, monetary. It is therefore in the fitness of things to make room for those who are dispossessed, and have been systematically dispossessed throughout India's recorded history, so that they can gain a measure of self-worth and basic, socially valuable, assets that will enable them to compete and relate to others as equal citizens. This is the fundamental justification for reservations, and the Constitution of India was the first to give it full scope on a firm, judicial basis before any other nation-state even contemplated such a measure.

Turning the Clock Back

Rural India is not however made up of Scheduled Castes alone. A bulk of the population, perhaps even a majority, comprise earthy peasant communities belonging to castes such as Okkaligas, Thevars, Jats, Gujars, Yadavs, Gounders, Reddys, and so on.

When the Indian Constitution provided reservations for Scheduled Castes and Tribes it also added that in due course of time similar legislation ought to be devised for the Other

Backward Classes (OBCs). The founders of the Constitution, however, made clear that caste was not to be the sole criterion for the notification of OBCs. This is ironic because today, as the 'C' in OBC refers not so much to class but, because of rather questionable political practices, to caste. A commission was set up in the mid-1950s under the chairmanship of Kaka Kalelkar but had to be abandoned. Attempts to identify a criterion or a set of criteria to determine backwardness proved too intractable. The empirical reality was far too complicated and multifaceted to allow a clear and just notification of OBCs.

This however did not satisfy power-brokers from different organizations. They were much more comfortable talking about caste than class, especially when doling out patronage to aggressive electoral blocs. So they maintained the pressure, which resulted in the formation of the Mandal Commission in the late 1970s. Unlike the first OBC commission under Kaka Kalelkar, the Mandal Commission had no difficulty in formulating their criteria for identifying OBCs and listed a number of castes who it felt qualified to be included. Through a clever sleight of hand, Mandal fudged caste for class and the first assemblage of OBCs were rolled out, ready for reservations. It was in 1990 that Mandal's recommendation became the basis of State policy and 27 per cent of all educational seats and government jobs were to be blocked for OBCs. This was the beginning of the justification for large-scale caste politics which soon occupied centre stage. This is how the clock was steadily being turned back.

The population of these so-called Backward Castes is difficult to estimate, and the figures range from 25 to 52 per cent of the total population of India. These Backward Castes generally comprise peasant and other agrarian communities. In terms of their socio-economic standing, they are generally placed between the traditional 'forward castes', such as Brahmans, Banias, Kayasthas, Rajputs, etc., and the Scheduled Castes and Scheduled Tribes. The forward castes constitute anything between 15 to about 36 per cent of the population. There are no clear numbers for this either. We only know with some degree of certitude that the Scheduled Castes constitute roughly 17 per cent of the population and the Scheduled Tribes a further 7 per cent or so.[4] However, because the Supreme Court ruled that as no more than 50 per cent of seats can be reserved, 27 per cent were reserved for OBCs as the remaining 22 per cent had already been slotted for SCs and STs.

Caste Virtuosos Call the Shots

The grounds justifying OBC reservations never sounded convincing but this policy carried a great deal of political weight. When in 1990 V.P.Singh, as prime minister, introduced reservations based on the Mandal Commission recommendations to outwit his rivals he put in place a retrograde system that will probably hold back both the development of citizenship and the economy for decades to come. Caste by itself is not that much of an obstruction to democracy as it can be pushed back from the public domain. Indeed, this is what the founders of the Constitution intended. However, the caste politics played out by politicians today in the wake of the Mandal commission is another matter and a deep source of concern.

Why are these reservations for the so-called OBCs regressive but those put in place by Ambedkar earlier progressive? The OBC reservations were to benefit the better off in rural India and not, as with SC/ST reservations, to help those without any assets whatsoever. Indeed, in the case of the Mandal reservations, those with rural wealth and economic power successfully pressurized the State to grant them jobs and educational placements in the urban sector. This has nothing to do with uplifting those who are marginalized and discriminated against, but everything to do with power politics.[5]

Whereas the earlier 1955 Kaka Kalelkar Commission found the task of drawing up a list of OBCs near impossible as the facts on the ground were too complicated, the Mandal Commission did not let the niceties of empirical evidence deter it from announcing that there were over 3743 castes, and counting, that qualified to belonged to the OBC category. As the late Rajiv Gandhi pointed out, in spirited opposition to the Mandal Commission on the floor of the Parliament on 6 September 1990, the Mandal Commission went ahead with its recommendations although the three eminent sociologists it had asked to advise the panel were against the identification of OBCs on the basis of caste. In addition, the information base for the commission's recommendation was extremely scanty. Out of approximately 500,000 villages, the Mandal Commission surveyed only 810—that too conducted by junior-level government officials without the assistance of any sociologist. Yes, towards the end of the report, Justice Mandal himself accepted that most states had not provided the information that was requested from them, and therefore the report was by no means 'an academic exercise'. It might have been greatly wanting in academic rigour but it certainly made up for this with political imagination.

Now let us see how blatantly political calculations entered the designation of OBCs by Mandal. This commission listed three major criteria for backwardness, namely, social, educational, and economic. So far so good! It then chose castes as the basis of looking at these criteria (needless to say that was unconstitutional) to determine backwardness. There is however much worse to come.

These major criteria also contained several sub-criteria within their rubric. Each of these subsets of criteria carried different weights and were assigned different points. It was then decided that any caste that scored eleven points or more was to be considered an OBC. Interestingly, social backwardness received the highest number of points as each of its sub-criteria carried three points each. Education came next with its own internal criteria carrying two points each. Last, the economic criteria had the lowest number of points, and if a caste were to score on each of the three criteria listed in this subset the maximum tally would only be three points. That is, the entire set of criteria under economic backwardness carries as much weight as a single criterion in the subset under social backwardness. One would have thought that economic

backwardness should have had top billing, especially when
calculations are being made on grounds of backwardness. This
is where the political machinations of Mandal, and of V.P.
Singh, its implementing hand, become apparent. The criteria for
backwardness was so overwhelmed by intangible and unverifiable
social criteria that it allowed the economically well off to sneak
in and be included as backwards.

What then were these social criteria that carried so much
weight in the Mandal scheme of things? The first social criterion
had to do with manual labour. If a significant number of men
and women, both in rural and urban settings, were engaged in
manual work then the caste would get three points. Likewise, if
a significant number of women of a particular caste worked
then that would yield another three points. If a caste was
viewed disparagingly by other castes then it would again get
three points. The cherry on the cake is the last of the four social
criteria. In this case, points are actually being given for breaking
the law. According to this criterion, a further three points are
given if, in a caste, 25 per cent females and 10 percent men in
the villages marry before the legal age, (10 per cent and 5 per
cent respectively for their urban counterparts).

It is not very difficult for any rural caste to score on all
these criteria. To begin with, no caste thinks well of any other
and a major characteristic of the caste order is 'mutual repulsion'.[6]
To score three points on this criterion can be taken for granted.
As for manual work, any proud landowning caste, say Jat, Gujar
or Yadav, will happily claim that they are hard-working peasants.
They would indeed, go the extra distance to make the point
that it is their ability to work with their hands that separates
them from soft city types or absentee landlords.[7]

To continue, the Mandal Commission hands out a further
three points to castes where women help their families by
performing manual work as well. This is an easy one too, for a
large number of women, even from well-to-do farmers' homes
are busy through the day milking, weeding, and performing
other sundry chores. This is a common enough phenomenon in
large parts of India and not a practice that is specific to poor

communities and those discriminated against. Age at marriage? Now that is tricky. Marriage records are rarely maintained in villages, so it is anyone's guess who got married at what age.

On each of these four criteria for social backwardness a caste can get three points each, a total of twelve points. As a caste only requires eleven points to belong to the OBC category one need not consider economic and educational backwardness at all. A clever move! With proper massaging of data, a caste can be home and dry as a fully certified OBC on grounds of intangible, non-measurable social backwardness criteria. Obviously, the whole scheme was designed in such a way that the well-to-do rural castes could easily escape scrutiny and receive the benefits of OBC reservations.

The judges of the Supreme Court stepped in at this point to impress upon politicians to create a filtering mechanism within the OBC reservation scheme that would deny benefits to those who may belong to the right caste but belong to the wrong class. What these judges probably do not realize is that the Mandal recommendations so carefully crafted the points system precisely to benefit this better-off section of society, as the formula carefully shields OBCs who are educationally and economically well-endowed. All political parties, from the left to the right, opposed the Supreme Court's attempts to thwart the ambitions of the rural rich by introducing the concept of the 'creamy layer'. Moreover, it is difficult to assess the 'creamy layer' in terms of rural infrastructural possessions as data on agricultural incomes and assets cannot be easily estimated or certified. Such figures are not only difficult to ascertain but are also open to manipulation by those who are well-connected in the rural sector.

Jats Become OBCs

If we examine the case of how the Jats manoeuvred to be included among the OBCs my contention regarding the use and abuse of Mandal by the powerful rural classes will become clearer.

After the Mandal Commission list was published a whole host of castes, including the powerful and prosperous Jats, Kayasthas, and Lingayats pressed to be included. Their sole justification was that they are nearly as poor as the Ahirs and Gujars who have got in, so why should they be excluded. In fact, at one point, the Haryana Backward Classes Commission set up on 7 September 1990[8] was faced with the Jat claim that they were below the Scheduled Castes too in terms of the Mandal frame of reference; that is the degree of Mandal's malleability.

In the matter of being disprivileged, only the Jats from Rajasthan had a specific complaint relating to as far back as the 1930s when the Rajputs did not allow them to ride a horse. There is nothing about not being permitted to enter temples, to draw water from village wells and other such humiliations that were the stuff of the everyday life of the ex-Untouchables. Time and time again Jat representatives complained about shrinking landholdings and rural distress, as if that is something that concerns only them. As the Haryana Jat Sabha from Hissar complained, 'The economic condition of the Jat community has become pitiable in the last fifty years.' Well, in this context the Jats are not alone. Rural distress is widespread with about 65 per cent of the so-called 'forward castes' earning less than Rs 525 a month.[9]

It is true that in Rajasthan Jats are economically below Rajputs and suffered feudal ignominies under them, but that was true for only one state. In Haryana or UP where there are significant Jat populations there were no other castes that could bully them into submission. Punjab and UP had Jat kingdoms and members of this community were always considered to be the most powerful in the region. Mandal politics is all about wielding power, and that is why the numbers of OBCs continue to increase under political pressure. To give a measure of how politically useful it is to be a member of the OBC, the number of castes in this category has progressively gone up from a mere eleven in 1883 to over 3000 today. When will it stop?

In the hearings held by a two-member Bench in 1997 on a

petition submitted by the Jat lobby it came to light that two Jat sub-castes listed as OBC by Mandal did not even exist. Nobody had heard of either the Gutka Jat or the Chillon Jat, and yet these names were there.[10] Clearly, as Rajiv Gandhi had contested, the Mandal Commission had not done its homework correctly.

Eventually, the Jats won their case bolstered by the many powerful advocates and strong-arm politicians on their side. Today, Jats are officially OBCs. The Solanki Rajputs are powerful in Gujarat so they make it to the OBC list too. There were other castes however who, for want of political clout, failed to make it into Mandal's list. There are many Vishwakarmas in UP who are politically well-connected so they are declared backward there but not in Maharashtra where they are not that prominent. For the same reasons the Boyas are among the OBCs in Tamil Nadu but not in Andhra Pradesh. There is, therefore, compelling evidence that it very often takes power and politically potent networks to be considered an OBC.[11] It is often said that OBC reservations have worked best in south India with positive social results. It has long been acknowledged that apart from Thanjavur district in Tamil Nadu, in no other region do the Brahmans come even close to the affluence and power that OBCs exercise in other regions of the state. Indeed, south India was privileged because the raja of Travancore and Cochin put in place an enlightened educational policy that allowed those from indigent circumstances to become literates. In fact, according to the 1921 census, the percentage of literates was 38 per cent, which is higher than in many districts of Bihar and UP today.

If however we take away the initial advantages that came to south India because of such provisions then we find the gap in the literacy rates between Tamil Nadu and the other states is closing. Between 1901 and 1921 male literacy in south India was 40–50 per cent higher than in the rest of India. By 2001 however the difference had narrowed down to a mere 8.3 per cent.[12] Even after years of reservations for the OBCs in Tamil Nadu, the conditions of the SCs have not significantly improved. For example, in the 7 plus age group 37 per cent of SCs and 59 per cent of STs are still illiterate whereas the figure is only 24 per cent for the rest of population.[13] Incidentally, Tamil Nadu has not had a single SC chief minister in all these years; even UP has done better on that score.

A further reason why the south India model of OBC reservations is to be viewed with suspicion is that the educational qualifications and capabilities vis-à-vis the OBCs and the so-called 'forward castes' is next to negligible. This demonstrates that in real terms the OBCs are not backward at all. For example, in the 2005 MBBS admission results for aspiring doctors in Tamil Nadu the cut-off marks for the open category was 294.83 and for the OBCs it was 294.59, a difference of only 0.08 per cent, or 0.24 marks out of 300. Consequently, as can be expected, the OBCs also dominate the places in the open category and corner the reserved positions as well. This gives them a much higher representation overall, belying their supposedly backward status.[14] In 2004 the 'forward castes' managed only twenty-eight seats out of 1224 in the government medical colleges of Tamil Nadu, though they comprise 12 per cent of the population. Not to put too fine a point on it, only four members in the Tamil Nadu Assembly are from the 'forward castes', though in terms of their share of the population there should have been around thirty.[15]

In the light of all this it becomes clear that what the votaries of OBC reservations have in mind is very different from the aims and intentions of the founders of the Constitution when they made room for SC and ST reservations. For Ambedkar and others, reservations were intended to rid India of the dreadful scourge of caste. In the case of Mandal the guiding motto is not the extirpation of caste but the representation of it. That is why, while the first aimed at creating greater fraternity, the latter was about nurturing sectional economic niches that could be exploited for all time.

So, if caste has entered politics today it is because of the steadfast campaign in its favour by privileged politicians from privileged backgrounds who want to corner chunks of State largesse by cynically flogging the reservation format. This is what the privileged caste virtuosos are busy doing, while the majority of their fellow caste members see no advantage in this for them as they are far too poor and far too unschooled to think in terms of high-end jobs in the private or government sector or places in higher institutions of learning. The root of the problem lies in the fact that while reservations were once intended to create fraternity they are now designed to give representation. That conveys the impression that caste passions inflame the breast of every voting Indian, while the truth is that caste is being strategically deployed by the well-to-do rural communities to enlarge their range of assets, from rural to urban. Finally, it must be remembered that when reservations were first conceived it was not as an anti-poverty scheme, but primarily intended to energize the cause of fraternity by giving the historically oppressed a leg up.

Creating Fraternity

Why did the founding figures of the Constitution worry about 'fraternity'? Let us take a good, close look at this concept. In his much cited speech of 26 November 1949, B.R. Ambedkar said that India was wanting in its 'recognition of the principle of fraternity'. What does fraternity mean? It signifies a sense of belonging to a citizenry with everyone enjoying an equality of opportunity in real and not just legal terms. The virtues of liberty by themselves do not create fraternity. For this to happen we must attend to the details of how the past affects the present so that those who come from less fortunate backgrounds are not held back merely because of their historic misfortune.

Before proceeding further in discussing the specifics of caste and reservations in India it is worth recording that liberty and equality can sometimes be contradictorily positioned. That is why it is important for democracy to redress these community-based grievances within a framework that does not violate liberal principles. While the individual needs to be protected, individuals in certain groups and communities need safeguards and support. After all, it must be remembered that communities do not create citizens, but that there are citizens within communities. Also, while it is quite risky to say that communities have rights, there is no doubt at all that within liberal democracies, individuals have rights. Indeed, these rights were secured historically so that individuals did not have to be burdened by community and ascriptive pressures on them. Democracies are often forced to take this important step in order to correct the ills of the past to serve the present.

The rationale behind affirmative action is that it releases suppressed talents and expands the pool of social assets in society for the general good. It was precisely this enlargment of the social pool of talents that recommended equal treatment for women and the acceptance of the Chartist demands in early-twentieth-century Britain. When women are repressed there is a 'loss of all the elements in the common stock which the free play of the woman's mind would contribute'.[16] By increasing the sum of realized talents in society, individuals can actually gain greater inter-subjectivity in their everyday lives. As the *set of resemblances* between them is now so much larger, they can practise the moral precept of participating in one another's fate.[17] This conception of resemblances is about citizens being equally able to avail of institutional facilities that ensure their acquisition of those skills that are considered to be *socially valuable*. In other words, social opportunities exist for individual self-expansion, and it is only individuals now who can exclude themselves. If grinding poverty comes in the way of acquiring such socially valuable skills, then those blocks should be met by developmental interventions, and anti-poverty programmes. However, the eradication of poverty should never, on any account, be made synonymous with reservations. Reservations are only meant to generate a measure of confidence and dignity among those who didn't dare dream of an alternative life. Anti-poverty programmes have a different rationale and a different target group.

The resemblances that are being advocated in the context of affirmative action should not be interpreted in terms of homogeneous 'sameness'. Sameness is what medieval religious fundamentalists aim at. On the other hand, the set of resemblances in a constitutional democracy enhances equality and not sameness by providing identical opportunities to all for self-expression and development. Citizenship is not about the sameness of lifestyles or of income. Marshall's notion of citizenship as a status that tends towards equality should be interpreted in this light. The equality that citizenship guarantees should be the foundation on which other kinds of differences can develop.[18]

It will no doubt be the case that differences will exist even after a minimum set of resemblances is established, but these will no longer be outcomes of accidents of birth. Affirmative action is instrumental in enlarging the scope of difference and diversity, but it succeeds in doing so by first ensuring that citizens resemble one another at a very critical level, namely in their ability to acquire socially valuable skills. Every other policy should arrange itself around this.

Caste Politicians Strike Back

A policy of reservations, however, loses course once it steps beyond providing the assetless with assets to enhancing the assets of those who already possess them. This is where politicians come in to exploit the public exchequer and institutional well-being in the name of caste.

As anyone will easily attest, India is the most stratified society in the world. There are caste distinctions over and above the huge differences in lifestyles and wealth. These phenomena naturally refuse to stay boxed in this or that social niche of social life but pour all over and pervade many aspects of everyday life, but not with the same degree of emphasis.

After the zamindari abolition came into effect, adult franchise and the land-to-the-tiller programme together forced the earlier landed castes to gradually cede ground in the villages. Soon, however, traditional peasant castes such as Ahirs, Kurmis, Koeris, Lodhs, Rajputs, and Jats began to dominate the political landscape of northern India.[19] In the southern state of Tamil

Nadu, the Vanniyars and Thevars have become assertive, and in Karnataka control was wrested in the mid-1950s from the traditional rural élite within the Congress party by the Okkaligas and Linagayats.[20] In the north Indian Hindi-speaking belt, upper caste members of Parliament fell below 50 per cent for the first time in 1977. The challenge to the established Congress was mounted in Uttar Pradesh quite effectively in the late 1960s by a coalition of peasant castes led by Charan Singh. In Bihar too there was a significant decline of upper caste members of the legislative assembly after 1977.[21]

The Yadav politicians led the charge in Bihar and Uttar Pradesh. The Samajwadi Party in Uttar Pradesh is headed by Mulayam Singh Yadav, and in Bihar the Rashtriya Janata Dal has Laloo Prasad Yadav at its helm, and they both put caste in the forefront. It is not always the case, however, that other peasant castes such as the Kurmis and Koeris unfailingly rally behind either the Janata Dal or the Samajwadi Party. In these parties Kurmis are not as widely represented as the Yadavs. In 1996 only three per cent of Samajwadi Party members of the Legistalive Assembly (MLAs) were Kurmis.[22] In Bihar the numbers were higher but still not more than around 8 per cent of MLAs were Kurmis in the Rashtriya Janata Dal.[23]

Notwithstanding the fact that these peasant castes had become powerful in rural India and many have ridden high on the crest of the Green Revolution, things are no longer looking quite as promising for many of them. With rural India in economic distress, the villages are hollowed out, and these powerful peasants who once constituted the 'dominant caste' are no longer in that position of privilege. They are now looking for a way out of rural poverty and inertia and, quite reasonably and predictably, the way out is to get urban jobs. Many of them however lack the skills and the networks to get there as they were for so long content with their rural dominance. That is when they hit upon the idea of using the constitutional provisions for Other Backward Classes in their favour and that is how politics and caste got so closely identified in the popular press and imagination.

Two considerations escape many uncritical applications of reservations as affirmative action. First, reservation-type affirmative action must resist any tendency by its beneficiaries to become vested interests; and, secondly, a measure of its success should be its own dissolution. While the second may be far away, it is by paying attention to the first issue that it is possible for affirmative action to eventually annihilate itself. Paradoxical as it may appear, only when this happens will the reservations policy have finally triumphed.

The successes of reservations become visible when those who benefit from it owe it to society to put in their newly acquired social assets to the service of the collective pool so that others who have so far been outside the reach of reservations can now qualify for it. This would both release and add to the social and material resources required for the continuation of the policy aimed at the enhancement of resemblances. By increasing the numbers of those who possess the minimum set of resemblances, the society has now a larger wealth of talents in a variety of fields and specialities than it hitherto had. This is how reservations eventually improve the lot of everybody in society. If, on the other hand, caste or other markers of historic deprivation become permanent considerations then that would inhibit fraternity and sow seeds of a caste society in perpetuity.

The resources for reservations come from placing the assets of the better-off in a collective pool, not for redistribution, but to create the infrastructure that is required to enhance the minimum set of resemblances necessary for substantive citizenship. With the aid of this capital, socially valuable assets are now created where none earlier existed. This measure has a strong practical dimension, for out of this collective pooling, new assets are being created. The creation of such new assets is possible because the initial aggregation of the assets of the privileged section of society allows the society as a whole to underwrite the expenses incurred for the establishment of certain baseline similarities for all. This is how fraternal citizenship is developed in truly liberal–democratic societies.

Reservations and Affirmative Action

It is worth putting in perspective the differences between reservations in India of the Ambedkar variety and affirmative action in America. In the former the emphasis is on *extirpating* status markers based on birth, while in the case of the latter the key feature is the representation of minorities and of the underprivileged. If the accent is on representation, then the ascriptive factor becomes a permanent badge that can never be overcome. To cope with this, the American programme does not allow for quotas and this makes the system more flexible. As there are no quotas, standards need not be sacrificed and only when other things are equal does a minority or disadvantaged group receive the benefits. Otherwise, representation by itself runs the risk of turning one's primordial identity into a perennial political resource.

However, the great similarity between the two forms of preferential policy is that in both cases it is in the public sector that positive discrimination is effectively realized. In America, the state encourages private-sector units to employ people of diverse backgrounds without specifying quotas for different races. If these enterprises can show a fair racial mix then they can get preferential contracts from the government. The State cannot force any private-sector unit to implement affirmative action. It is a combination of goodwill and rewards that carry forward affirmative action in the American private sector. For example, Bob Jones University does not receive any public funds and, therefore, refuses to accept affirmative action, even of the most muted kind. It is only when organizations depend on State funding, or when they want to be rewarded by the State, that policy of affirmative action comes to life.

Why then is it that nobody says that race dominates American politics as caste is supposed to do in India? There are two reasons for this. The first is that Blacks constitute only about 12 per cent of the population of the US, whereas Indian society is shot through with castes, vertically and horizontally. That is why it is possible, in the latter context, for professional casteists and caste virtuosos to come to the fore and advocate their cause in a finely segmented fashion. As everybody belongs to one caste or another one can always hope to play on identity anxieties for political mileage.

Even so, this does not tell the full story. There are hundreds of castes, and nobody knows just how many: there are over 3,700 castes in the OBC rubric alone. It is not very difficult, however, to name castes that are in the political forefront, such as Yadavs, Jats, Gujars, Thevars, Okkaligas, etc., for these are the powerful ones. The hundreds of poorer castes have little to do with the machinations of these better-endowed rural communities. That is why when word goes around, as it did that evening with Chris Patten, that India is held back by caste passions, it is so unfair to the millions of poor, rural Indians who have had nothing to benefit from the caste politics of the rural rich. The world of the politician in India is so far removed from that of the rest.

11

BLAME IT ON THE NATION-STATE

MANUFACTURING ETHNICITIES AND MINORITIES

If caste is played behind the backs of Indian voters is politics any different when it comes to exploiting religious sentiments? Though one's caste affiliation does not change, parties that base themselves on these identities have good days and bad. There is therefore something obviously beyond caste that determines electoral outcomes. This was the story of the previous chapter.

It now remains to discuss if religion too is used by politicians for electoral gain. Do politicians ride on the wave of anti-religious feelings that well up at the popular level, or are such animosities created? Is it that Indians can barely restrain their base religious passions so that they are ever ready to fly at each other's throats at the slightest provocation? Or do politicians stoke this sentiment? On a routine basis Hindus and Muslims live side by side in grudging acquaintance, Pakistan remains a threat, and yet the rise and fall of the right-wing Hindu BJP cannot be predicated on either of these factors. It is one thing not to openly admire another community, and quite another to be willing to go out and kill. Ethnic enemies are not always the natural givens of history, nor condemned by incompatible beliefs to be in eternal opposition. The manner in which Sikhs were attacked in 1984 in Delhi and, before that, south

Indians attacked in Mumbai in 1966 clearly demonstrate that politics can make an enemy of the closest friend.

Ethnic Violence and Political Manipulations

Just as with the ephemeral careers of caste leaders, there are times when the Hindu right is popular only to be dumped unceremoniously soon after. This is true not only at the national level with the BJP, but also at the regional level with organizations like the Shiv Sena in Maharashtra and the Akali Dal in Punjab. In one election they are up, and in the next they are out of sight. The Shiv Sena won tremendous victories in the Mumbai municipality elections, but also lost several times. It partnered the BJP and came to power in Maharashtra but was soon out and the Congress took over. In 1975, when Indira Gandhi declared emergency rule in India, the leader of the Shiv Sena went out of his way to make peace with her fearing the decimation of his party. Likewise, the BJP came to power in 1997 and then went out quite suddenly in 2004. All those who made a career by writing about India's relentless march towards fundamentalism, suddenly fell silent.

When Khalistani militancy swept across Punjab demanding secession from the Indian union, the Akali Dal, an established and moderate Sikh religious party, was helplessly in power. The extremists got their ideological charge by accusing the Akali Dal, including its clerical leader, Sant Longowal, for not adhering to fundamentalist Sikh values. Even so, in 1985, without yielding an inch to Khalistani seccessionism, Rajiv Gandhi came to power in Delhi. He then executed the famous Rajiv–Longowal accord on the basis of which a popular election was held in Punjab in 1986 that brought the Akali Dal back to power. There was a record turnout in that election though militant Sikh secessionists had called for a boycott of the polls.

V.P. Singh, the next Indian prime minister, made a triumphant entry into Punjab and was met by tumultuous crowds though the militants had again ordered a boycott. In 2001 came the greatest surprise. The Congress narrowly beat the Akalis to capture power in Punjab. Who would have thought this was possible after the bloody violence Sikhs faced in Delhi and elsewhere in the wake of Indira Gandhi's assassination by her own Sikh bodyguards? Undoubtedly, Sikhs had other things on their minds than to nurture a wounded cultural hurt, or a religious passion, in perpetuity.

These are just quick glimpses that indicate the volatility of election results and how public sympathy shifts from party to party without leaving an enduring trace of their past visitations. The fact that religion and caste do not determine political outcomes does not mean that people are above these considerations in other spheres of social life. It would be completely incorrect to argue that fundamentally Hindus and Muslims are in each other's arms and that this accord is broken by politicians. That is far too romantic a picture.

Throughout human civilization, economically advanced or not, the fundamental anthropological tendency is to divide and stratify. In India too, at the mundane, quotidian level, Hindus and Muslims live apart and their mutually incongruous food taboos and forms of worship flag the differences between them. In Muslim-dominated estates the temple cannot be allowed to dwarf the mosque and in Hindu-controlled regions there would be no question of giving in to the Muslim demand for cow slaughter, even during certain festive occasions.[1] To top this, in recent years, Pakistan is an added irritant as it often threatens India's borders and there have been several wars already between these two countries.

Let us not forget how traumatic the Partition has been on the Indian side as it had to dismember itself for the creation of Pakistan. In Indian history books for school-children, Partition is seen as a dark chapter in the otherwise glorious march towards independence from the British. This is one deficit of the otherwise impressive anti-colonial struggle that has not been creditably accounted for even by the most charismatic of Indian nationalist leader of those times.

Notwithstanding these long-held prejudices, the fact remains that ethnic violence does not take place simply because anger boils over into the streets in an uncontrollable torrent that takes days, even months to control. It is another matter that Hindus would not normally invite beef-eating Muslims to their homes, but even this issue is not all that simple, though much is made of it.

If beef-eating were such an insurmountable social barrier for Hindus then why is it that they have absolutely no problem in inviting any number of Americans and Europeans to eat with them, attend their wedding festivals, and on the like? There have been numerous occasions when I have seen Europeans or Americans being literally cajoled by the relatives of the bride or bridegroom to join the wedding feasts even though they had never set their eyes on them before, let alone knowing their names. This usually happens when the wedding is held in a hotel, for then there are so many white Western tourists that one can easily grab one or two to adorn the occasion with a 'foreign' cachet. How is it that beef-eating does not matter at all in such circumstances?

With Muslims then, it is not just because they eat beef that they are kept at a distance by most Hindus. What we need to factor in is the history of confrontation between these two communities over a very specific political turf, both prior to British colonialism and after. As long as the Muslim rulers stood well above the populace, Hindus had no problems in assimilating to their ways of life, stopping short, of course, at eating beef. Raja Rammohun Roy, who later became a proponent of English values of rationality and a considerable savant of the European way of life, was earlier, under Muslim rule in Bengal, fluent in Persian and a member of the Turki establishment.

Unlike the Europeans, poor Muslims lived in close proximity to Hindus. They did not stand apart from the rest like the British colonial rulers did. Poor Muslims, who were numerically the most preponderant, lived in the same regions as the Hindus and performed rather menial tasks. The Muslim was the neighbourhood butcher, barber or weaver, among other low-grade service occupations. In addition, these self-same Muslims were, until relatively recently, once indigent Hindus of poor, subaltern castes who had since converted to Islam. This memory is quite alive in the minds of Hindus, though Muslims, quite naturally, want to forget about it. It is in this context that 'beef-eating' became a big cultural divider between the two faiths, and not simply because Hindus revere the cow and Muslims eat beef.

British supremacy in India led to a new equation. From the days after the 'revolt of 1857' (often termed the 'First Indian War of Independence'), the British carefully nurtured the Hindu élite at the expense of the earlier Muslim aristocracy. During this period too texts were written by both Hindus and Muslims extolling their respective virtues. The jockeying for power began between these two communities, and British rule provided the stage for such rivalries to be played out, and they often resulted in full-scale violence. Later, after the Indian National Congress entered the picture with ambitions to unite Hindus and Muslims against British rule, the colonial powers fought back by equating the Muslim League with the Congress as representatives of Islamic and Hindu people respectively. The British rulers refused to recognize that the Congress had both Hindus and Muslims in its fold, and that it was by far the most representative political organization in the country. This further exacerbated the atmosphere between these two religious communities leading, as we all know, to the partition of India in 1947.

It is easy to blame the British for everything, but we should accept our share of the blame for what happened. Of course, the British, as a colonial power, would divide and rule: to act otherwise would be foolish. They were an outside power with allegiance to a faraway northern isle and with no social roots in those regions of the tropics they had subjugated. It is, therefore, to be expected that they would use every stratagem available and elevate the policy of divide and rule above all else. In this endeavour, it must also be said, the British perfected the art more than any other colonial power that the world has seen.

Franz Fanon had once said that when the ruling, alien power is too strong to be dislodged the subjugated turn upon themselves, thus heightening pre-existing tensions between them. This process of 'internal dialectic' provided the ground that enabled the divide and rule policy to flourish. The tensions lurking under the surface came to life and set off a spiral of mutual suspicions on which the British could adroitly capitalize.

Agents of Hatred

Even a cursory glance at Hindu–Muslim relations during the British period shows that anger does not boil over spontaneously and unaided; a political setting enables the process. Though some leaders, especially the secular wing under Jawaharlal Nehru, noticed this fact, many others in the national movement actually played into this communal divide. After Partition, in many states of India, notably UP, Muslims began to be discriminated against and their numbers in public services dropped sharply. It was almost as if the Muslims who had stayed back in India were to pay for those who worked for Partition and had left for Pakistan.

This territorial divide became a major rationalizing force in perpetuating Hindu–Muslim tensions ever since. The Shiv Sena resorts to it, the Vishwa Hindu Parishad constantly harps on it, and the Bharatiya Janata Party continues to demand an Undivided India (*Akhand Bharat*), which basically amounts to the denial of Pakistan. Partition is clearly a very valuable political resource for these parties and they have mined it extensively to ferment many communal riots in India. On these bloody occasions the cry that Muslims should return to Pakistan is frequently heard on the streets and also among political leaders. Sadly, even those who are not overtly part of this saffron Hindu fold remain suspicious of Muslims, and this suspicion is a great demotic divide.

For most of us the manner in which British divided and ruled Hindus and Muslims is not part of our public memory. The agency behind breeding this hostility has historically vapourized under the euphoric heat of Independence, leaving behind only condensed hatred. That is why, in riot after riot, most of us were willing to believe that these were pure symptoms of popular anger that could not be dammed because prejudice was so supreme. I began to question this wisdom after the Sikh killings in 1984, as did many others. In my case, I was a slow learner for I had earlier witnessed the Bhiwandi riots in the early 1970s in Maharashtra where the Shiv Sena played a huge role. It, however, needed the Sikh massacre after Indira Gandhi's assassination to drive home the point in my head that without a protective agency there are no riots, no matter how deep-seated the hostility.

In the perfervid days following the killings of 1984, we saw the naked display of agency. Congress was in power, and Congress functionaries roamed the streets inciting violence, hiring anti-social elements to loot and kill, and drawing the all too willing police into their larger design. As a member of the Peoples' Union for Democratic Rights (1984) I was privy to a number of horror stories where members of the ruling Congress party were instrumental in the killings and maiming of Sikhs, not to mention the looting of their homes. Yet so powerful was the secular image of the Congress that these findings often met with disbelief from among those who had simplistically divided their political world into the secular and left-leaning Congress and the communal right-wing Bharatiya Janata Part (at that time the Bharatiya Jana Sangh).

However, before long it was clearly established that Congress had indulged in a clear case of political cross-dressing. The way in which Congress let loose squads against the Sikhs shell-shocked the traditional right-wing Hindu BJP into inaction. When I saw how goons descended from trucks in organized platoons, how victims' homes had been clearly marked in advance, and how the police actively encouraged killings and lootings, I was also compelled to re-think some basic received wisdom. I went to many of my family members and asked them about Partition. I had been brought up to believe that members of my family left East Pakistan after Partition because the Muslims wanted them out and would stop at nothing to expel them. Now I began to question this narration and was on the

lookout for tell-tale signs of plotted violence. Was it Muslim
anger boiling over, or were those killings too orchestrated? I
pointedly asked my relations: 'Who came to attack you? Were
they your neighbours? Were they people you knew?' In all
cases the answer was that they were other people who came
from outside, sometimes in vehicles, probably from a long
distance. This led me to conclude that even the Partition riots
did not just happen: they too were engineered.

The pieces of the puzzle fell into place and I understood
more clearly how politicians use human failings, that perennial
anthropological failing to spontaneously divide, to help
themselves to positions of power. After 1984, the next major
incident of this sort happened in Gujarat in 2002. This time
around it was not the Sikhs but the Muslims who were targeted,
as they have been in most such massacres in Independent India.
I visited Gujarat with my eyes wide open and I saw the same
level of official and administrative involvement in inciting riots,
protecting the killers and looters, and finding justification for
all this in the name of popular passions that are so hard to
control. Just as in the killings of Sikhs, once again Muslim
homes were marked out, and hoodlums and anti-social characters
were recruited to indulge in no-holds-barred violence.

After the Sikh killings of 1984 and the massacre of Muslims
in 2002 I found a clear pattern emerging. My memories of what
I saw about three decades ago in Bhiwandi in Maharashtra took
on a new dimension. I now recalled vividly how Shiv Sena
rioters set off for Bhiwandi as if they were heading for a
daylong picnic. They were laughing and joking, calling out to
neighbours and friends to join them, rushing back to pick up
weapons before hastily rejoining the cavalcade of vehicles setting
out to teach 'a lesson' to the Muslims of Bhiwandi. I saw the
same expressions on the face of rioters in Delhi and I realized
then that the picnic atmosphere was because the rioters were
assured of safe passage back and forth and a good time in the
killing fields. Rioters are bullies who happily 'kill for a cause'
but would never die for one.

It is not as if high-level encouragement of religious conflict is of recent origin nor is it just an Indian or Asian peculiarity. Consider, for example, what Lord Acton said over a century ago:

> Fanaticism displays itself in the masses, but the masses were rarely fanaticized, and the crimes ascribed to it were commonly due to the calculations of dispassionate politicians. When the king of France undertook to kill all the Protestants, it was nowhere the spontaneous act of the population . . .[2]

Those in power, and those hungering for power and more, often play the religious/ethnic card, for in many ways it is collective action without responsibility. If their ploy works they have the world to gain, and if it does not, it is no big loss for them. The lives of ordinary people are inconsequential.

When Conspiracy Theories Count

In recent years I have found a few other social scientists from the West endorsing what a large number of secular activists in India had already learnt from their close encounters with incidents of communal violence.[3] We now know that conspiracies are continually being hatched but are not always allowed to leave the political nest. These plots get room to express themselves only when political rewards are to be had in terms of general or local elections.[4] This sounds like a conspiracy theory but that is no reason to cast it aside. It must be taken seriously if we are to infuse our political life with a true secular attitude, something that is tough and unrelenting. Some grand facts would stand by us if were to adopt such a position. For example, how can we ignore the hand of the ruling party and the connivance of the administration in each of the major incidents of communal killings I have just talked about?

If these grand facts cannot be ignored then the element of conspiracy has to be entertained. The only thing one can say is that conspiracies do not often end the way the conspirators planned. We should however also learn from the fact that while riotous mobs roam the streets in one area, in another there is inter-faith peace. The difference between these instances is that in the former the rioters have active administrative support and in the latter that agency is missing.

In 1984 for instance, West Bengal and Karnataka remained peaceful and the Sikhs in those states were safe and unharmed. This is not for want of trying by interested parties, but the regional governments stood in the way. We however need to accept that conspiracies and conspirators often come to unpredictable ends, or else Indira Gandhi would not have been assassinated.

In fact, the tragedy that came upon the Sikhs post-Indira Gandhi's assassination also has its beginning in another conspiracy. This one was plotted by Congress to unseat the Akali Dal from power in Punjab. It is common knowledge now that Congress, in spite of its so-called secular reputation, went out of its way to encourage and patronize a Sikh fundamentalist hothead named Sant Jarnail Singh Bhindranwale. According to Congress calculations, Bhindranwale would be encouraged to outdo the moderate Sikhs in the Akali Dal, thus destabilize Punjab and make it easier for Congress to walk in and take over the state. As it transpired, the mission was partly successful, but only partly. Both Bhindranwale and Indira Gandhi died soon after as a consequence of this conspiracy.[5]

A good five years later, the killings of Muslims in Gujarat again provided fresh evidence of high-level political involvement. Details of administrative involvement and connivance from the top are still coming in although several years have passed. Interestingly, however, the BJP-led government in Gujarat under whose aegis the killings were conducted was re-elected handsomely in the elections that were called soon after the riots. This once again leads us to consider how ethnic killings are timed so that they pay electoral dividends.

The Limits of Popular Ethnicity

The Gujarat story has however another lesson for us all, provided we take leave of our usual stereotype of secular versus communal. Today, Narendra Modi, the chief minister of Gujarat and the conniver-in-chief of the killings of Muslims in 2002 is still a popular leader. Does this mean that Modi is playing to a hysterical and deeply prejudiced Hindu electorate in Gujarat, or is something else also afoot?

Recent reports suggest that Modi's continuing popularity is due not so much to his intractable and unrepentant Hinduism as to his successes in the secular arena. Under Modi's leadership, Gujarat has progressed economically and large sections of the population believe that he has directly contributed to their welfare. According to one datelined report, widespread acclaim for Modi in small villages in Gujarat is based on them now receiving piped water and no longer needing supplies from water-tankers. In addition, irrigation facilities have improved vastly in that region because the village councils there have, with state support, constructed a number of small dams. This has changed the fortunes of agriculturists in what was till recently a near perennial arid zone. In addition, in villages such as these, Modi's government is also commended for setting up telephone exchanges, power stations, and better transit systems that link town and country more effectively, crucially important for the poor rural Indian.

Secular parties should learn from this. For the ordinary Indian who comes from the majority community of Hindus, what happens to Muslims periodically is of no great interest. During the killings the Hindus may become very Hindu, but that does not sustain them over a long period. Even as their Hindu sensibilities are sharpened an overwhelming majority would not step out to kill Muslims but would look kindly upon those who do so under state support. However Modi has not remained in power only by organizing riot after riot, but also by attending to the secular interests of those in Gujarat.

If secular parties have to mount a sustained attack against communal and ethnic organizations like the BJP and governments like those of Narendra Modi, it is not sufficient for them to keep digging up tales of religious horror and intolerance. They will have to better Modi in the economic and administrative arenas too. Without this backup all protestations against Modi's ethnic intolerance and his deeply prejudiced notion of Hinduism will not arouse any resentment against him from amongst his voters. In fact, they might also be tempted to buy into Modi's Hindu chauvinism precisely because he delivers in other areas.

Secular parties therefore have a greater, much greater, responsibility than governments and organizations such as those presided over by Modi and others like him. In order to establish a bigot-free and non-majoritarian rule they have to excel on issues relating to the public delivery of public goods, and not just limit themselves to considerations of one-dimensional economic growth. If Modi can perform at these levels, secular parties have to do it even better. This is because voters do not usually go to the ballot boxes as professional Hindus or Muslims but as concerned parents, husbands, wives, daughters and sons. For members of the majority community again, attacks against Muslims do not occupy them beyond a very limited point. They easily return to normal routine and often find it difficult to recall how and when it all began. What happens to Muslims is quite removed from their daily concerns.

Muslims, of course, cannot forget the hurt and the violence unleashed against them. We also know that many Sikhs still chafe at the memory of what they went through in 1984. However if secular parties really want to secure a safe place for their religious minorities, so that these sections can function without the constant fear of their basic human rights being violated on a political whim, they must do more than just ideologically rail against ethnicists. They also need to excel in meeting the economic and developmental needs of the electorates. That is why the ethnicists get stronger every time the recognized secular parties falter and fail to deliver to the public on these issues. Voters see in parties, like the BJP, a viable alternative for the future although they do not necessarily subscribe to the anti-minority stance. Anti-incumbency cuts both ways.

When the BJP-led alliance won in 1997 I know of many otherwise secular individuals who voted against Congress because they wanted a change to a better and more effective government.

Their subsequent disappointment with the BJP was not because of any riot that BJP had presided over during its tenure but because it too failed to live up to its 'secular' promises of bettering social and economic standards of living. Therefore, while the electorate swings from one extreme to the other let us not buy into the facile argument that these transitions are on account of the ebb and flow, wax and wane of religious passions.

Nevertheless, there is no doubt that the political leaders of the BJP, the Rashtriya Swayamsevak Sangh (RSS), the Vishwa Hindu Parishad (VHP), and other assorted Hindu ethnicists obsessively think of and harp on religious conspiracies. However, it does not follow that the voters are equally besotted with paranoiac arguments. Modi, the BJP chief minister of Gujarat, is reinventing himself as the provider of economic well-being, and that is why secular parties have a job on their hands. We should recall that the BJP floundered and lost in the parliamentary elections of 2004, but it did well in Gujarat and may return to power again in that state. Thus the ability to deliver on the ground outweighs pure loyalty to the ethnic ideology.

Rethinking the Indian Nation–State

Why is there a prevalent view in most intellectual quarters that India is continually prone to religious conflict that could tear the nation-state asunder and, by extension, also the economy? The paradigmatic grounding for this exists in the many idealized versions of the nation-state claiming that a true prototype grows naturally through the bonds of religion and language. Therefore, as India has many languages and religions, ethnic and linguistic riots are inevitable.

To begin with, we need to challenge the popular view of the nation-state. This make-believe tale was spun in the West long after their nation-states had secured themselves, often on a multi-religious and multi-linguistic basis. It has been so long since then, sometimes a century or more, that they have lost their collective memories of the painful process through which their nation-states were wrought.

Contrary to this well-thumbed view of the nation-state, neither England, nor France or Italy, the exemplars of this idealized version, came into being effortlessly. It is not as if they were eased into history greased by a uniform cultural sentiment. There were differences in all these nation-states not just in terms of diverse, often divisive, cultural and religious pasts, but, believe it or not, also by linguistic differences. The more one forgets how one's nation-state toils its way into existence, the stronger the myth of its natural origins appears. Ernest Renan will tell you no French citizen knows if he is an Alan or a Visigoth, nor will he remember the thirteenth-century massacres on St. Bartholomew's Day in the Midi. The problem is when a mythified notion is passed off as the ideal, or the most authentic direction for the emergence of a nation-state.[6] Such an idea would imply that the sentiments that underpin successful nation-states (particularly those in Western Europe) slumbered for centuries till they were awakened by the gentle persuasions of democracy.

Language and religion did not easily combine to form a nation-state. In England, the English language gradually emerged with many twists and turns, aided and abetted by the agency of the printing press, to gradually become a national language.[7] When France became Independent less than 20 per cent of its people spoke French. Soon after the Risorgimento had accomplished its task, Massimo d'Azzeglio famously exhorted: 'We have made Italy, now we must make Italians.'[8] He was pressured to say this because when the nation-state of Italy came into being less than two per cent of its population spoke Italian. Even Metternich, who was fashioning the state of Germany, said that Italy was a 'mere geographic expression'.[9]

Recall too that the Irish spoke English for the longest time, that Norwegian closely resembles Danish, that Danes also speak fluent Swedish, that, German nationalism notwithstanding, the Mecklenburgers spoke a dialect closer to Dutch than German.[10] None of this implies that any of these nation-states are wanting in authenticity. Indeed, nobody remembers enough to level such a charge today. Likewise, if in Pakistan they also speak Punjabi and Urdu, as millions do in India, or if the majority population in Bangladesh and West Bengal speak Bengali, then that should not diminish the nation-state authenticity of any of these countries.

Even so, when India was struggling to become independent it was not just individuals like Churchill who said that India would not last as an entity without the British standing guard, but also certified historians and scholars, including recent ones like Percival Spear and Ainslee Embree, argued along similar lines. As India emerged as a free, independent nation-state following its own peculiar path, so did other Western nation-states. There is no single yellow brick road to nationhood. As Renan remarked with characteristic candour and scholarship, every defeat that Italy suffered strengthened the Italian striving for a nation-state, and on the contrary every war won by Turkey 'spelled doom for Turkey'.[11]

Centripetal Forces and the Nationalist Sentiment

After India became independent the great divide occurred with the emergence of Pakistan and immediately consolidated the view that India was staring in the face of its demise. India weathered that storm. Around the 1950s a different threat seemed to threaten India, with the emergence of the demand for linguistic states in the union. Maharashtra wanted its own state and did not want to remain within the existing bilingual state of Bombay. Likewise, there was a similar demand that sought the separation of Andhra Pradesh from the state of Madras, again on the basis of language. This led many to conclude that India would soon break up into a balkanized geographical mess.

That, however, did not occur. Once Maharashtrians won Maharashtra and Gujaratis, by the same token, got Gujarat, the matter ended. It was not as if the creation of these linguistic provinces fireballed into the demand for sovereign states. In fact, the Congress high command in Delhi too overestimated the popular sentiment that Indians nurture against another Partition and opposed the formation of these linguistic states for they too feared the worst. Although Congress initially opposed the demand for linguistic states in the 1950s, it had, during the anti-colonial struggle, promised that once they won independence India would be zoned into different linguistic states for a better, and more democratic, form of governance. The leaders of the party later resiled from their earlier decision because they now feared that Partition would repeat itself, so horrific was the memory of 1947. They need not have worried, for once these linguistic demands were met the matter ended. Indeed, the formation of linguistic states within the union of India brought about an increase in democratic participation.

If we were to examine the discussions in the Constituent Assembly soon after Independence we find that the Assembly took three major decisions that have a bearing on culture, language, and the nation-state. This august body decided that there would be no further Partition and thus debunked the whole idea of national self-determination. The creation of Pakistan, post-Partition, was obviously a wound that still hurt. The Constituent Assembly also agreed that there would be no further administrative demarcation of the various states that make up the Indian union. Finally, Hindi was to be the national language. Clearly, many of the members of the Constituent Assembly had also uncritically accepted the textbook notion that a nation-state needed a single language to cement its political structure.

As it transpired, despite the great charisma of the leaders of the Independence movement and of Congress, the suggestion that Hindi be the national language and that there would be no further demarcation of states on linguistic grounds drew voiciferous objection on the street. The only issue on which there was unanimity was the inviolability of India's territorial possessions. On this issue the popular consensus was remarkable. That is why no objections were raised in any significant political quarter when Sardar Patel, as home minister, integrated the former princely states into the Indian union, or when the government enacted the law that any attempt at further partitions would be considered seditious and hence liable to the most grievous punishment.

Thus, if India remained one it was not as if the charismatic leaders were pulling in one direction towards unity and the people at large were straining in another towards division. During the sixty years and more in the career of independent India we find that one of the favourite tactics of right-wing Hindu fanatics was to accuse Muslims of fomenting another Partition, or even partisanship with Pakistan (and they usually amount to the same thing). This ploy usually works when the timing is right. Even the Congress in the 1980s cast the Sikhs as secessionists keen to partition India yet again, and quite predictably won the support of Indians nation-wide. It is not as if this kind of nationalist jingoism is healthy, but again is there any nation-state in the West that is devoid of it. Do we not see that tendency in the US, in the UK, in Germany, in France, and elsewhere?

I return then to the original proposition that religious fanaticism on the streets does not naturally flow from the peculiar character of the Indian nation-state. If the Indian nation-state has many languages, then let us recall that linguistic differences did not block the formation of Western nation-states either. The only difference is that by the time India became independent the idea of liberalism had also grown in all democracies, and hence the question of suppressing languages just could not be entertained. Therefore, rather than weakening the Indian nation-state, the prevalence of multiple cultures should in fact strengthen it.

Now we are ready to answer the question of India as a nation-state, looking at it more clearly in the eye. If there are massacres on the grounds of religion in India it does not necessarily mean that the foundation blocks of the nation-state are in some ways deeply flawed. Instead, blame should be laid at the doors of politicians who create inter-faith discord for their selfish pursuit of power. The problem is not so much with spontaneous surges of religious hostility at the popular level but with a careful nurturing of primordial sentiments by political leaders for their own political ends.

It is an élitist inclination to easily blame the people, the poor and the illiterate, for the frequent bouts of caste and religious politics in India. Politicians play on this predisposition and make it appear as if they are just responding to popular feelings. Unfortunately, intellectuals and journalists play into the hands of these power-wielders primarily because they spend too much time with them. This ideological cover that politicians receive from otherwise respectable quarters gives rise to the false alarm that religiosity and a rural/caste bent of mind is holding up the nation. When asked the question whether India can fly or fly high enough, the answer often is that it might, provided Indians can overcome their primordial passions of caste, kin, clan, and religion. That is where the commentators go wrong and that is how politicians and party functionaries escape closer scrutiny. They are not really held responsible, either for casteism in politics or for religious displays of mass intolerance.

12

DO WE DESERVE OUR LEADERS?

WHEN POLITICIANS BECOME A CLASS FOR ITSELF

Democratic politics only allows those candidates to survive who can stand, and indeed add, to the heat of politics. This heat is generated through the combined combustible energies released by money and violence. This raises the entry price for those who want to enter politics. No politician can make it happen by relying on good behaviour, or even good will. To count in politics as a viable contender in India, the candidate must have huge funds and the power to unleash violence and protect oneself from it.

Recent elections campaigns in the US too have demonstrated in bold print that presidential candidates must be able to raise massive endowments to fund their campaigns. That is why, beyond a point, they dare not offend business interests, religious organizations, and the more powerful lobbies that in the corridors of Washington. This makes Hillary Clinton waffle when it comes to the Iraq war, and Mitt Romney swallow air when asked if he believes in every word of the Bible. The American people do not matter. There is also a bipartisan agreement on a trillion-dollar bailout of failed banks in America. Tax payers and rank-and-file Republicans and Democrats, however, resent the handing of golden parachutes to greedy Wall Street CEOs.

The Entry Price to Politics

Just because we live in a democracy does not mean that we deserve the leaders we get. It is true we choose our leaders in a highly festive, often carnival-like, atmosphere. Notwithstanding the festoons and speeches, posters and ballots, charisma and chicanery, we are really constrained to vote for one or the other candidates that are up in the electoral market-place. We cannot choose our ideal candidate because that individual figures nowhere on the ballot paper.

Why is that so? There are frequent comments in the media and also among idle gossips that good honest citizens should join politics and cleanse the democratic system of the accumulated filth of decades of administrative malpractice and misrule. Why don't such people turn up? This is after all a democracy. Where are they hiding? And why? Don't educated people have a sense of commitment to their country?

True and false. We live in a democracy but that does not mean that just anyone with a gold nugget for a heart can enter politics, part the waters, and lead us to some promised land. Just as a monopolist raises the price of competition in a 'free market' through advertising, among other things, politicians too raise the price of joining politics by introducing violence as a basic qualification. Anyone in this business must have the ability to control, inflict and resist violence. Without this attribute one cannot even think of taking the first baby step towards political activism. Money does not suffice to make the political mare go; in addition one needs a whip in hand. This is particularly true of newly emerging democracies where the electoral spirit is willing but democratic institutions are weak. It is against this background that the rise of dynastic politics can be best understood.

Pakistan has a population of over 150 million, and India is famously a land of a billion people plus, and yet we constantly depend on certain families to provide us with political leadership. The reason clearly is not that we are lacking in drive and resources as individuals but we lack the wherewithal to cope with violence to make the political grade. While India can boast of a million enterprises booming every year, this does not translate easily into the realm of politics, for violence stands guard as the gatekeeper to political fortunes.

After the assassination of Benazir Bhutto the leadership of the Pakistan Peoples' Party (PPP) could have sought a candidate outside the Bhutto family, but this was not to be. If Bilawal has taken over the reins, even though he is a political ingénue, it is simply because his family can control violence, sustain violence, and ride on violence. This is true of other political families in the region too. How many can rise after a cruel assassination of a loved one to enter the political fray and risk everything? It has to be someone who has lived alongside violence, seen it from close quarters, and is not alarmed by its entry into their private spaces.

When we hear of a father grooming his daughter, or a mother her son, or a husband his wife it is really to inure the initiate to violence. I have heard it being said, and not just in the case of Benazir, that those who inherit the mantle from their dead ancestor or spouse, have lived, breathed, and thought politics for the better part of their lives. This is certainly true. It is not however as if they learnt the craft of administration, the skills of statesmanship, diplomatic finesse, or whatever, but rather the ease with which they can handle violence and live alongside it, that qualifies them for the job.

It is not as if dynastic politics only happens at the top. Take a look at political satraps in India. From Sharad Pawar, to Karunanidhi, to Mulayam Singh Yadav, to Deve Gowda, everywhere, in every corner of India, we see the familiar sight of fathers pushing sons and daughters, and husbands grooming wives, to take to politics. The principle of open competition, so that the best get into politics, is easily subverted because only certain people of exceptional social upbringing can handle violence as calmly as a routine phenomonon. A mother dies, the son steps in, a husband killed and the daughter walks in; this has become such a familiar routine that it must depend on the exceptional qualities of these people. It is certainly not brilliance, foresight, erudition, or heart, but rather the experience of living with violence, facing it and using it, that separates political families from the rest.

It matters little then if Bilawal is still under-age and cannot vote. He nevertheless qualifies for appointment as chairman of the PPP. What sets him, and others like him, apart is his upbringing in a political family where violence is a familiar intruder forever leaning against the doorbell. This is a rare background and does not come easy. Politics is not for the faint-hearted or the honest do-gooder and that is why we almost never get the leaders we deserve.

When a ghastly assassination happens at the top, such as that of Benazir, it raises the entry price into politics, by that much more, all the way down to the lowest functionary. This effectively shuts out the good guys and the field is left only to those who can handle violence with ease. That all of this takes place under a supposedly 'democratic' system should not blind us to the fact that the players out there in the middle are not our ideological representatives or our points of inspiration, but are patrons in command or in waiting. If violence is the key political qualification, then law-abiding citizens can only function from the sidelines, now casting their vote for one patron, now for another. The choice is extraordinarily constricted.

Patron politics is not incompatible with electoral politics. We can democratically choose our patrons and swing from one extreme to another in search of someone who will deliver and address some of our aspirations. By definition, a patron, in Indian politics, is one who either breaks or lives on the edge of the law, or else the person is of little use. What violence does is that it makes the system all the more susceptible to higher and higher levels of patronage politics. It does not matter if the PPP comes in or Shah Nawaz, violence is now endemic in the system, and assassinations, such as that of Benazir Bhutto, only reaffirms this tendency.

Every time a political leader is killed we must mourn not only for the departed patron but also for the further diminution of democratic politics in the substantive sense. Elections can still be held but it will be a contest between people who can control and inflict violence. To believe that after a leader has been brutally murdered there will be a lot of soul-searching in the political realm is wishful thinking. We have heard it said that after Benazir was shot, Pakistan politicians are taking a long hard look at the role of violence in order to root it out of the political system. This was also said when Indira Gandhi and Rajiv Gandhi were killed. Indeed, this is a standard, protocol announcement made by those who have survived the assassination or have been touched by it as political activists. In reality, just the opposite occurs.

The truth is that after every such incident the level of violence rises significantly as the price for entering politics. That too is indeed why we never get the leaders we deserve.

Politicians as a Class

Politicians are perhaps a class by themselves and tend to see their interests as separate from the rest. This at least can be vividly demonstrated in the Indian case, and yet we expect the Indian phoenix to fly. Sample the following list of activities, positions and policies to which all politicians from the left to the right in India susbscribe:

- *Acceptance of the Mandal Committee Reservations for OBCs.* This policy has been accepted by all political parties though it is widely known that it was formulated hastily and without adequate research. No major political party recognizes that the Mandal recommendations are giving an entirely new twist to what was the original design of reservations by the founding figures of the Constitution. Strangely, while they voice private disagreement with the Mandal recommendations, they cry hoarse in its favour publicly.
- *Receipt of parliamentary privileges, retirement benefits, travel and upkeep allowances.* These are really lavish. Parliamentarians become eligible for retirement benefits the moment they get elected. Length of service does not matter. Once a parliamentarian, the person is entitled, for

life, to travel in first-class carriage, with a companion. Parliamentarians are allowed to annually make 100,000 telephone calls, consume 25,000 units of power and wash down 2,000 litres of water. This would mean roughly 275 phone calls a day. Recently it was also reported that the members of Delhi's Legislative Assembly met only for twenty days throughout 2007 and did business for precisely sixty-two hours in that entire year. In other words, each member of the legislative assembly in Delhi costs the exchequer Rs 40,000 a month for a ten-minute workday.[1] All these privileges are over and above what they receive in terms of free junkets, housing, and other kinds of funds for a variety of unaccountable expenditures.

- *Hostility towards the judiciary.* Parliamentarians are upset that the judiciary has made them accountable by allowing public interest litigations. The Supreme Court came down heavily against politicians for not paying attention to environmental issues and eventually in a show of judicial activism it banned diesel buses in Delhi. This measure was opposed by all political parties as they were connected to the transportation lobby. More recently, all political parties resented the Supreme Court's action requiring the government to explain the justifications for the Mandal recommendations regarding OBC reservations.

- *Against the eradication of undemocratic laws that curtail civil liberties.* All political parties have subscribed to laws that allow for detention without trial for long periods of time. Even the Janata Party which came to power after overturning Indira Gandhi's emergency regime went ahead with the maintenance of such provisions in law. Very often the name of the ordinance is changed but the substance remains the same.

- *Supporting the establishment of Special Economic Zones (SEZ).* This policy, providing land for economic development, has won unanimous support among politicians from the left to the right in Parliament. As of 29 August 2007 there are 142 SEZs, up from just sixty-four only fifteen months ago. What is interesting is that at least eighty-six of these are single unit, intended to benefit just one entrepreneur. Nobody asks why there should be SEZs at all. The system began in China to find a way out of China's socialist system. There is no reason for SEZs in India, unless of course one wants to avoid labour laws and the scrutiny of those who are supposed to uphold the normal democratic laws of the land. Incidentally, the number of SEZs in China is still in the single digits. In India only one SEZ is over one square mile in area, while about 60 per cent of the total[2] are below even fifty hectares. The land for all these have been acquired by the government for the benefit of private entrepreneurs. This again is different from the Chinese case in which government land was given for SEZ development. The phenomenal growth of SEZs in India, and the manner of its expansion, provides a glaring example of crony capitalism.

- *Allowing non-performing assets.* No political party has so far advocated the pursuit of those who have defaulted on bank payments, causing Indian banks to accumulate massive non-performing assets (basically loans that have not been repaid) to the tune of Rs 17722 crore, of which Rs 14561 crore relates to public-sector banks. These figures pertain to 2005-06, and are therefore quite recent. Interestingly, it is the the public-sector banks that suffer. These are the banks that use our money, and from whom the rich borrow and do not repay. The list of debtors who owe massive sums to these banks is like a corporate Who's Who which has never been made into a political issue. We have come to accept that the state will be corrupt and that is why NGOs and multilateral agencies are having a field day in countries like India.[3]

Anti-incumbency as a Market Corrective

In all fairness, the Indian voter is not consumed by caste or religion to the degree their leaders are, and it makes sense.

They constantly confront mundane issues, like getting food on the table, sending their children to school, paying hospital bills, and so on. The worrisome immediacy of these matters tends to preclude feverish concern with large questions of religion or caste. However, these questions absorb the leaders from whose ranks the electorate is forced to choose their so-called representatives. That is why the election pendulum swings so rapidly, and the term 'anti-incumbency factor' has won such wide currency and acceptance.

Pundits and politicians alike take the 'anti-incumbency factor' into account in all elections, for it is well known that governments exhaust their store of popular goodwill during the course of a single term in office. The power-wielders are clearly callous to the needs of the public that elect them, and contrary to being servants of the people; they soon make people their servants by taking on the role of dispensers of patronage. The leaders do not represent views and opinions as much as they put themselves up as patrons and potential patrons by resorting to primordial partisanship to win clients and to distinguish themselves from their rivals.

However, if voters with their pressing quotidian concerns discover that they are not getting what they want from a particular regime, why should they not turn from it? This is how millions of voters calculate. Hence, the 'anti-incumbency factor' is shamelessly trumpeted by politicians in order to explain away victory or defeat.

Representation or Delivery

There is no doubt that Indian democracy seeks to represent the interests of a diverse section of prominent political interests, so long as it is not strictly about poverty. The emergence of coalition governments in India over the past three general elections have led some to value *representation* as a virtue in itself without asking what happened to the *delivery* aspect of politics.

Indian political parties strive to represent as many interests as possible, some real, some false, and some imaginary. The real ones have to do with extending the interests of those who have significant social assets, such as wealth, power, or intellectual resources. The false ones are so blatantly transparent that they don't need to be spelt out. Every election promises better schools, better hospitals, better roads, in short, better public goods, but an elected politician is hardly ever interested in these. The public health and public education systems, for example, have remained a national embarrassment for decades.

The advocacy of imaginary interests is best seen when inter-faith conflicts are notoriously propagated by different political parties. The Congress did this in 1984 when it minoritized the Sikhs and the BJP did it in 2002 in Gujarat by singling out the Muslims—the Partition of 1947 is still resource-rich for a large number of jingoistic political operators. We must also admit here, among imaginary interests, the utopian belief that it is possible to create a 'perfect' society of complete equals.

When Indian politics seeks to represent, it does it best, and least harmfully, when advocating the stated interests of those classes with socially valuable assets. No longer can money be seen as the only such asset, though it still probably holds a leading position. In addition, however, there are other social assets, such as intellectual and political resources.

While these interests are balanced out in a give-a-little-take-a-little spirit of compromise, nothing is really done in terms of relieving the conditions of the very poor, except what happens by default or seeps through in the normal process of entrepreneurial engineering. The quantum of such benefits is minuscule if one cares to recall how many poor people still struggle for a living in India. However, a number of informed political scholars continue to see a positive virtue in the mere fact of representation without asking what happened to the *delivery* of public goods.

The reservations for the OBC are an example, *par excellence*, of representation. The conditions of schools and hospitals are not on the agenda as what matters most is that the politics of 'equality of opportunity' is freely accessible to people and communities with socially valuable assets. This is what politicians claiming to be spokespeople of castes such as Jat, Gujar, Okkaliga, etc., fought for and won. However, delivery at the national level still remains to be accomplished, but does anyone remember that any longer? Unfortunately, most Scheduled Caste *representatives* are also more concerned in finding positions in high places rather than insisting on better *delivery* of quality health, education, and other public goods to the poor, including the poor in their own communities.

The principal of representation without delivery is a cardinal feature of coalition politics. I do not want to limit the concept of 'coalition' to mean just a formal arrangement between different parties. In my view this term could apply effectively even in a situation when a single party aspires to represent diverse interests under a single umbrella. This is akin to what the Congress party was in the early days, but today it is an ideal that most parties try to emulate. There are thus coalitions within parties and between parties. This double dose of coalitions drives the issue of delivery completely out of view and off the table.

Why are coalitions and representative politics inevitably doomed to ignore delivery? I imagine an answer to this is necessary, but it will be one that takes a somewhat meta-theoretical detour in order to reason by analogy. Though representation is obviously different from translation there is a significant similarity between the two as they both seek to represent: one a people/community and the other an author.

A translation may be a form of representation, but it happens only under the constraining voice of the author who lays out the primal script. The translator might take liberties in terms of the original text, but that would be in order to attempt to remain true to the spirit of what the original author wanted to say. A translator cannot stray too far away from the text without losing credibility, and yet a good translator is always recommended for the ability with which the tenor and timbre of the author's voice is retained.

When it comes to political representation the matter is quite different. A translator is supposed to give the best possible representation of the author's voice, which is a preexistent and preeminent reality. Political representatives do not work on an already resonant voice. Instead, they create a voice that is a combination of many inchoate utterances of the community or class chosen for representation. However, the final manifest product always bears the imprimatur of the politician, and the politician alone, which is what marks it out as the master narrative for representation. This is how caste and ethnic virtuosos are created. They become representatives in themselves and begin to constitute a *separate* class that is above those whose interests they are supposed to protect. On occasions, even trade unionists can be seen as virtuosos of sorts, especially when they lead their followers towards imaginary interests that almost invariably come to grief. They are the specialists of the kind that Roberto Michels warned us against in terms of the 'iron law of oligarchy'.

The anti-incumbency factor is the dominance of representation over delivery. A new cast of politicians is chosen each time an election is held, but not on the basis of actual delivery, but because a new beginning is proposed. Because of the monopolistic tendencies of the political market-place, one can choose between one set of representatives or another in the hope that if one does not deliver perhaps the other will, and so the cycle of hope and despair continues.

Most parties like to be internal coalitions too, for then the imperative to deliver is blunted. The politics of reservation is largely about representation for it has not delivered to the masses of the poor of all castes in India as a whole. That is why even as politicians promise to represent this or that class or faction, the final voice is that of the virtuosos.

We truly do not deserve the leaders we get.

13

AGAINST ROLLING BACK THE STATE
THE LIMITS OF NGOs AND MULTILATERAL AGENCIES

Well, if we don't deserve our leaders, can India then at least afford to roll back the State? Advocates of the Washington Consensus constantly call for this. They are echoed by those who believe that the State refuses to free the phoenix of the ashes of the past.

However the question could well be, is it possible for the State to roll back any further? As things stand, to advocate such rollbacks means little more than relieving the State of all obligations of accountability and responsibility. The State is already sufficiently rolled back; that is why our education and health services are execrable and millions of the abjectly poor desperately scratch to make a living. The lack of infrastructural and social security facilities helps the merchant producers more than anything else. Other developed countries also spend much more than India on the public delivery of public goods. In fact, the Washington Consensus should have commended India as the capital of the free world.

Instead of rolling back the State, and letting its functionaries indulge in full-scale corruption and worse, it is imperative to push for greater State activism accompanied by greater accountability.

233

Learning from the West

The route I regard inspiring is that which Western countries trod about two hundred years ago. It is not as if India today is what Europe was in the 1800s, but history offers valuable lessons and if these ideas are logical, and seem empirically sound, there is no harm in adopting them, albeit with some tropicalization. One major feature of the Western world is State investment in the delivery of public goods such as health, education, housing and energy. It is worth reminding the neo-liberals and proponents of the Washington Consensus,[1] that Western states, including America, did not 'roll back' when they were in the early stages of development. On the contrary, they stood firm to put in place social benefits and services. The development of 'citizenship' can be traced to precisely the State's investment in public goods, which filled out the notion of social rights in a democratic society.[2] Incontrovertibly, this gradual escalation in State funding helped generate sustainable industrial, even capitalist, growth.

The genealogy of State-backed policies for public welfare in developed Western societies is impressive. One must laud the well-recorded salutary effects of interventions such as those in the 1870s by the Third Republic in France; Roosevelt's New Deal in the 1930s US; State expansion into health care in the UK and Canada; or, Nordic Europe's comprehensive social cover. Europe has a long history in State-led welfare programmes. In Britain, Whig aristocrats like Lord Grey, Durham and Russell, as well as Tories, like Melbourne, Palmerston and Stanley, initiated several reforms for the working people. This included the landmark 1897 Factory and Workshops Consolidation Act. In the 1860s in Italy, an important strand in the Risorgimenti advocated Owen-style 'free schools'. In France, the 'socialist' Napoleon III wanted to settle colonies for the poor and provide loans to the unemployed. In fact in Germany, Bismarck is widely acknowledged to have been the founder of social insurance policies in Europe for his vigorous championing in the 1880s for maternity leave and accident compensation.

Ironically, although the US today advocates the rolling back of the State to most countries, including India, it did just the reverse to set up the most powerful economy in the world. Critical State intervention, in the social services sector or in the provision of public goods, not pure market economics, is actually the US model. Let us recall the huge subsidies that the US gives its farmers. In India, the farmer is subsidized to the tune of roughly US$66 per farmer, whereas it is over forty-four times higher for each farmer in US. Public investment in public goods even in the US today is way above the Indian State's contribution in this sector both in percentage, and obviously also in real terms. Yet, instead of advising and enabling countries of the developing world to make their governments more responsible and efficient, the message from the West is to cut back on public financing.

Joseph E. Stiglitz, no enemy of globalization, has written persuasively about the important role the State must play to set up an economy and ready it for world-class competition. In the nineteenth century, the US government actively helped to develop transportation, communications and markets countrywide. It regulated commerce and set minimum wages and working conditions and provided a host of unemployment and welfare legislations to cushion the harshness of the market.[3]

Although the US inveighs against workers' bodies in the post-war period, as many as one-third of its non-agricultural labourers were unionized. It pioneered the 'Great Society' that sanctioned health care and unemployment benefits on a scale that the US might be embarrassed to acknowledge today. John F. Kennedy visited the Appalachian region from Virginia to East Kentucky in the early 1960s and promised the miners hospitals and the establishment of an anti-poverty programme. After his assassination, Lyndon B. Johnson honoured most of Kennedy's promises and put these policies into practice, including free school-lunches, reminiscent of our midday meal programmes. These measures were in place till Ronald Reagan cast them aside, and from then on America's 'secret history of capitalism'[4] became more and more difficult to penetrate.

It was again in the US that a Federal National Mortgage Association was founded because the private market provided mortgages at rates that poor- and middle-class families could not afford.[5] Likewise, financial markets were regulated in Western societies till as late as the 1970s, when they were already well into becoming advanced industrialized countries,[6] and America continued with National Banking until the Clinton administration relatively recently reversed this policy.[7] Yet America and the IMF want poor countries to follow this path now when they are desperately poor and capital hungry.[8]

Around 1875, America realized that State funding was essential if it was to progress in education and research. It sent its best people to Europe and the UK to learn the latest in science, a process that continued till the Second World War. Thereafter, the US gave refuge to Europe's best scientists. This move escalated the intellectual capital of the US and certainly contributed to its present leadership in science and technology R&D. Today, about 48 per cent of all expenditure on education is State-funded in India, and this is gradually declining,[9] while in the US it is between 75–80 per cent.[10] From the 1950s to the mid-1990s the US government funded as much as 50–70 per cent of the country's R&D.[11] Incidentally, Sweden and Finland spend a larger percentage of their GDP on R&D than even the US.[12] Scandinavia has truly demonstrated how state intervention can strengthen private enterprise and innovation.

In fact, public funding of education in America inspired the great Jules Ferry, when he was premier and later minister of public instruction from 1879–85 in the Third Republic of France. For Ferry, democracy would certainly not live up to its potential if a mass of the people were not educated and therefore unable to participate as real equals. In his considered opinion, France would do well to learn from the US where free education is provided to millions of children.

'The budget for public instruction in America is not the budget of the American republic, but is the budget of the various states, and, above all, the budget of the townships. Do you know what its total is? It is

tremendous: free America spends annually 450 millions
for public schools; and by means of these 450 millions
they generously open the great sources of learning to
seven million children and they give to these children of
all classes instruction which is received only by a small
number of children of the bourgeoisie of France. And
that is not all, gentlemen: there is not only free
instruction, common and public; there are enough great
colleges, academies, universities, special foundations, to
make us hide in humiliation. In America, the rich pay
for the instruction of the poor. And I am prepared to
find this just.'[13]

As a result, the Third Republic is reputed for its insistence on
public education by recruiting schoolteachers nicknamed *Hussards
Noire* or 'soldiers in black', wearing black coats and spreading
quality education across the length and breath of France. If the
French could learn from America in the late nineteenth century
then let us in India be instructed by this experience too, albeit
over a hundred years later.

When we come to health services, we find that here too
almost 77 per cent of all expenditures in India are private, with
the State providing only about 23 per cent of health costs.[14] In
the US, on the other hand, about 40–45 per cent of health
expenditure is public. The State participation in health in the
US can be linked to the Hill-Burton Act along with the
Commission on Hospital Care; these led to the gradual advocacy
of comprehensive medical care in America[15] and in 1954 this
was extended to include long-term and ambulatory care facilities.
In Canada the State funds 70.6 per cent of all health
expenditures.[16] A nutshell review: 6.1 per cent of the US GDP
is spent on health. The proportion is 8.1 per cent in Germany.
In India it is an abysmal 0.9 per cent.[17] Surely by now we have
adduced enough evidence to say that in India the State
involvement in matters of public welfare could not be any more
negligible and negligent than it is at present. One, at least,
hopes not.

The great Scandinavian model is even more helpful to refute the popular notion that State interventions are contrary to an economy's health. Across Scandinavia, the State is at the centre of job creation, providing social service benefits and long-term health and old age insurance cover. It also allows for comprehensive workers' representation, and 80 per cent of its workforce is organized. What is really inspirational is that this has led to immense prosperity in Scandinavia and a remarkable egalitarianism in the lifestyles of its citizens.

Enter NGOs and the Degradation of Civil Society

America's prescription to the rest of the world is not in keeping with its own experience during its developing years. When it comes to India, many influential contemporary thinkers, both at home and abroad, stridently recommend that the state should be rolled back allowing NGOs, community participation and private initiatives to take over. Such alternatives to State involvement can appear quite attractive in relation to the sloppy and inefficient State bureaucracy in India. After the initial post-Independence years, the defects of the government machinery brought well earned disrepute to the public sector and socialism. The Indian State, like many others, had become overbearing, callous and self-absorbed with its superstructure of functionaries and minions. The State machinery existed solely to aggrandize and perpetuate itself. This meant, inevitably, such a vacuum of agency that alternative interventions could acquire the sheen of a new legitimacy. NGOs and community participation drew éclat because they appeared to promise compensation for the State's ineptitude. This is the context against which we should note the promotion of culture-based explanations at the expense of sociological ones. The most significant among them is the reinvention of the term 'civil society' which has now come to mean NGOs.[18]

Civil society today denotes the exact anti-thesis of what it meant to de Tocqueville, Ferguson and Hegel. In the classical version, the democratic state provided the essential scaffolding for civil society. Without the State, aspects of basic freedom would be impossible to realize at all levels: from the family to the corporation. The impulses of democracy are fully realized only after the State creates institutions that help realize freedoms and the basic equality between citizens. These institutions are critical because they link the State to citizens and not to individuals or beneficiaries. State interventions in public goods delivery were important landmarks in the development of civil society. NGOs, or popular participation at community levels, do not significantly figure in this scenario.

The contemporary inversion of the meaning of civil society makes it synonymous with NGOs. Now civil society connotes agencies outside the State and even hostile to it. While many NGOs do, and must, make common cause with this or that government, their ruling ideology is anti-State. This has two major consequences. The first is that the State is exonerated in toto of its responsibility to perform and deliver public goods to citizens. With NGOs squatting in the middle, State and citizen cease to be in a relationship that could, even formally, define them in mutuality. These developments attract any poseur who wishes to profit (even if not in the conventional commercial sense) from the conflation of civil society with the exercise of a form of philanthropy. This is such a tempting proposition for the ruling élite in backward and developing societies that many of them have joined the NGO brigades.[19] The inversion, or rather the perversion of the term civil society, enables the élite to gain much face without losing an inch of place. They, and members of their families, have found both alternative vocations and sources of funds. The community, qua community, is too poor, uninformed, bereft of social network skills, and most of all deeply fractionated. This enables the élite to rise once again as the vanguard and claim through their *très chic* NGOs to be the self-anointed oracles, if not messiahs, for the deprived masses.

The second consequence of the NGO anti-State ideology is that, as the State's vacation from responsibility is extended, NGO-style interventions evade demanding audits and are apt to be judged with kindly latitude in a piecemeal manner. It is no longer possible for an NGO to provide micro-credit, health services, education, and energy resources under one coordinated thrust. Even if several NGOs were to get together, such an eventuality is impossible to achieve as their energies, provenance, and social outlooks are different. NGO efficacy is seen in terms of isolated exemplar efforts as they cannot be replicated in a coherent and comprehensive way at a societal level. Even successful single-pronged NGOs come up against functional resistances as the other correlates of development are beyond their scope and competency. Undoubtedly, some well intentioned NGOs are forced to pick up the slack because they see so many hopeless cases around them. Guilt drives them to participation, but as with lawyers and used-car salesmen, 95 per cent of NGOs give the remaining 5 per cent a bad name!

Even so, this non-State alternative has gained ground. The large-scale expansion of NGOs is justified as an inherently better alternative to the State for third world countries like India. Foreign funds are not all that sustain these organizations and, given the extent of government patronage to NGOs in terms of financial grants, the Indian state too seems to have been convinced by this point of view. Around 21,000 NGOs are registered in India under the Foreign Contributions and Regulation Act. It is anybody's guess how many thousands have not registered themselves under this act that allows them to obtain legitimate donations from abroad. The Indian government granted about Rs 6,000 crore to NGOs in 2006-07.[20] Domestic funds that the State should have used to discharge some of its duties to citizens are disbursed instead to agencies to help them exercise a fascinating new form of *noblesse oblige*.

Development in the West, from the Third Republic in France to welfare regimes in the US and UK, was made possible because the agencies of the State worked hard at it. Why then should India not follow the same recipe? The answer, very simply is, yet again, culture. The fatalistic thought runs that Indians are notoriously prone to patron–client relationships and to interactions that are informal and face to face. Impersonal agencies like the State, or large cross-cultural themes like secularism, leave the ordinary Indian not just unmoved, but positively alienated. The argument goes that countries like India, which are poor and rural, do best in warm, fuzzy contexts at the community and village level. What we end up with is a cultural justification of NGO-style civil society. Recommendations and dispensations of this kind would find no purchase in any major western European country; nevertheless, many of them eagerly push for and fund NGOs in developing societies. Obviously, what is good for the West is not good for the rest. Well-heeled developmentalist agencies working in, and on, India tend to argue that only through the medium of NGOs can this society be nudged forward. What is the historical basis of this judgment? For starters, would it not be worthwhile to pause to ask the simple question whether NGOs were part of the Western developmental experience?

Admittedly, most Indians find the State a distant institution and the idea of secularism much mangled and capricious. Why should this be so? Must all this be explained away as cultural when there are in fact good empirical and historical reasons behind them? Can one not find cognate phenomena of the kind that bedevils India elsewhere in other climes and at other times? Western-oriented development agencies believe that Indians can only act in informal huddles and in patron–client combines so it is best that they displace the 'bad' patron (the State) and come in themselves instead as 'good patrons'. Both the modern nation-state and the liberal idea of secularism appear hostile to the natural bent of Indians/South Asians.

Reflecting a position that S. Radhakrishnan articulated well before him, T.N. Madan writes:

> '... secularism in South Asia as a generally shared credo of life is impossible, as a basis for state action impracticable, and as a blueprint for the foreseeable future impotent. It is impossible as a credo of life because the great majority of the people of South Asia are in their own eyes active adherents of some religious

faith ... Secularism is the dream of a minority ... a social myth that draws a cover over the failure of this minority to separate politics from religion in the society in which its members live.'[21]

If, as Radhakrishnan had argued, Indians live their everyday lives on a religious basis, then Madan can perhaps stretch it to say that secularism is an alien concept to the Indian mind.

Ashis Nandy, however, does not mince words on this subject and is quite ballistic on the matter:

'Secularism ... is definitionally ethnopobic and frequently ethnocidal, unless of course cultures and those living by cultures are willing to show total subservience to the modern nation-state and become ornaments or adjuncts to modern living, and the orthodox secularists have no clue to the way a religion can link up different faiths or ways of life according to its own configurative principles.'[22]

What are these authors saying? Though they are not arguing the same point, their positions are supportive of those who despair at India's inherent ability to be modern. Their stance is, in sum, that Indians should not aspire to a liberal democratic State and all that goes with it. Democracy, secularism, and the nation-state are stellar features of modernity, and on all these parameters Indians are not up to the task, and in any event their tradition was much better and more congenial. Instead they should cavort and carol in telegenic fields or huddle around the well and the *chaupal* in the name of community bonding. It is not as if scholars who urge Arcadia on Indians belong only to the developing world. The American sociologist Amitai Etzioni (1995) has, of late, emerged as a guru of communitarian thinking, but regardless of his advocacy, few takers in his own society would advocate NGO-activism for themselves or even a retreat of the State. Thus, only countries like India are candidates for experiments at revivifying traditional culture and bonding.

Giving Primacy to Culture

If perchance interpretations of the past curdle relations between faiths, as it has happened on innumerable occasions, the thing to do is not forsake tradition but to idealize it even further and push it up to its farthest heights. Rather than attack tradition for the damage it has caused humanity over centuries, the attempt here is to re-invent it as a benign and rarefied phenomenon, completely disapproving of what is happening on the ground in its name.

It is no coincidence that developmentalists too generally glorify an orientalized Gandhi as a source of inspiration for India-based programmes. Villages need to be revived, and had not Gandhi himself advocated such a strategy? They not only overlook the modernist side of Gandhi, but there is no mention of Nehru anywhere either. Indeed, Western developmentalists from the Ford Foundation to Oxfam and UNICEF ritually lambast Nehru. It is no surprise that these organizations project the village as a *gemeinschaftlich* cultural entity. These multilateral agencies are willing to advocate a range of measures, from micro-credit to self-help groups, to barefoot doctors, and the stranger they sound to Western ears the more funds they receive for the east from European and American donors. They believe that this would answer the deeply cherished values of Indians, namely to regenerate village life, and recreate vanishing crafts. This would encourage tradition and return people to their authenticity so that they can blend into the rural landscape.

There is no evidence so far that any of these measures have actually helped in development. Micro-credit institutions may reduce poverty for some privileged and targeted families, but they are not stand-ins for development. Vijay Mahajan, a leading figure in world of micro-credit and the crucial person behind Basix, said quite categorically that 'microcredit pales into insignificance as a "solution" for poverty-alleviation and promotion of livelihoods'.[23] One of the major reasons for credit is still medical emergencies and straitened family circumstances. The small sums of money that women Self-Help Groups (SHGs)

244 THE CAGED PHOENIX

generate cannot help launch a business enterprise, let alone sustainable development. Moreover, I have also found from my own experience that SHGs do best when its members have kin and family who are earning a regular income from an urban, non-farming job. Without this added help from outside, SHG members would be hard put to pay back even what little they borrow from their meagre savings.

As for traditional crafts, these do well only when they serve an external market managed by hard-nosed business people. Millions of women make embroidered cushion covers, carpets, sequined clothes, mirror and lacework garments in conditions worse than those of sweatshops. Designed by huge Western buying houses, their handiwork makes a good display in foreign stores. Occasionally these items are advertised in Europe and America as products made by poor women from destitute surroundings. Buyers find this so heart-wrenching that they willingly empty their pockets and pay over a hundred times more than the poor rural artisan actually received from the marketing agent.

Selling Culture

Poverty certainly makes for an excellent advertisement, especially if the commodity is produced by calloused hands in conditions of extreme scarcity. This strategy would not work as well for goods manufactured in the West. They would be slammed for a host of civil rights violations and for producing under inhuman conditions. It is however all right for things that come out of countries like India. This little bric-a-brac was made by a starving family, that little thingummy by a cyclone victim, that bauble by an orphan, and so on. It appears that the Western buyer has a near-insatiable appetite for such curios though they are made under very iffy conditions. What excuses it all is that these items are thickly doused in an imagined Indian culture.

What sort of cultural blarney camouflages the violations of labour laws? If a worker, still a minor, is slaving full time, without any opportunity to go to school or for recreation, the excuse is that rural children do not understand recreation, vacations, or the meaning of education. Therefore, to exclude them from a full-time job would be a form of discrimination. This line of reasoning would not pass muster in the West, but it succeeds here.

Alternatively, take the issue of denying the right to representation. Western buyers are not keen on pushing this idea anyway for it has tones of socialism. They however find a neat rationale for looking the other way when gross violations occur in this area. The local supplier hands out the story that workers look up to the management and come to them in times of need just as they would do to the elders in their family. This is in accordance with Indian culture. If these familial conditions hold at the workplace, surely there is no need for formal trade unions or other forms of representative bodies for the workers. They would find that extremely stifling and inadequate to meet their multiple personalized needs.

As nothing can be formalized along rational lines, the developmentalist never looks to the State machinery as the first choice of agent for change and growth. Neither is the State structure a favourite with foreign buyers who usually patronize NGOs of various descriptions when they think of doing something by way of Corporate Social Responsibility. In New Delhi in 2006 I heard the chief economist for South Asia of the World Bank advocating that India learn from Bangladesh and rule itself through NGOs, as that is the only way South Asians can relate to welfare-oriented schemes. What an example to proffer! How many NGOs are doing the rounds in Washington? Would Americans be pleased with such advice? For that matter, would any self-respecting country? Indeed, had this World Bank person consulted normal Bangladeshis on this issue he would have been in for a surprise.

Developmentalists are so wrapped up in their certitude regarding the cultural motif that they do not feel the need to ask their supposed beneficiaries what they really want. They assume that the objects of their attentions are juvenile in their ignorance of what is best for them; horror, they might even decide to up and leave the country for the town. The idea that this might not be a bad thing is anathema to developmentalists.

Nevertheless, the Industrial Revolution in Europe was made possible by the rush of hungry peasants to cities, ranging from London to Petrograd. This is how the poor reacted in Europe, and this is what successfully fed the Industrial Revolution there. They rushed to the industrial towns much more readily than the towns would have them. At that time, some Western scholars resented this transition too. It was seen that the move away from rural community life would bring about 'a retrogression in the culture of the individual with reference to *spirituality, delicacy and ideals*'[24] (emphasis mine). This point of view was soon discredited, but it holds firm with developmentalists in the Indian context doggedly refusing to learn from Europe's past. In India the developmentalists' song is all about 'spirituality, delicacy and idealism'; Indians cannot live with the 'inconsiderate hardness'[25] of formal procedures, which is why their natural bent is towards village life, community solidarities, and *patres familias*. They might say something to the contrary on the spur of the moment, but one must overlook such childish exuberance.

As the developmentalist knows best, and as Indians are endearingly mired in their strange ways, the need of the hour is to work around their customs and sneak in a rational measure that would help them in spite of themselves. The suggestion is never seriously entertained that members of these target groups may want a different life for themselves and for their children in order to escape crushing clientelism and agrarian servitude. The developing world is to be addressed in terms of needs that the West knows all about. They should not have independent and out-of-the-box aspirations for they belong to the 'other' world where culture determines all.

Multilateral Agencies and the Communitarian Agenda

Some anthropologists, especially those who study Asia, Africa and Latin America, tend to view culture as a road map, a recipe, a grammar, that its adherents are bound to follow or be banished to the sidelines in their own societies.[26] To a considerable degree, this perspective skews intellectual enquiry in India, and, with it, the instruments of public policy. For a long time the term 'civil society' was a highly respectable one till, as we mentioned earlier, UN organizations, the Ford Foundation, and other multilateral agencies and think-tanks around the world decided that it needed revision. As these organizations have more money than any Indian academic institution, and as there is no longer an intellectual stigma in collaborating with such agencies, they have aggressively altered the intellectual agenda in India.

Sample a few Ford Foundation projects picked at random. The Asset Building Community Development Project aims to find 'solutions to problems of poverty and injustice', no less, 'by helping low income people and communities build the financial ... social and natural [sic] assets they need to overcome poverty and injustice'.[27] If only eradication of poverty and injustice were so simple. No mention of the State anywhere. In the Knowledge, Creativity and Freedom Programme the aim is to examine how religious traditions can help in 'creating a just, healthy and pluralistic society'.[28]

However, the moment America figures, as in the project on Peace and Social Justice, terms like state and local governments, budget and tax issues, and electoral reforms begin to appear.[29] For the developing world, the focus is all about community, vulnerable sections, religious and faith-based reforms, appropriate technology, and the preservation of the arts and crafts (as in Ford Foundation's Asset Building and Community Development Programme). The distinction between the West and the Rest for social interventions/engineering is very clear. For the West State, citizenship, and public welfare are critical variables, but for the East one must only nurture community and tradition.

In some cases the Foundation's efforts border on the utterly precious. In the project entitled Peoples' Commission on Environment and Development, the Foundation's aim is to use community-based participation to encourage 'organic farming'.

This is a first-class pipe-dream. Organic farming is the most expensive technique of farming conceivable, and to imagine that those who can barely farm cotton without being pushed to suicide will switch to this high-priced and risk-prone method is clearly utopian. Incidentally, why is this project not based in US? Why are American examples not cited?

Oxfam has a similar point of view but there is a slight difference. Oxfam promotes community participation, no doubt, but it also believes that NGOs (of which it is one) should have a greater presence in government decision-making or else things will go wrong. Incidentally, Oxfam openly states that NGO leadership in development is the one sure ticket to survival and success for developing societies. It states that development can occur only through 'improved access for civil society to policy-making and implementation'.[30]

NGOs and Western aid agencies of different hues have not only successfully distorted the term 'civil society', the statements and activities of these organizations warp civil society and community in order to force them into a marriage of convenience. The reality of rural life is ignored in favour of an imagined community existence without even a rumour of disharmony. Civil societies are continually encouraged to build community resources and community participation, but where is this community on which NGOs harp? This question does not stop organizations like Oxfam whose *Oxfam in India* brochure advocates the need to '(b)uild community organizations, assets and infrastructure'. One wonders what kinds of assets these communities hold in common? Or, for that matter, even infrastructure? Now a host of research institutions and university departments legitimize and participate in this kind of 'community' action and research.

As Western institutions tend to loosen their purse strings for academic endorsements of this new *ersatz* civil society, the rigours of real research on the subject are gleefully abandoned. Disciplined research, something that takes years, even lifetimes, is supplanted by the vastly more enjoyable activity of networking. In other words, in this dispensation, academics can and should safely and profitably turn themselves into lobbyists for NGOs. The Ford Foundation, for example, has projects on democracy which do not even ask for a tangible outcome in terms of a written paper or a report. All that is required is that there should be evidence of 'networking' with distant like-minded people. It would be rare for underpaid academics in a developing country to refuse such easy pickings.

Democracy, as these civil society activists put it, is not about claiming rights as citizens but in winning access to education and health in selected areas through the more convenient means of networking. Is this how liberal democracy established itself in the West? Of course not! Why then is it advocated here?

The madeover idea of 'civil society' can be used to undermine struggles for citizenship, mass activism, and the need for State accountability. These things are fine for the West but not for India. By orientalizing perfectly respectable universal terms like 'civil society' and 'community', democracy has been replaced by NGO patronage, the State by community associations, and the public by people in target groups. Oxfam is willing to work with any government of any poor country regardless of whether it is a dictatorship or a democracy. That is because the State is of no consequence except to give access to Oxfam and its cohorts. Can women's labour rights be sustainably enhanced in a dictatorial regime? Can we imagine actually listening to the 'voices of the poor' in countries where elections cannot be held?

Community Medicine as Appropriate Technology

The 'community' song is not only part of the NGO repertoire but is also a loop sample in the policy prescriptions of the World Health Organization (WHO) for 'third world' countries. From the days of the 1978 Alma Ata declaration, the WHO has favoured a populist health policy where health initiatives should be left at the level where the 'people' are most comfortable. To begin, WHO have nothing, or little, to say about quality medical care at the curative level in hospitals. According to this declaration, what developing countries need most is 'Primary Health Care'. It is as if poor countries are ravaged only by dysentery, whooping cough, polio and other 'common diseases and injuries'.

So, how is this programme of 'Health for All' to be accomplished? WHO categorically states that it should be with the 'full participation of the community' and 'at a cost that the community and country can afford . . .' Should the Indian state be excused for letting over 80 per cent of its health care expenditure to be privately funded on the grounds that it is a resource poor country? If so, should health care programmes be dependent on passing the hat around and hoping for the best? WHO officials should note that in 1995-96 as many as 24 per cent of rural patients and 21 per cent of urban ones had to forego medical care because of lack of funds. Less than ten years previously the figures on this ledger were 15 and 10 per cent respectively.[31] If a society were to depend on what it could afford then a large chunk of its poor would go unattended when sick. Would the West ever countenance such a suggestion for itself? If the WHO declares health a fundamental human right, why should standards differ across the world for different countries?

In keeping with the culture-laden sentiment lavished on the East, WHO holds that the onus for health care devolves to the community. Primary health care 'requires and promotes maximum community and individual self-reliance and participation in the planning, organization, operation and control of primary health care.[32] Technology used for this purpose has to be appropriate and must also include traditional practitioners. Appropriate technology is clearly a low-level and untested technology; how else can traditional nostrums be advocated without proper clinical trials? Would WHO advocate this line of action for primary health care in the West without being laughed out of court? However, no-one laughs at these suggestions when they are bestowed on India. Poor people get cheap diseases that require only primary health care. Rich countries have expensive diseases like heart ailments and cancer that require specialized medicine. Clearly, the human body is not the same in different settings.

Incidentally, WHO's Alma Ata declaration of 1978 was meant to accomplish *Health for All* by 2000. Our health situation today is perhaps worse than in 1978, but the drawbacks and failures of WHO have never been closely examined. Instead, WHO keep advocating the same policy of community participation in different forms, even extending its sweep from primary health care to palliative health care. The quality of palliative care is far less important than its spread even if standards are sacrificed in the process. Manjeli and Mallapuram in Kerala are advocated as models where volunteers with little to no expertise roll out palliative care, which is no better than holding hands and sharing sorrows. Palliative care is a very specialized branch of medicine. It has to do with pain relief, symptomatic chemotherapy, bowel interventions, cauterizations, and the like.[33] You cannot expect your neighbour to have the expertise to provide all this!

Clearly, Western medicine is neither appropriate technology nor one that the community can afford. This then rationalizes the coexistence of two types of medicine—one for the rich and the other for the poor. Western allopathic medicine is for those who can afford it and community-led health care is for the poor. What poor villagers therefore need is a host of semi-literate barefoot doctors, and this would raise India's health status and standards of medical care.

If only this were the whole truth! Undoubtedly MBBS doctors are urban, even élite by Indian standards, but even Indians suffer from a range of diseases beyond dysentery and malaria. They have typhoid, leprosy, cancer, heart ailments, multiple sclerosis, and everything else to which the average American or European is susceptible. It is a waste of medical resources to send degree-holding doctors on anti-diarrhoea missions when paramedics and auxiliary health staff can effectively undertake the task. There is little need for doctors to go on immunization and inoculation missions. This can be undertaken by the same paramedics. This is exactly the Western pattern. Neither Europe nor America wastes doctors on ailments that can be attended to at a lower level; yet in no Western society is it ever said that there should be a reduction of emphasis on high level medical training, or that doctors and super-specialists are a waste of time and resources. Why then should this be said of India and by the very people who enjoy these advanced health privileges in their own country? Is this because of the pernicious idea that Indians do not suffer from complicated diseases, they probably do not live long enough or are too poor to obtain treatments for difficult diseases anyway? In 1987 the representative of Voluntary Health Association in India, a body that is heavily financed by Western funds, said in my presence that 'cancer was a disease of the rich'. This was his remarkable response when a cancer survivor asked him if, as a cancer survivor, she could be of some use to his organization. I was left aghast by his remark. Surely he must be aware that cancer is class blind; in fact, poor people are more susceptible to it as their immune systems are already compromised by a diet insufficient both in terms of caloric and nutritional value. Why would a man with some background in medicine not know such an elementary fact? I probed him further to try and follow his reasoning and concluded that he viewed health care for the poor in India as a voluntary affair undertaken by part-time professionals and neighbourhood angels. Cancer, however, requires expensive treatment by medical specialists. As only the rich can afford such an elaborate medical regimen, by extension, only the rich contract cancer.

I know of a very poor parent who came to the All India Insititute of Medical Sciences, New Delhi, with his son who was suffering from cancer. After diagnosing the child the doctor prescribed a regime of drugs that was less expensive, and less effective, because he knew of the distressed economic condition of the family. The father of the child objected passionately: 'Don't look at me as a poor person, see me as a father. Tell me what my child needs to get well and I will find the money somehow. That is my responsibility. I am first a parent.' Can anyone think of anything nobler, more caring, and human than this? The doctor was immediately contrite, realizing the cultural stereotype under which he was labouring.

It is true that cancer care is enormously expensive and for a poor person the diagnosis of cancer is almost like a death sentence. Even so, such a person has dignity. The State policy should be to ensure that the poor can access quality medical care instead of providing them with separate second-class treatment? The parent who protested with the doctor for viewing him only as a poor person and not as a father taught the doctor, by the latter's own admission, an invaluable lesson.

I also learnt from another touching experience what the role of the family (even the community) should be when dealing with a patient. They should not take over the job of providing medical services and curative therapies but act as supportive structures. A doctor instructed a grandfather to tell his ailing grandchild the exact nature of his ailment and the procedure to be followed. The elderly gentleman however saw no reason why his grandchild should know all the details of his illness. In his view, what the child needed to know, feel and experience most completely was that no matter what, his family would love and care for him. He said that it was this certitude that a child needed to know and experience. It was this knowledge, that he was loved, regardless of circumstance, that was going to help him the most. This was how the family could most directly help him fight the disease. At the same time, the grandfather would not compromise on the medical care for his grandson. He taught me in a few simple words that there are two kinds of care, both useful within their own spheres of operation.

Can health be a purely voluntary affair left to barefoot-doctors? WHO nurses a blissful oblivion of the lessons from China, the only country that really implemented the barefoot-doctors programme on a grand scale, when it lauds non-formal health care. Initially, the barefoot-doctors' programme, introduced by Mao, met with resistance from ordinary people as well as the Chinese Medical Association. However, once they were introduced there was a greater demand for hospitals as health expectations were raised.[34] After years of turmoil and popular dissatisfaction with barefoot doctors and the extreme politicization of medicine, China was compelled to seriously rethink the programme. In 1957 the Chinese government effectively devalued the barefoot-doctors' programme by calling for a doubling of enrolment in regular medical colleges.[35] Zhou Enlai played a sterling role in dismantling Mao's populist health policy. He emphasized instead that both rural and urban areas should have access to quality medical care.[36] It is not as if the superior doctors in the Chinese Medical Association could overrule Mao's diktat; it was the people of China who did. Again, in contrast to what Mao said and what WHO consistently suggests, Zhou argued in favour of high-level medical research. According to Zhou: 'Basic theoretic research exerts a far-reaching influence on scientific and technological progress and we must pay sufficient attention to this field as well.'[37]

Intellectual quests should not be abjured in the name of expediency, and worse, of poverty. It is baseless to argue that high research is of no consequence to poor people. To say this is to assert that the poor and the rich do not have the same basic anatomic and physiological features. After all, what is the point of saving someone at the age of two from dehydration and schistosomiasis infection, and have him die a few years later from something as treatable as a ruptured appendix?

WHO specialists are of no use, whether for curative medicine or palliative medicine. The truth is that most people in India, rich and poor, go to the allopath when they are seriously ill. A quick trip to any public hospital would easily demonstrate the distance poor people travel in order to get to a specialist allopath. One really does not need research studies to demonstrate this. However, the number of hospitals per hundred thousand population is a mere fifteen.[38] This of course raises the prospect of patients experimenting with grandmother's remedies, ayurveds, and unanis, neighbours' suggestions, and so forth. However, once they are convinced of their illness and ready to adopt the 'sick role',[39] they do not readily go to a traditional healer. Regardless of their class background they tend to stay with the allopath, but the chances are that when the disease is chronic or terminal the economically disadvantaged are compelled to choose interventions that are less than helpful. For the poor, a visit to non-medical practitioners is necessitated by the fact that Western medicine may be more expensive and unavailable. Surely, the reason behind why, in India, a large number of people go to alternative medical practitioners, is not because of diehard 'cultural preferences'. True, the poor tend to go to alternative therapies more than the better off. This is when they are not able to access more efficacious interventions. In this they are not so different from the rich or the Westernized elite. One has only to look at the mushrooming of 'alternative therapies' in the Western world to realize that their attraction arises primarily when Western medicine fails the patient.

Élite Advocacy of Community and NGOs

A subscription to the multilateral and NGO doctrine of community and civil society perfectly suits an operational context shot through with corruption and administrative opacity. NGOs and multilateral agencies need high-level government functionaries to oil the wheels of the bureaucracy. The authors of red-tapism are favoured by these community-driven NGOs and multilateral agencies just to undo what they themselves have done. The entire cycle of exchange works in perfect synergy. It would be instructive to see how many of those employed by multilateral international agencies in India thrive on official and political connections.

It is impossible to roll the State back any further. To believe that the State should not, need not, or cannot actively contribute to the development process is inexcusable. Worse, it is profoundly damaging to the all-round development of India. This fact is conveniently set aside when people cursorily read growth statistics and the picture of an upward spiral bolsters their misplaced and misinformed optimism. In my view, it is dangerous to exonerate the State in the name of preserving Indian traditions. But to avoid this danger, we need an unadorned and clear examination of Indian society. Any short cuts in this matter will keep us from achieving useful perspectives on our present economic situation. The nature of India's current economic advance should neither be viewed in purely cultural terms, nor as an oddity which curiously grew from nowhere. Nevertheless, these points of view are frighteningly collusive and exercise a powerful hold on our critical faculty. To recognize this is a necessary, though not sufficient, step to an alternative and more cogent perspective, and thereby to interventions that will not be maquillage for a corpse.

Let us look away from developmentalists and Indophiles and study what the social sciences tell us about culture. Sociology and social anthropology cannot be accused of ignoring culture because that is one of their staple concerns. In recent times even history and political science are taking culture seriously, without however being culturally determinist. This is how some of the most eminent Western sociologists analysed culture. Culture was to be understood in terms of evolving structures of social relationships and not as an independent phenomenon, least of all one that is determinant in nature.[40]

All cultures tend to look at other cultures as if they are analogues of nature.[41] The European views non-European cultures in this way, and this is exactly how Africans, Asians, and the native people of the Americas look at 'white people' and their culture. The 'other' is always fixed and immobile, while one's own culture is flexible, open to reason, and based upon very sound and straightforward premises. If other cultures are always fixed and rigid, it is logical to infer that they must be inferior to one's own. Now we, as good products of the Industrial Revolution, would certainly not expect the !Kung people, with their Stone Age economy, to believe that they are the best. Alack for our vanity, but they do. The Kachins in Mynamar know that there are Shans and Burmese around, but they are convinced that their neighbours have not yet fully evolved. The Pueblo Indians have a similar view of those around them, as do also the Chinese of the Middle Kingdom or the Hindus of India.

It is not only other cultures that are seen as inferior in general. This downgrading goes all the way to physical appearance. When the famous eighteenth-century British traveller, Richard Burton, went to Africa he recorded the pity the so-called tribal African felt for Europeans: they had thin mouths, big noses, and the skin colour of an albino. Till recently, East Asians too took a very dim view of the European appearance. In the aesthetics of the Bismarck Archipelago of Melanesia, beauty clearly meant a large mouth, strong white teeth, flat noses, and pierced ear-lobes.[42] All this may now have changed because the idea of beauty closely follows the reality of power, and that has tilted inexorably towards the West.

The moral of the story is that cultures spontaneously tend to naturalize other cultures, and that is why they find the ways and aesthetics of the stranger inferior to their own, and always in need of explanation.

Levi-Strauss, the great and inspirational French anthropologist, once said that members of his profession were like the ragpickers of history. As lowly ragpickers, anthropologists ferret out from the past and present, the humblest of phenomena, and see in them answers to the most endurable riddles of humankind. History glorifies itself by claiming totality, but leaves out tiny details for the ragpicking anthropologist, who makes much of them. These leftover bits and pieces actually lead us to an appreciation of some of the most fundamental truisms of humankind. We are invited to see the exotic as variations of something that we routinely practise. Armed with this determined universalism, we are better equipped to approach some supremely mundane matters of Indian society and to remove the patina of exoticism. We will see how these matters have been rendered mysterious and exotic, seemingly immune to query, apparently intractable paradoxes. In the process, we will be able to recall the disciplined enquiry of Indian social matters from exile.

The Hindu Conception of Dirt

This must be the rarest of paradoxes: how is it that Indians are so fastidiously clean, but India so incredibly dirty? A recent *Forbes* magazine survey ranks India as a major dirt capital of the world. In fact, two of our blue-chip metropolises, Delhi and Mumbai, figure among the twenty-five dirtiest cities listed in the study. It might take a herd of wild horses to keep an Indian from a morning douse, so complete is our fidelity to ablutions, but just outside our homes filth accumulates as though it were complying with a law of nature.

Can this duality be explained in terms of Hindu other-worldliness? Or should we seek a key to this riddle in our backwardness? Before we rush to an answer let us remember that it is only in the subcontinent that filth forms so spontaneously around us. Hindus cannot beat Buddhists at other-worldliness, yet Vietnam, Mynamar, and Sri Lanka do not display dirt with the same gritty brazenness as India does. Nor is there a straight correlation between poverty and filth. In comparison to India, many poor neighbourhoods all over the world, from Latin America to Asia, look quite spruced up, never mind their straitened circumstances.

Hindus do have an idea of dirt, but it does not square up with modern/Western notions. The anthropologist Mary Douglas once clarified that dirt was simply 'matter out of place'. Food on the plate is the way it should be everywhere, but becomes dirt when it is on the floor. Shoes on one's feet are fine, but if they are placed on the table one has dirt. American kids have no problem going to bed with their shoes on, something that would horrify most Hindus.

It is a question of how Hindus define dirt, or 'matter out of place'. Hindu conceptions of dirt draw their fundamental justifications from deeply ingrained notions of caste. According to the caste principle, all routine substances that come out one's body, like perspiration, excreta, and menstrual blood are polluting even to oneself. By the same token, hair is also polluting. The traditional roles of the barber, washerman and scavenger were directly and precisely intended to absorb specific pollutants so that members of the upper castes could remain 'clean'.

Whatever can be expelled from the body must be brought out. The chorus of gagging sounds one hears every morning is because Hindus want to ensure that their sinuses and bronchial passages are squeaky clean. It would be quite unlikely for a non-Westernized Hindu to carry a handkerchief, for the idea really is to blow one's nose in the air and let the pollutants fly in the breeze. Using a handkerchief for this purpose is like recycling pollution and causing ritual damage to the self. A soiled handkerchief in the pocket is dirt, but not garbage outside one's door. It is perfectly fine to skirt around such filth and not be offended at their sight. Once such substances are out of the home they are quite in place, and hence no longer dirt.

It is not then that Hindus have no notion of dirt, just that it is different from the way it is viewed in the West and in medical treatises. Every civilization has its own understanding of both dirt and hygiene, strange as it may sound to outsiders. As the ideology of caste runs across religious divides in the subcontinent, it is not surprising that *Forbes* magazine should have found so much dirt in Dhaka, Karachi, and Mumbai.

What, after all, does dirt outside one's home have to do with a good life? A lot in fact, once we work in the notion of citizenship which also implies the responsibility of the State to strictly enforce the law and adherence to 'public' norms. As we found, the Hindu notion of dirt may have a logical consistency, but it certainly does not respect the idea of a 'public' where others count as a limiting constraint on the self.

It must also be stated for the record that though Europeans are not votaries of the Hindu notion of dirt, Paris and London were filthy till the last decades of the nineteenth century. In fact the Western notion of dirt and hygiene evolved gradually over a little more than a hundred years ago. It is the rigid enforcement of the norms of public hygiene that brought about great changes in Europe, and by extension in America. Nineteenth-century Cincinnati was known for the heaps of garbage in the street, not to the left or the right, but in the centre. Pigs were let loose to clear up the mess, but such a situation is unthinkable now. I can do no better, in this context, than recommend Norbert Elias's monumental contribution in the *Civilizing Process*[43] in order to allow readers to appreciate how far Europe has travelled in its understanding of what dirt is.

Doesn't all this sound vaguely familiar with what we see in spiritual India?

The Ragpicker at Work

Three stock questions about India: Why do Indians revere godmen? Why do they worship the cow? Why are they vegetarians?

There are usually two very tired stock answers to questions like these. The first is the Indians' abiding belief in karma and rebirth, and the second is the hold that the other world has on Indians, Hindus in particular, which makes all 'this worldly' considerations irrelevant. Those who use these grand explanations usually flit from one to the other. This is easily accomplished, for in both cases the intangible (either karma or the other world) provide the ground rules for the imagination. Notice too how alien such systems of thinking are to the straight, normal, and rational modes that prevail in Western societies. This is also, perverse though it may seem, what makes Indian culture a trophy that can be carried home for display. Some years ago a British traveller, after returning from a harrowing car ride from Jaipur, asked me in a quavering voice: 'Now how does karma actually work?' He could think of no other explanation for the rash driving on Indian highways.

The ragpicker thinks differently. The ragpicker looks for what is acceptable in the universal market-place. Plastics can be recycled, cloth and paper can be put through the grind for born again pulp, bits of wool and dirty linen can always be washed to look good once more, and so on. Nothing is strange, unique, or unusable if we carefully juxtapose contexts and seek parallel utilities, which may, at first glance, appear unworkable. How would a ragpicker regard these three so-called Indian issues that challenge Western credulity and whet their appetites for 'exotic India'? It is entirely possible to show that India is not a riddle wrapped in a mystery inside an enigma.

First, we can scrutinize the passion for godmen to see if it implies some unique Indian predilection for the mystical. Is the adulation for godmen in India all that strange or unique? It is true that Indian godmen look different from Billy Graham and Jerry Falwell. It is also true that the languages of address are different. It is true that the parables, the clichés, the kinesics and the dramaturgy sound and look different. What is categorically not different is the fact that the evangelist and godman are both showmen, skilled in whipping up collective effervescence, skilled also in verbal pyrotechnics or crude shows of legerdemain. In America, I was struck by the mesmerizing, near shamanistic, impact evangelists exercise on their audience. The element of gaudy shows, of playing to a gallery, is in ample evidence not only in the televangelist shows of Joel Osteen and Robert Schuller in America, but also in Indian cable-television channels like the Hindi-language Aastha and the UK-based English-language channel with the rather charming moniker of GOD TV. This raises the question: are Indian godmen all that different or is the difference just an unusual variation of a phenomenon that is familiar elsewhere? Both in the West and in India there is a place for godmen who claim superior knowledge of the divine, and they are not just straightforward ritual specialists.[44] Also, one does not need to be a Hindu to be susceptible to these strange religious figures. Rajneesh, Sri Sri Ravishankar, and Mahesh Yogi became popular in India once they were discovered by celebrities in the West. Remember the Beatles and Mahesh Yogi, and the sitar strains in *Sgt Pepper's lonely hearts club band?* George Harrison, Richard Gere, Steven Segal, and Mia Farrow are, or have been, happy to be high-profile groupies of one or another purveyor of spiritual snake-oil.

If the parallels between Indian godmen and Western evangelists are not convincing, we could note the unexpected similarity between the godman and the psychoanalyst. The godman speaks and the audience listens to his lengthy *pravachans* (discourses), an assortment of bromides and misquotes from ill-read texts. The psychoanalyst soothes the febrile temperaments of middle-class Americans; they speak, the certified listening post-cum-confessor listens, occasionally interjecting a question.

The settings are different, the roles seem different, the purposes of the interfaces seem unrelated. But after the session is over, the analyst, like the godman, collects the fee for services rendered and sets up a date for the next tryst.

Second, let us shred the much-embroidered idea that Hindus deify the cow. Why do Hindus worship the cow? Well, why shouldn't they? After all, the cow was their only ticket to survival for the longest time. The male calf would soon grow to be a hardy ox, so necessary for traction in the fields. Cow's milk was a source of necessary nourishment, and cow-dung was used as fuel. Even when the cow died its hide could be put to use. Here is the unmistakable this-worldly attitude, marked by remarkable cruelty, of the Hindus to 'Mother Cow'. If there are too many female calves then a bracket is put around its head so that she cannot get to her mother's udders and gradually dies of starvation. Then the calf is stuffed and placed near the lactating cow so that her milk flows easily.[45] Surely, there is a great difference between the theory and practice of cow-worship.

Third, we can say outright that the idea that Hindus are vegetarians is a pure occidental myth. Three-quarters of this country comprises meat-eaters and only a small proportion (primarily Brahmans and Baniyas) are vegetarians. Kashmiri and Bengali Brahmans are hearty meat- and fish-eaters respectively, though it is true they don't eat beef, at home anyway. Vegetarianism is a minority feature that has been inflated to encompass all Hindu food practices. This is because vegetarianism was and is such an oddity in the Western mind.[46] Of course, as an oddity from the East it has also assumed grand moral and spiritual value for those who can afford to walk into a well-stocked supermarket and decide at leisure which foods would not cause them moral dyspepsia. A large number of poorer castes in India could not afford to be vegetarians. They ate cattle carrion, rats, and other moving creatures because of their desperate poverty. These communities turn to vegetarianism when they make a little money and want to be upwardly mobile. Vegetarianism is much more expensive than eating rats and carrion, and to alter their diet in this way is also to signal that they are not amongst the lowest and most despicable castes. Further improvement in wealth and status will alter their dietary practices once again. Now they will turn to expensive meat and fish products like chicken, fish and lamb. No more rodents, no more mongoose, no more beef carrion, no more of strict vegetarianism either.

What is worth noting in this context is that in a large number of vegetarian communities, eating habits are being challenged by members of the younger generation. Baniya and Marwari youth are eating meat today. Such a practice horrifies their elders. In tradition it is precisely their disapproval of the Brahmanic/Vedic animal sacrifice that led them to carve out a separate identity of their own. However, the youths who have broken with food taboos have not forsaken their caste status; their reaction against vegetarianism is cognate with their opinion of meat-eating as a hip oddity. In this one sees that the hip Marwari meat-eater is the mirror-double of the hip vegan and vegetarian in the West.

Marking out the Modern from the Contemporaneous

The notion of 'the public' emerged full-blown in Western societies. The opposition between 'public' and 'private' is very recent and is quite different from the opposition of 'open' and 'secretive'. These latter terms are of much greater antiquity. In India the second set still prevails in the main, primarily because we have not yet been able to fully step into the time zones of modernity.[47] India lives next to, and is coeval with, Western societies where practices that are properly 'public' are more fully developed. As different temporalities still jostle one another in India, it will take a while before this society too truly enters the modern age.

This should not appear inexplicable, for everything contemporaneous need not be modern. There is no doubt that with the passage of time India too will change, but for that to happen it will need a strong middle-class to emerge. Where there are great differences in wealth and status, the 'public' takes a long time to emerge. Democracy, in particular, liberal democracy, works best 'in a situation of mild scarcity'[48]. This is not to cover up for Indian inadequacies, but to position them in context so that urgent interventions can be set in place to correct them instead of throwing up one's hands and saying everything Indian is incorrigibly cultural and obdurately enigmatic.

In India as we discovered, just three per cent of households can afford to live a lifestyle that the Western middle-class take for granted. This makes liberal democracy hard to get off the ground.

I have heard well-to-do Indians complain angrily against the poor for everything that ails India. From disease and pestilence, to poverty and over-population, the poor are held responsible for all our ills. This vast discrepancy between classes tempts the view that even within one's own society there are these 'others' who are fouling things up. The poor are considered to be lazy, to breed like rabbits, and to be given to all kinds of irrational beliefs. They cannot be changed for the better as they are naturally constituted of some particularly adamant substance. It is not as if one must belong to another country, culture or clime to regard those who live round the corner as aliens and pure execrations of nature. Poverty is also a great divider and the longer stark discrepancies exist in lifestyles, the longer it will take for citizenship to evolve in India. It is not just the Europeans who stereotype India; Indians also inflict this on each other. The better off in the IT sector and in the financial world and in the assorted garment industry would have led a much deprived lifestyle had it not been for the existence of the very poor around them. If they did not get cheap labour, what would they have exported with such success?

Affluent Indians complain that if the poor were rational they would have smaller families and our population problem would be at an end. The ragpicker would then ask when the small family norm emerged in the West. Did it accompany lower infant-mortality rates? Did family size begin to shrink in

Europe around the same time that industrialization and urbanization grew along with public medical care? If all this is true, the mass of Indians have still a long way to go. Finally, till the early decades of the twentieth century even in Britain the very rich and those at the bottom had large families.[49]

Public Services and Citizenship

In all my years of fieldwork the two most depressing sights in rural India have been its schools and hospitals. I recall going from village to village in Jharkhand, UP and Bihar, and being appalled at the level of public services available to the rural poor. There were two hundred children in two rooms and an open field with two teachers carrying stout twigs in their hands to frighten their students into submission. I always asked these teachers what their timetable for the day was. The answers were often made up on the spur of the moment. This was to be expected as there were children bunched together in the open who should have been separated into three or four different grades. However here they were all sitting together with the teachers intermittently asking them to write or read something at random. Would I send my child to such a school? Would you? But then, do the rural poor have any choice?

Poverty induces a certain amount of recklessness when it comes to family size. It is not as if with fewer children the educational or health status of the family would rise. Schools are either non-existent or of such poor quality that they do not make a difference. Most people cannot send their children to private schools because they can neither afford them nor do they have any expectations from education anyway. What will their boy do with a school education? He too will end up as a labourer, just like the father. On the question of health, the matter is much more tragic. While one can still live and earn something without going to school, there is no hope of surviving a serious illness without going to a doctor. That is why medical emergencies are one of the major reasons for the poor in rural India to take loans.[50]

Given a shot at an education that is half-way towards quality education, even poor villagers will opt to send their children to a private school somehow. Private schools are not the preserve of the rich.[51] As many as 20 to 51 per cent respectively of families below the poverty line (BPL) in rural and urban areas somehow manage to enroll their children in private schools. Remember that the poverty line in India is determined by whether or not a person can afford to buy food items to meet basic calorie requirement for survival. So when we talk about families below the poverty line, we are really talking of utterly impoverished households.[52] For the poor, even Rs 40 a month (or just US$1) is quite a drain.

It would be grossly inaccurate to even suggest that the average Indian villager is not a risk-taker or does not think of a better, non-agrarian future, if not for himself then at least for his children. It should be borne in mind that if the poor do not send their children in adequate numbers to school and if there is a high incidence of poverty and school dropouts, these have nothing to do with culture or the rural mindset. The low quality of education in government schools takes away from the urge to see their children through a proper education much more than does the cultural upbringing or the brute force of poverty. The same survey found that in rural India 63 per cent of children in private schools could read compared to only 51 per cent in government schools. This has little to do with levels of education at home. In private school, 47 per cent of children who come from families which have had no education can read as against only 37 per cent of those who come from the same category of families but are in government school.[53] To complete the story, there are many kinds of private schools in rural India to suit all kinds of budgets with fee structures from Rs 40 (or less than US$1) to about Rs 150.

In India there is no dearth of private schools and hospitals catering to the rich. There is also no dearth of cheap labour that the well-to-do can employ as household servants, cooks, drivers, ayahs, sweepers, gardeners, contract labourers, and the like. If the affluent here can live a life of leisure it is because there are so many poor people to look after them. This reality is easily ignored and that is why even though different classes live in close proximity, there is this great divide that is almost continental. We don't have to go very far to begin exoticizing our own kind.

Alternative Rationalities

Admittedly, poverty induces certain preferences. The inaccessibility of public goods and services makes one vulnerable to informal sources of health, education and credit. Even so, what surprises me is how this grinding poverty does not fully confine people in cultural straitjackets. This is the most amazing aspect, and that is why it is so necessary to give poor people their dignity as human beings.

I am not romanticizing the poor. Nor do I feel, like the English anthropologist Verrier Elwin, any urge to serve the poor, feel their pain and to experience 'greater toil and fuller suffering'.[54] Instead, I feel an immense injustice is done to them in India by typifying them as irrational, unimaginative and unwilling to go beyond what has been laid out by culture. I feel angry rather than pained for I know the shallow ethical positions from which such judgments are passed on those who were born in unfortunate circumstances. With such desperately impoverished people in such numbers, even a low-paid clerk can afford to keep an undernourished child from the village as his kitchen boy. It is bad enough that the poor are systematically and cynically degraded by the better off, but my anger wells up when they are also belittled as being intellectually and culturally wanting. Far from the poor being galvanized by primordial sentiments for political purposes, it is instead the leaders who are prone to such persuasions.

My accumulated field experiences have convinced me that innovation, adventure, hard work, rationality, and all that is good and treasured, exist as much among the poor as among the privileged. The difference is that these attributes are expressed in ways that are unfamiliar to us who, on account of the randomness of birth, are fortunate to occupy a far better position in the social scale. If however we pay attention to small details and are convinced about the oneness of humankind, a different vision suddenly pops up, and then we wonder why we were so blinkered to something so obvious for so long.

On the face of it the poor may appear to be 'rural idiots', or as even Marx had said 'potatoes in a sack of potatoes', but these same people think hard about making ends meet, picking up a number of skills at whatever levels that are available to them, travelling long distances in order to find work. We saw the effects of this in the social character of the small-scale factory worker and we also learnt why they were being pushed out of the village because of a failed rural economy. I have seen that the village poor travel thousands of miles on a prayer and a song with barely a promise of a job somewhere. The risks they take in migrations of this kind would terrify anyone else who is better placed. Perhaps an adventurous few would undertake such missions, but the poor are doing it all the time and in huge numbers. The latest count tells us that the Indian Railways carried over five billion passengers a year, just going by the official tally. Entire families, including old grandparents and women nursing their babies, travel crammed into the stinking, airless lavatories of the euphemistically named 'general compartments' (the third-class carriages) of the Indian Railways. In their effort to get some work, they travel from as far as Kashmir and Bihar to the southernmost parts of the country in this manner. They sleep on tiptoe, kept upright, sometimes fainting in the sheer crush of people who are unable to afford even a third-class ticket, and must travel in this way. They cannot move from their positions, or they would lose their precious few inches of sitting or standing space. One will not find their intrepid critics in these superheated birdcoops. One will not find them quelling their nausea at having to lean forward, one hand on a wall for balance, twenty-four hours at a stretch, over an excrement-dripping toilet bowl. However, there is an excellent possibility of finding these eloquent orators in the airconditioned bogies, just a few feet and some strong steel doors away, fulminating about the filthy hyperproliferating brutes who crawl with lice, stink to the high heavens and steal everything that is not nailed down or locked up.

The latest manpower statistics show that maximum migration occurs for reasons of employment. In 1999-2000 this accounted for 42.45 per cent of all causes for migration. Interestingly there has been a near 15 per cent jump on this account during this period.[55] The bulk of this migration is from rural India and those from poor regions, like UP and Bihar, have the highest rate of out-migration.[56] There is an undoubted correlation between poverty and migration in search of work, and this stands to reason. Why should somebody who is well looked after at home go far away to start life in unfamiliar surroundings?

By seeking parallels and juxtaposing contexts, the burden of culture is lightened and the structure, history and empirical details that were earlier not sought for now become research enterprises. I need to illustrate the way new facts come to light under a comparativist scrutiny at some length later by relying on my first major rural research venture. I learnt two important lessons from this experience which confirmed my ragpicker's approach and distrust of cultural explanations.

Farmers' Movements or Peasant Culture

In 1987 I began my study of the Bharatiya Kisan Union (BKU). In the 1980s and early 1990s this was a strong political organization of owner–cultivators, particularly in western UP. The more I examined this phenomenon the clearer it became to me that far from being rural idiots, these farmers were neither 'pre-political' nor 'pre-ideological'. These negative characterizations came from highly respected scholars like Eric Wolf and Teodor Shanin,[57] who in turn, spawned many more culturally oriented studies of rural people.

I found, on the contrary, farmers heatedly arguing politics in the BKU and weighing different options in terms of alliances and parties. While the official position of the BKU was that they were 'non-political', I realized it meant something quite different. Not unlike the contemporary trade unions of today, both in the East and in the West, the BKU felt that they were better off by not officially attaching themselves to any political party as that would enhance their bargaining power with the State. They sent out signals to all, and whoever picked them up, became their ally for the day. It however required a degree of perseverance on my part to uncover this, but I found that very rewarding. The famed notion of the peasant's inability to look beyond family, kin or clan was easily discredited, and the cultivators of western UP appeared so much more normal.

While engaged with this study I came across other researches in cooperative sugar factories in the western state of Maharashtra. What was most interesting about such investigations was the attempt to plot the reasons why cooperatives fared so well in Maharashtra. After considering a range of literature on this subject I found that the most authoritative ones also resorted to a culturally oriented argument. The explanation in this case was that the pragmatic and secular culture of Marathas had led to the success of the cooperative movement in Maharshtra.[58] Clearly Indians cannot handle success either without succumbing to cultural explanations. This argument was in need of an inter-contextual makeover.

I went to Maharashtra soon after and met some of the notables in that region, and the sugar barons in particular, and found that they were vastly dissimilar to the cultivators I had become familiar with in west UP. However, before I come to the differences, let me sketch the similarities. The dominant caste in Maharashtra was Marathas, and in western UP it was the Jats. However both the Jats and Marathas were proud to be farmers, scoffed at Brahmanical pretensions, and believed they had a martial past. What made these parallels more striking is the fact that both Marathas in south-west Maharashtra and Jats in western Uttar Pradesh grow sugarcane.

Now for the differences; the most glaring is that Maharashtra has successful, buoyant sugar cooperatives, whereas in western UP sugarcane generally goes to private companies. Like the

Marathas, the Jats are also pragmatic and egalitarian, and yet, most of western UP is devoid of cooperatives but for one or two emaciated examples. Thus, the well-established cultural answer for the success of sugar cooperatives just will not work.

In the course of my field trip to Maharashtra I had the occasion to meet a large number of sugar barons and realized how different they were from Jats, even from Jat leaders in the BKU. Those who controlled the sugar cooperatives in Maharashtra were people feared in their localities and were clearly members of the élite. What may have foxed researchers is that Marathas, rich and poor, high and low, have very down-to-earth lifestyles and aesthetics and in that they share many attributes with a large number of villagers. Like the Jats, it is difficult to distinguish that some of these 'peasants' are actually quite rich. This is where the optical illusion of Maratha egalitarianism originates.

A taxi driver whom I asked to take me to the home of a sugar baron entertained no such illusions. He was genuinely petrified when he learnt my final destination. He realized that his bargaining capacity with regard to the fare had become virtually non-existent. He was in fact quite willing to drop me off, gratis, and put as much distance as possible between himself and this imposing cooperative boss. On a separate occasion, the appointed minion of another sugar cooperative calmly stopped a state transport bus midway with a wave of his hand, so that I could board it. This kind of pure power would be impossible for a Jat to exercise routinely: perhaps against a few poor castes, but not as freely and widely as can the powerful Marathas.

I then realized what made sugar cooperatives work in Maharashtra. It was not because of so-called Maratha egalitarianism, but the precise opposite—because Marathas were stratified in terms of rich and poor, high and low, power-wielders and ordinary folk. The sugar cooperative bosses were all from leading Maratha families, with clearly discernible social and cultural capital. A well-heeled sugar baron, also a member of Parliament, kept his leg up on his desk through our entire conversation, imperturbably disregarding any social niceties towards a visitor. As members of the élite they were able to win State support and could also control the market. Their unchallenged supremacy made the small cooperative member cower in his presence and this led to a peaceful and orderly exercise of power. Nobody wanted a coup, and no voices were raised at the meetings of the cooperative's shareholders.

The Jats of western UP were different. They were really equal with little to separate one from the other. Very often they would give me the *sirhana*, or pillow side, of their string charpoy for me to sit on as a gesture of courtesy. These Jats were primarily small landowners in a sea of small landowners. They were not desperately poor but separating them along class lines was difficult. This equality did not breed bonhomie; rather it made them bitter rivals as one could not stand the relative and wafer-thin prosperity of the other. Contrary to what journalists made of BKU leadership, I witnessed that in many organizational meetings the leader had to bleat out his position amidst angry protestations from the assembled gathering. They joined ranks[59] against the outsider who did not share their difficulties. Left to themselves they were a fractious lot. How could cooperatives work in such an environment?

Now we see that the Marathas and Jats are normal people and not cultural confections. It is not Maratha culture or Jat culture that alone determines why there are cooperatives in one instance and not in the other. The answer does not lie in the stars, but on the ground. Structured relations between classes and communities are outcomes of historical forces whose origins may well have been a chance occurrence; a lost war, an unexpected flood, an administrative *ukase* could wholly alter the trajectory of a set of relations. In all cases however they can be nailed down to something empirical, and hence amenable to a ragpicker's special skills.

According Respect through Universal Categories

It is easy to misunderstand my argument so far by interpreting it to mean that there are no differences, or at least no notable ones, between India and the rest of the world. That would be an unkind cut and far from fair. To admit to differences is not the same as exoticizing; to seek to make the other 'normal' does not mean that all societies are the same.

There is no doubt that India is different from other societies, indeed even from its neighbours in Pakistan and Bangladesh. Notwithstanding the similarities in language and some ritual practices, it would be incorrect to overlook the many institutions and practices that separate us from other countries in South Asia. When I go to Pakistan or Bangladesh I am struck by the numerous divergences between us and them, but I know that if I had the time I would find perfectly good empirical reasons, with their historical accompaniments, to explain these variations.

Most often the normal tendency is to view other cultures with other lenses and not through the normal optic with which we view ourselves, and other people like us who we accept as 'normal'. Very often one hears that to understand India one needs categories that are native in character, or the conceptual armory needs to be peculiarly designed to explain the peculiarities of just this society. The principal consequence of de-exoticizing India is that it can now be apprehended through universal categories and does not require a suspension of empirical judgment. This also extends respect to the people one studies, for they are now much more than just respondents. They can also teach us a lesson or two, and it is about time we learnt these. Properly done, it is only by examining societies that are different that one can get to know more about one's own. As the Kipling ditty goes: 'What should they know of England who only England know.'

Universal terms and concepts are put to the test only when they are placed in unfamiliar conditions. This is plain methodological commonsense. Why should we have universal categories if they only apply to the West, or perhaps, to a part of the West?

A theory of marriage that is conceived for monogamy is useless for polygamous societies or where the practice of levirate union prevails, and is obviously weak from the outset. A study of doctor–patient relationships that cannot accommodate the indigenous medical practitioner, even the witch doctor, is urgently in need of help. If a concept or theory evolved in the West does not work elsewhere then it is not the fault of the elsewhere but of the theory itself. If a theory of economic growth clearly bypasses India, or a study of political mobilization leaves the subcontinent cold, it is not because special and incommensurable categories are required to appreciate our specifics, but because the theory and the terms it has employed are just not good enough; cannot last the wash.

It is true that many Western scholars write about their own society as if expressing universal verities. For example, unlike most of us who are always urged by our publishers to introduce a subtitle clearly demarcating our empirical field, a Western scholar can get away without this form of finessing. When Talcott Parsons wrote *The Social System* (1964) he did not insert a subtitle such as 'A Study of the Middle Classes in the Eastern Sea Board of United States'. In my view, though this book, or the even more inaccessible, *The Structure of Social Action* (1959), or the deeply inspiring work by John Rawls simply called *A Theory of Justice* (1971) were all inspired by the New England region of America, they were all sufficiently powerful to generate credible universal categories. In a similar way, the work of scholars examining the specifics of caste, religion or village life also contribute to universal theories and not to special regional bodies of knowledge. True scholarship is evident when theories make sense and illumine lives in regions far away from their place of nativity. Therefore, like Parsons and Rawls, other scholars working on the subcontinent or in sub-Saharan Africa should also feel encouraged to write a book without subtitles.

A good theory is one that has room to expand, finesse, and accept fresh empirical data. This might mean some rearrangement of the furniture, but it would be all for the better. It is with this methodological view that I have written this book on India's development and sought to link the apparently disparate rural with the urban. I hope I have been able to explain with some degree of adequacy Indian realities and demystify some of its most enduring mysteries with the aid of universal categories. India has secrets aplenty, but they are not impervious to disciplined sociological attention. Good theory that is keen on comparative research would easily unlock these mysteries.

Incidentally, a good theory would say things as they are, stand up to popular myths of the day, and, in this process, function as an invaluable guide to social development.

14

CONCLUSION
HELPING THE PHOENIX TO FLY

What will it take to release the phoenix? Unfortunately there are no no easy answers here, because we are talking about the phoenix and not a songbird caged by design. In this case we need to fundamentally rethink the fundamentals, and it is not as if the resources for that are untraceable. It will however need to be a multi-tiered approach starting from a rigorous rejection of cultural otherness and the spontaneous tendency to exoticize those who are not like us. This is especially so if these others happen to be poor and less well-endowed than us in terms of socially valuable skills. This intellectual bent need not always originate from the West, or be a pure emanation of colonialism; it can also be nurtured to full bloom under local hothouse conditions.

If this intellectual trait comes so easily to many Indian scholars, policy-makers and commentators, then it is because of the wide gaps that exist in this country between the rich and the poor, and even between the not-so-rich and the not-so-poor, and all the way down. This, more than anything else, inhibits us from seeing other lives as connected to our own. We have already noticed that the levels of poverty in India would be unthinkable even in the poorest Western society.

In this book I have inveighed heavily against elitist culturological explanations of everything Indian. The reason why I tend to reiterate this, both at the beginning and towards the end, is because I hope to wear down the opposition with as many examples as I can muster from everyday life and letters. I think the intellectual can contribute meaningfully to a country's development by advocating an academic perspective that is always on the look out for something to criticize. This often offends the general public who want to rejoice in something, instead of finding fault with everything. But the task of criticism is an intellectual's true job and we should do it without fear or favour. If we succeed then we will have damaged, if not demolished, every ivory tower in the vicinity.

Intellectuals often undermine their position which is why every so often they are willing to be political journeymen. But they would perform a huge service to society and, indeed, to all of human kind if they would stand up and point out the limitations of our impressive growth rate, of the inadequacies of our poverty removal programmes, of the nexus between politician, bureaucrat, contractor and merchant producer and, most of all, how the rich live well because the poor barely live.

If one is thinking of ways of making a difference in the lives of one billion plus Indians then a start can only be made if intellectuals realize the many problems, and constraints, of things as they are. If they too buy into the popular myths then there is no way to make a difference. Of course, we need better infrastructure, better schools, hospitals, roads, energy provisions, housing and water. Everybody knows that, but why is little done towards making such public goods available? Among other reasons, it is because intellectuals have shied away from calling a spade a spade and have sided with one or the other popular constructions of reality.

It is hardly a Copernican revelation that all such popular notions of what is real begin from one's own self interest. Like Karl Mannheim, I believe that an intellectual should stand apart and have no interest, other than safeguarding the intellectual profession. What an intellectual's profession demands, more than anything else, is the readiness to criticize and analytically show the way forward. Johan Fichte has remarked that the human condition is one of perpetual toil for every achievement erects a fresh barrier. This process is unending. As every thesis sets up its own anti-thesis there is just no resting place. Whilst Marx and Hegel subscribed to Fichtean dialectic, they believed that it could be put to rest in the fullness of history. It is the lapse in their judgement that led to some of the execrable outcomes of actually existing socialist states.

Intellectuals always win, but it takes a while. So this job is really for the long-distance runner as it is quite lonely and requires a lot of stamina. A society may appear to have a rock hard carapace that can never be cracked to liberate its contents, and yet there is a moment of intellectual magic waiting to happen. It happened with the birth of democracy in the West and the East, with the fall of Nazism, with the liberation from Stalinism and Maoism, and it happened when Spain came out of Franco's shadow. As a Spanish scholar once told me, 'Under Franco, Spain was in black and white, but today it is in colour, and it is because of us'.

India, sadly, continues to be painted in black and white. About 836 million people, or 77 per cent of our population, earn less than US$2 per day.[1] Three-quarter of India's non-agricultural workers are either landless or marginal farmers.[2] As much as 80 per cent of all health expenditure is out of the individual's pocket, the state picking up only the remaining 20 per cent. This is the lowest in the world, as every other State (with the probable exception of Iraq) spends a greater proportion of its country's total health expenditure. Roughly 23 per cent of Indians forgo medical treatment as they do not have the resources for it. The litany continues: poor public education, transportation, and energy infrastructure, irresponsible patronage-style politics.

There are no ready solutions at hand, but we can make a beginning if we accept that the rich are just a small fraction of the population and their wealth is intimately tied to the poverty of the many. We must also realize that the rich have prospered the world over only when the general standards of livelihood have risen across all social classes. That is how a country moves from 'black and white' to 'colour'.

The Information Technology sector employs but three million people and we showcase, brag about, and delude ourselves with the contribution of this tiny sector. Every time it stamps its tiny feet and pounds the floor with its little hands, we stand to attention. What we need to appreciate is that the major source of non-agrarian employment is actually in the informal and unorganized sector where sweatshops dominate. The bulk of our export earnings come from these unorganized and informal units, and as much as 92 per cent of India's workforce is to be found in these places. Admittedly, this is not the kind of thing one happily writes home about, but we cannot ignore this reality for long and only discuss our amazing growth-rates.

These informal units employ largely unskilled, or barely skilled, villagers who are desperate for a job and will even settle for less than minimum wages. Villages are imploding from within as agricultural growth is either stagnant or creeping up at the rate of less than 2 per cent per annum. Subdivision of holdings has led to a serious agrarian crisis and farmers are committing suicide at the rate of a little over a thousand a year. In fact, we may have to re-classify the rural character of Indian villages, for easily 35 per cent, if not more, of its economy is non-agricultural. The agricultural crisis has also released millions from the villages who are eager to rush to the cities which have not yet readied themselves for such an influx. This near impossible contradiction has led many to romanticize the village, but the villagers are not among such romanticists. They want to get to the cities faster than the cities will have them. For now, however, they can only find openings in enterprises akin to sweatshops where their skills are tested at the lowest level. The Indian informal sector is full of such shallow water-wells.

The Indian rich, whether in the ITES sector or in the informal industries, are prospering primarily because they are exporting cheap labour, and not quality products. In the case of the ITES sector, it is cheap sub-baccalaureate-level intellectual labour (with a few stars thrown in), and in the many processing and manufacturing units it is primarily cheap manual and semi-skilled labour, with barely a redeeming feature. There are obviously a few exceptions to the rule, but as in all such cases, exceptions happen to prove the rule. Obviously this is a bitter pill, for most of us want to feel good by thinking in terms of growth statistics alone. Of course, the *percentage* increases in the super-rich category and in the purchase of consumption goods from motor cars to lipsticks are impressive, but given India's size these figures are utterly minuscule. In addition, as most of the graphs on wealth and consumption are calculated from such low baseline levels, the existence of prosperity even in a tiny sector shows up as a steep incline.

Under these somewhat depressed conditions it is often tempting to lapse into a species of extremism. Either one advocates the nobility of poverty because conscience has already sent in its calling card, or gung-ho consumerism hoping that the goodies will eventually filter down. The answer does not lie in either of these approaches, but in accepting the fact that in spite of appearances there is a profound connection between the rich and the poor. The unfortunate part is that their fates are contrarily intertwined. That is why in the short run it is tempting to look away from the dishevelled crowd and concentrate instead on people like us.

It does little good to blame caste and religious differences either for our economic and social backwardness. So much of this is primarily a consequence of patronage politics and pandering to cultural virtuosos rather than taking hard decisions to drive democracy down to the poorest citizen. Caste and ethnic mobilization are the fluff with which politicians blind us, but as I have sought to demonstrate, people rarely ever get the leaders they deserve. This is truest in democracies that are characterized by extreme scarcity and where the temptations of 'representation' drive out the need for 'delivery'.

That is why this book pays so much attention to intellectual conditioning without which long-term planning will never be taken seriously. If the connection between the rich and the poor is more than just coincidental, then interventionist policies that raise the substantive content of citizenship must be put in place. This would however demand a huge amount of public investment and involvement, but unfortunately the Indian State has not exactly covered itself in glory in its earlier attempts at social engineering and economic regeneration.

That need not, however, necessarily be the case because we have the European and American examples, particularly of the nineteenth and twentieth centuries, to act as our historical guides. Governments must efficiently deliver health, education, and other public goods, and they cannot be relieved of this essential task. The private sector can come in later, but only after the state scaffoldings are ready, replicating the European and American model. The presence of multilateral agencies is nearly always a distraction, so it is indeed a pity that our State and our pampered classes think so highly of them.

If we wait endlessly for the long term to work its magic then the cage may rust one day, but by then the phoenix will have died again. We have an impressive human-resource base even now, but if we are not careful, it will soon become a thing of the past. Research and high levels of knowledge production are still possible, but we are allowing our institutions of higher learning to rot, mesmerized as we are with our service-sector miracle. It is wrong to believe that a poor country needs only poor intellectual offerings, from nuclear science to medicine. In truth, it is just the reverse. A poor society requires the highest levels of intellectual investment, for alternatives have to be found that are scientifically true and yet cost-effective.

We were very fortunate that our country was twice-born. Its first birth was with the attainment of Independence in 1947. It was born again in 1950 when we crafted one of the most superior Constitutions of the liberal–democratic world. Here again, however, we need to be extremely cautious. We have already allowed far too many amendments to our Constitution to serve sectional and group interests (such as reservations for OBCs). If we drop our guard here, before long our Constitution will be denuded of its many sterling features that encourage fraternity and citizenship.

There is no doubt that in the past sixty years or so, we have made several errors as an independent nation-state. Our resources could have been augmented more rapidly had we stayed close to the original constitutional promise of creating a fraternity of citizens. This would have brought home, with greater clarity, the realization that the lives of the rich and those of the poor need not be negatively related. A positive bonding can be forged, but for that we must be ready to take hard decisions and think in terms of the whole, not just the rich or only the poor. Just as the trickle-down theory has problems in spreading the benefits of enterprise; a theory that glorifies the poor does little to raise working class standards.

If the phoenix can struggle through the ashes of our feudal and caste-ridden past, a past that was degraded by considerations of a closed and unjust agrarian economy, then it is in our interest to recognize the strength of its much-abused form. In spite of the strikes against it, India is not just a democracy, it also has a liberal Constitution that is infinitely more than a piece of paper. We have shown that we are capable of instituting progressive norms (for instance, our legislations against untouchability and in favour of minority rights), we have a strong indigenous intellectual and literary class, and we are still a united country. India has several faults, but also undeniable attributes that many societies crave. It is about time then that we opened the cage and let the phoenix fly.

APPENDICES

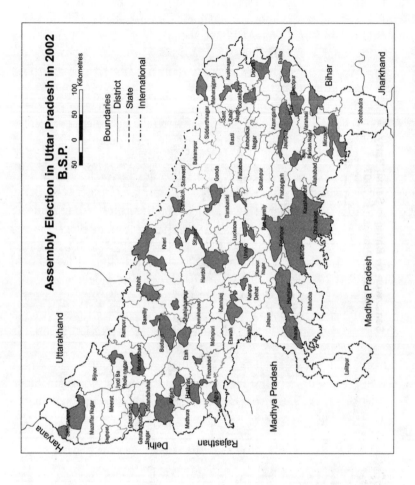

Assembly Election in Uttar Pradesh in 2002
B.S.P.

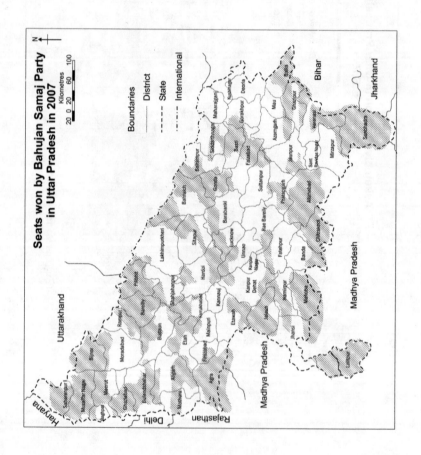

Seats won by Bahujan Samaj Party
in Uttar Pradesh in 2007

284

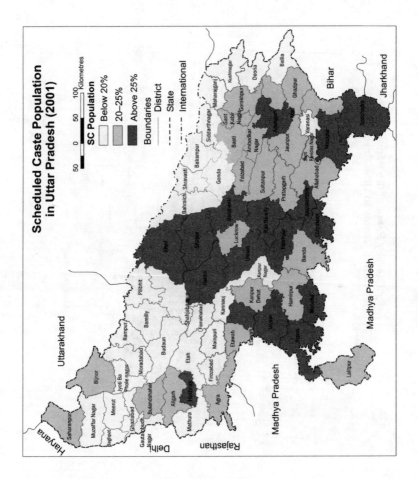

Scheduled Caste Population in Uttar Pradesh (2001)

SC Population
- Below 20%
- 20–25%
- Above 25%

Boundaries
- District
- State
- International

50 0 50 100 Kilometres

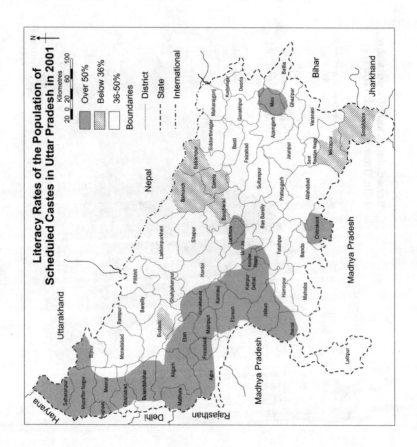

Literacy Rates of the Population of
Scheduled Castes in Uttar Pradesh in 2001

Over 50%

Below 36%

36-50%

Boundaries

District

State

International

Kilometres
20 0 20   60   100

286

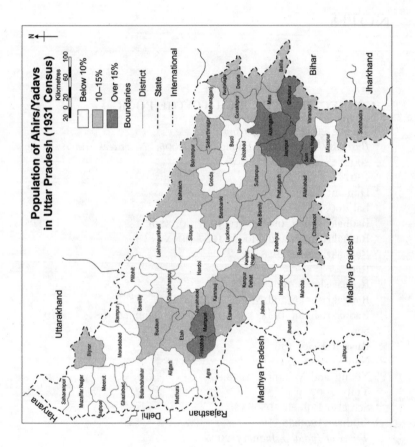

Population of Ahirs/Yadavs in Uttar Pradesh (1931 Census)

Kilometres
20 0 20 60 100

Below 10%
10–15%
Over 15%

Boundaries

—— District
------ State
-·-·- International

287

NOTES

2. CONNECTING THE RICH TO THE POOR

[1] Taeube 2002: 7, and *passim*
[2] *Business Week* 2007; Panagariya 2005; *Newsweek* 1997; Nayar 2006
[3] 2007
[4] Dumont 1988
[5] Lal 2005: 6, 27, 263, 295.
[6] Radhakrishnan and Moore 1957 (a): xxiii
[7] Radhakrishnan and Moore 1957 (b): xxx
[8] Radhakrishnan 1958:25.
[9] Ibid.
[10] Radharishnan 1957: 320
[11] Radhakrishnan and Moore 1957: xxiii
[12] Radhakrishnan 1958: 25; see also Pochhammer 1981: 278-79
[13] Sen 1997
[14] Russell 1950: 136
[15] Nandy 1989
[16] Young and Willmott 1973:85
[17] Tully 2007
[18] See also Russell 1950: 130
[19] Guthrie 1958:53
[20] *Times of India*, 1 January 2005
[21] Embree 1988

3. INTELLECTUAL CAPITAL AND MERCHANT CAPITAL

[1] See *Census of India 2001, Slum Population*: 3-4
[2] Rodrik and Subramanian 2005; Acharya, Cassen and McNay 2004: 208
[3] Kundu and Sarangi 2007: 29

[4] Durkheim 1956: 277

[5] Sengupta 2008

[6] ESCAP 2006, Table B-2, p. 199

[7] UNCTAD 2002: Table 7.3, p. 343

[8] Asian Development Bank ADB 2001: Table 13, p. 50

[9] *Statistical Outline of India* 2007: 261

[10] ESCAP 2006 Table B-11, p.217

[11] *Economic Survey* 2006-07: 149; Jhabvala 2005: 154-55, 163

[12] *Statistical Outline of India* 2007: 7

[13] Ibid.: 265; see also www. BasicEd.org

[14] *Economic Survey* 2005-06: p.146

[15] See *Economic Survey* 2005-06: Table 7.18, p. 148

[16] *Hindustan Times* 21 February 2007, p.26; see also *Economic Survey* 2006-07: 147

[17] *Economic Survey* 2006-07: Table 7.15, p.153

[18] *Handbook of Industrial Policy and Statistics,* 2003-05[37] (latest figures are up to 2004)

[19] *Economist* 2007

[20] NASSCOM 2006

[21] NASSCOM-IDC 2006

[22] Shankar Acharya

[23] Acharya 2006: 23

[24] Ibid.: 24

[25] *Economic Survey* 2006-07: Table 3.3, p. S-50

[26] Ibid.: p. S-50, table 3.2

[27] *India Key Data* 2007:2008: 64; see also *Economic Survey* 2005-06: Table 7.17, p 155

[28] *Manpower Profile in India 2005 Yearbook*

[29] Table 3.2.26, p. 174; see also *Statistical Outline of India* 2006-07: 7

[30] Down from 259, 380 in 1998 to 255, 357 in 2000 ibid.

[31] *Manpower Profile in India 2005 Yearbook 2004*: Table 3.3.28, p. 175

[32] According to the definition given by the National Commission for Enterprises in the Unorganized Sector (2007), the 'unorganized sector consists of all unincorporated private enterprises owned by individuals or households engaged in the sale and production of goods and services operated on a proprietary or partnership basis with less than ten total workers'. (2007: 2)

[33] Earlier the definition of small-scale sector was based on two criteria: they used power and had less than fifty employees, or they had between 50 and 100 employees and had power. In 1999 the definition was radically changed and small-scale industry now means units with less than Rs 10 million as fixed-asset investment.

But since this exempted cost of equipment such as tools, jigs, moulds and dies, research and development, generator sets, transformers, cable installation, cost of storage, even fire-fighting equipments, it was not difficult to fudge the records. The latest definition has raised the bar from Rs 10 million to Rs 50 million. A medium-scale industry can have as much as Rs 100 million in fixed investment, while a micro-industry is one that has fixed investment in land and assets not exceeding Rs 2.5 million (Office of the Development Commissioner 2008: vide S.O. 1642 (E), 29.09.06) Micro-enterprise has an investment of up to 25 lakh; small-scale of 25 lakh to 5 crore; and medium-scale of from 5 crore to 10 crore.

34 *Economic Survey* 2006-07, Table 7.11A, p. 149; see also *Statistical Outline of India* 2007: 62
35 *Third Census of Small Scale Industries Sector,* 2002
36 *Economic Survey* 2006-07: Fig. 7.3, p141
37 Ibid., p. 140
38 *Statistical Outline of India* 2006-07: 62
39 *Handbook of Industrial Policy and Statistics,* 2003-05 table 7.12: 177
40 *Handbook of Industrial Policy and Statistics,* 2003-05: table 7.5:182
41 *Economic Survey* 2005-06, p.S-25, table 1.23
42 Between 1993-94 and 2005-06
43 *India Key Data 2007: 2008:* 52
44 *Economic Survey* 2006-07, p-S 118, table 6.8
45 Ibid: S-57, table 4.6
46 Bidis are small thin rolls of tobacco leaves held together with a fine thread. They come in conical paper packages and are usually bought by the poor as they are much cheaper than industrial cigarettes, let alone cigars.
47 *Five Year Plan,* 2002-07, vol. 1, Annexure 5.3; see also *Statistical Outline of India* 2006-07: 35
48 Jhabvala 2005: 154
49 Ibid.: 154; see also the *Economist* 11 October 2007
50 Ibid.: 163
51 *Hindustan Times,* Business Section, 29 December 2007
52 *Manpower Profile of India* 2005: table 3.2.1: 143
53 Smith 2007: 112. Though India's exports are growing, their scale is still much lower than smaller countries like South Korea and Singapore. India's export earnings were US$55982 million in 2003, but Singapore's was US$145366 million, South Korea US$193817. Even Indonesia and Thailand had, at US$62631 million and US$80522 million, significantly higher export earning figures than India.

[54] See Damodaran 2008
[55] ESCAP 2005, p.247
[56] *Five Year Plan* 2002-07: 208, table 10.4
[57] *India Key Date 2007:2008*: 139; *Outlook*, 9 April 2007: 24
[58] See World Bank, 2007, *World Development Indicators*: 93, table 2.14
[59] Madduri 2006
[60] Singh and Mukherjee 2004
[61] *World Bank Human Development Indicators* 2007: 75-76, table 2.9; see also *ESCAP* 2003: 230,table III
[62] Source www.BasicEd.org
[63] BBC News 2007
[64] *Economist* 3–9 February 2007: 75

4. HOW MERCHANT PRODUCERS OPERATE

[1] See Ramaswamy 1990: 162
[2] Holmstrom noticed this feature in the 1980s well before globalization became a household world. See Holmstrom 1985: 212
[3] *Report on the Conditions of Work and Promotion of Livelihoods in the Unorganised Sector* 2007: 31

5. THE MIDDLE CLASS MYTH

[1] *NRI Reality News*, 11 January 2007; DeParle 2007
[2] Sengupta 2007; see also *Report on Conditions of Work and Promotion of Livelihoods in the Unorgaized Sector* 2007: 6–7
[3] See *Manpower Profile in India 2005 Yearbook* 2004
[4] Himanshu 2007: 497
[5] According to computations by McKinsey (IMA 2006: 23)
[6] Ibid.
[7] Taken also from the findings of a study undertaken by the Duke University School of Engineering
[8] IMA 2006
[9] *India Key Data 2007: 2008* 2007: 69, table 7.9
[10] NASSCOM-IDC 2006
[11] iWatch 2009, *1st Employment*, Mumbai
[12] *Economic Times* 27 August 2007
[13] See Sengupta 2007
[14] *Statistical Outline of India* 2006-07: 83
[15] *Economist*, 7 December 2006
[16] Friedman 2007
[17] *India Market Demographics Report* (National Council of Applied Economic Research 2002: 66-Table 8.1)

[18] *Statistical Outline of India* 2007: 85, table 97
[19] See also *Sarvekshna* Annex III: table 30U, p. 120, NSS 55th Round 1999-2000
[20] US Census Bureau 2005 *Highway Stastistics* (table 1066)
[21] US Census Bureau 2005 *Current Housing Reports*: table 964
[22] *Economic Survey* 2005-06: 141, table 7.11
[23] See also table 7.11, p. 141, *Economic Survey* 2005-06
[24] Working based on FADA figures mentioned earlier
[25] *National Council of Applied Economic Research* 2002
[26] *Statistical Outline of India* 2006-07: 85, table 97
[27] National Council of Applied Economic Research, *Market Demographics* 2002: 66-table 8.1
[28] Ibid: *2002*: table 7.8: 60–64
[29] See Phookan 2004
[30] Smith 2007: 106
[31] Compare, for example, the statistics on this from the forty-third to the fifty-seventh round for an estimate: see NSS Report–fifty-seventh round: pp. 37–39
[32] NSS Report no. 476: pp. 23, 26, 29, and 32; and NSS Report no. 480: pp.22, 25, 28, 31
[33] See http://wcd.nic.in/ub2007.htm
[34] Trevelyan 1951: 611
[35] See Guerard 1951: 693–7
[36] *New York Times International*, 27 September 2007: p.A-4

6. THE HOLLOWED VILLAGE

[1] Rao 2008
[2] Epstein 1973
[3] Kumar 2006: 5369
[4] Ministry of Agriculture, *Government of India and India Year Book*: 2003
[5] Small and marginal farmers own less than two hectares, medium farmers own less than four to ten hectares, large farmers have ten hectares and above. Obviously, it does not take much to be categorized as a large farmer.
[6] Ministry of Agriculture, *Government of India and India Year Book*: 2003
[7] http://dacnet.nic.in
[8] *National Sample Survey*, 2006: table 3.2
[9] *India Key Data 2007: 2008* 2007:35
[10] Ibid.: 48, table 5.22

[11] Between 1994-95 to 2001-01 (Acharya, Cassen and McNay 2004: 216)

[12] http://agricoop.nic.in /statistics stock2.htm

[13] *World Trade Report* 2006: 136, table 15

[14] 2001 *Census of India* estimates 29 per cent (see http://www.indiastat.com/india/Show Data. asp?secid=324). On the basis of the information in the National Sample Surveys fiftieth and fifty-seventh round Omkar Goswami concludes that about 35.2 per cent of rural households are non-agricultural. Goswami n.d; see also Lee, Dias, and Jackson 2005: 28.

[15] See Chadha 2003:55 for earlier figures

[16] Census of India 2001: http://www.indiastat.com

[17] Ibid.: 16

[18] Ibid.: 58

[19] Ibid.: 5

[20] Ibid.: 55

[21] See Parthasarathy, et al., 1998:141

[22] Simmons and Supri 1995:145

[23] Ibid.: 149

[24] Ruthven and Kumar 2002

[25] Parthasarathy, et al. 1998:149

[26] See Basu and Kashyap 2002: A-180-81

[27] For contribution of public utilities investments that have spurred RNFE Visaria 1995: 404

[28] Study of a UP village (Ruthven and Kumar 2002)

[29] Visaria: 404

[30] Basu and Kashyap 1992: A-181

[31] Ibid.: A-187

[32] See Gupta 1997

[33] Fertilizer Association of India 1988

[34] See Abbi and Singh 1997

[35] Narayanamoorthy 2007: 2377

[36] Ibid.

[37] Mitra and Shroff 2007: 73–77

[38] See Chandrashekhar and Ghosh 2005

[39] P. Sainath, lecture, 18 Janurary 2006

[40] See NSS fifty-fifth Round 1999–2000, 2002, ch. V, table V.1; see also NSS fifty-ninth Round 2005 Indebtedness of Farmer Household: 22

[41] Desai and Dubey, *Economic Times* 2007

[42] Ibid.:22; see also NSS Press Note 2005

7. THE CHANGING OF AGRICULTURE

[1] 17.96 per cent (Chadha 2003: 58)
[2] Parthasarathy, et al. 1998:140
[3] Mujumdar 2002: 3983
[4] Pradhan, et al, 2000: 2531
[5] Vaidyanathan 2001: 1814
[6] See also Deshpande 2002.
[7] See Cohn 1987: 213
[8] Inden 1991: 131
[9] See Rasul 1974
[10] Srinivas 1987: 59
[11] See Beteille 1980: 110–15
[12] Breman 1974
[13] *Village India* 1955, edited by McKim Marriot
[14] Ibid.: 171 Epstein 1973: 86, 99, 192
[15] Ibid.: 117
[16] Ibid.: 165
[17] Ibid.: 171
[18] Ibid.: 240
[19] D.N. Dhanagare wrote about agrarian classes 1983, Djurfeldt and Lindberg (1975), Bose (1991), Bandopadhayaya and Von Eschen (1991), Harriss, J (1982), Sahay (2001), Chakravarti (2001), and a host of other authors discussed tensions between agrarian classes, pointing to the severe asymmetry of rural social relations.
[20] See Beidelman 1959
[21] See Dwyer and Patel 2002: 63-64
[22] For a critique see Gupta 1997
[23] See Gupta 1997
[24] I interviewed twenty-six social notables and opinion-makers. Among them were leading politicians from different parties, journalists (print and television), advertising executives and influential public intellectuals. This took some time as they are all very busy people. Many interview dates had to be cancelled at the last moment, and on many occasions they had so little to say that it seemed pointless to continue the conversation. What was most remarkable was the overall lack of interest in rural India and the fact that they had to strain and think hard to respond to my poser regarding how agriculture should be regarded in the context of the Indian economy and culture. Even politicians who should have had such answers on their fingertips were floundering and snatching for an odd idea here and a phrase there to give body to their

comments. I remember that in the 1970s and early 1980s there were clear and forthright views regarding the village, and the lack of such visions today was the most enduring finding of my interviews.

[25] This is a play on the Congress Party's election symbol which is the 'hand'. The slogan therefore means that if you vote for the hand then this hand is for the poor.

[26] From *National Sample Survey 59th round: Some Aspects of Operational Land Holdoings in India*, 2002-03, table 3.2

[27] Kumar 2006:5367, 5369

[28] Kumar 2006: 5369–70

[29] *Hindustan Times*, 25 August 2007

[30] http://agricoop. nic.in/seedpolicy.htm

8. FROM VILLAGE TO VICINAGE

[1] NSS 2006, Chapter 2
[2] See *Hindustan Times*, Business Section, 29 December 2007
[3] Jain 2003

9. NORMALIZING 'CASTE'

[1] *UNCTAD World Investment Report* 2007, Annexe B tables B.1–3
[2] See *UNCTAD 2004*: table 1.1A, pp. 8-9
[3] Acharya 2006; see also Gordon and Gupta 2005:234–36
[4] See for example, Folgar 2007
[5] Tully 2002: 297
[6] Moffat 1979
[7] See Dumont 1988
[8] Leach 1969
[9] See Gupta 2000
[10] Gupta 2007
[11] Ibid.
[12] See Siddiqi 1978
[13] See Desai 1976
[14] Dumont 1988: 197
[15] Dumont 1988: 240
[16] See Marriot 1976
[17] See Gupta 2000 for more details
[18] See Chattopadhyaya 1976
[19] See Srinivas 1996: 101
[20] Ibid.; 102–05
[21] Cox 1970: 8

[22] Dirks 2001 : 10, 170-71
[23] See also Wagle 1998
[24] Rudolph and Rudolph 1987; Washbrook 1989; Sheth 2002; Weiner 2002
[25] Rudolph and Rudolph 1987: 52
[26] Ibid.
[27] Ibid.: 52-53
[28] See also Brass 1997: 205
[29] Srinivas 1972: 11
[30] See also Bose 1991; Frankel 1988, 1989
[31] Sharma 1997: 216
[32] Ibid.: 217
[33] Karanth 1996: 105
[33] Béteille 1965
[34] Chaddha 2003:55
[35] Goswami n.d.
[36] Desai 1976; see also Rao 2001: 82
[37] See Burra 1996
[38] Shah 2001: 212
[39] Vora 2004: 283
[40] Kolenda 1978: 121
[41] See for example, Narayan 2004
[42] See Gupta 2000 117–123; Babb 1998; Cort 2004
[43] Michelutti 2004
[44] Narayan 2004; Jodhka 2004; Deliege 1993
[45] Zelliot 1970
[46] See *Times of India*, 4 and 5 November 2001; *Hindu*, 5 November 2001
[47] For example, see Burra 2001
[48] See O'Hanlon 1983; Gore 1993: 180
[49] Jodhka 2004
[50] Karanth 1996: 89
[51] Sahay 2001: 117; see also Sahay 2004: 125-26; Kumar 2003: 3870.

10. CASTE VIRTUOSOS STRIKE BACK

[1] National Commission for Scheduled Caste and Scheduled Tribes and Ministry of Statistics and Programme Implementation, 2003; Ministry of Personnel 2005-06: 28
[2] National Commission for Scheduled Castes and Scheduled Tribes 1991
[3] See Galanter 1984

4 Based on figures for these communities found in the *Census of India*
5 See also Béteille 2000
6 Célestin Bouglé 1991
7 See Gupta 1996
8 See *Compilation of Documents* . . . 2006
9 http://wikipedia.org/wiki/Forward_Castes
10 Ibid.
11 The case of reservations in Tamil Nadu demonstrated this long ago. Ramaswamy Naiker, or EVR as he was popularly known, led an anti-Brahman (but not anti-caste) movement, which subsequently grew into the Dravidan movement, in the late nineteenth century. This movement advocated the cause of reservations for the powerful non-Brahman castes in the name of backwardness and was successful in doing so. These non-Brahman castes had a lower literacy rate than the Brahmans but were economically and politically much more powerful. Today, there is very little to differentiate between the educational attainments of the OBCs in Tamil Nadu but they continue to receive the privileges of backwardness because of their political power. (See Choudhary 2006: 34–39)
12 Choudhary 2006: 39
13 Ibid.: 40
14 Ibid.: 40-41
15 Ibid.: 46
16 Hobhouse 1911: 55
17 Ibid
18 Marshall 1977
19 See Jaffrelot 2003: 207-08; Sahay 2001:147
20 See Brass 1997: 205; Manor 1997: 267–70
21 Blair 1980: 67
22 Jaffrelot 2003: 376
23 Ibid.: 381

11. BLAME IT ON THE NATION–STATE

1 See Gupta 1996: 190
2 Acton 1985.
3 See for example Brass 1997; Wilkinson 2004
4 Ibid.
5 Bhindranwale soon became a genie out of the bottle and began to challenge his erstwhile patron, the Congress Party. This led to a gun battle between the Indian Army and Bhindranwale's Khalistani extremist supporters. Bhindranwale died in this skirmish and

Indira Gandhi was gunned down soon after by her Sikh bodyguards who felt that she had de-sacralized the Golden Temple by ordering the army to enter the holy precincts to hunt down Bhindranwale.
[6] If one were to go by the schoolbook version of the nation-state, all these European states mentioned will have to be considered 'inauthentic'. In none of these cases do language and religion, the primary markers of nation-states, fall neatly within geographical boundaries. To believe then that India with its multiplicity of languages and religions makes it especially prone to all manner of fissiparous tendencies would be to deny the true history of the emergence of European nations and nationalism.
[7] See Renan 1990; also Anderson 1991
[8] Hobsbawm 1988: 110
[9] Ibid
[10] See Gupta 2005: 168
[11] Renan 1990:11

12. DO WE DESERVE OUR LEADERS?

[1] *Times of India,* 27 December, 2007
[2] At least 87 SEZ
[3] *India Key Data 2007:2008* 2007: 89, table 9.6

13. AGAINST ROLLING BACK THE STATE

[1] See also Lal 1983
[2] Marshall 1950: 25; Marshall 1975: 129–42
[3] Stiglitz 2002: 2
[4] Chang 2008
[5] Stiglitz 2002: 55; Chang 2008: 51–55
[6] Stiglitz 2002: 31
[7] Ibid.: 69
[8] Ibid.: 65
[9] *Statistical Outline of India,* 2006–7:227
[10] See *National Center for Educational Statistics* in Internet site http://nces.ed.gov/pubs/elipid/4/asp
[11] Chang 2008: 55
[12] Becker 2007 Not in reference: 41–53
[13] Ferry 1964: 731-32.
[14] *Statistical Outline of India,* 2006–7: 227
[15] See Starr 1982: 348-49
[16] OECD 2007: 220
[17] Singh and Mukherjee 2004

[18] See Stromquist 1998: 62–67
[19] Ibid.: 62
[20] Kumar 2007: 114–15
[21] Madan 1998: 298
[22] Nandy 1998: 324
[23] Quoted in the *Hindu*, 15 November 2006
[24] Simmel 1978: 150;
[25] Ibid.
[26] E.g. Clifford Geertz (1984) and Pierre Bourdieu (1977)
[27] http://www.fordfound.org/programs/assets
[28] http://www.fordfound.org/programs/kcf
[29] http://www.fordfound.org/programs/psj
[30] Oxfam's *Poverty Reduction Reduction Strategies: A Guide*
[31] *National Sample Survey* 1995-96, 52nd round
[32] See Djuknovic and Mach 1973:105
[33] Gupta 2004
[34] Lampton 1977: 230
[35] Ibid.: 54
[36] Ibid.: 99-100
[37] Ibid.: 106
[38] Lok Sabha, unstarred question no.1996 (http:// www.indiastat.com)
[39] Parsons 195 : 428–70; Polgar 1963: 39; Freeman 1963: 112
[40] For L.T. Hobhouse (1911), Talcott Parsons (1961), David Reisman (1950), or Edward Shils (1981)
[41] Claude Levi Strauss, the great and inspirational French anthropologist
[42] Van Damme 1996: 33; see also Boas 1955: 9
[43] 1978; see also Lofland 1985
[44] See Nanda 2007:39–42
[45] Harriss 1989
[46] A padre friend of mine, who was properly trained in Rome, once told me in jest that God forbade the Hindus to eat beef and the Muslims to eat pork, so that Christians could eat well. He was obviously not paying attention to the dietary abominations that were once pronounced by Leviticus in the Old Testament.
[47] Gupta 2003: 56–69
[48] Rawls 1971
[49] Young and Wilmott 1973: 89
[50] See Misra, Chatterjee and Rao 2003, Desai and Dubey 2007
[51] Human Development Survey by the University of Maryland and the National Council of Applied Economic Research (2005)
[52] Desai 2007

[53] Ibid.; see also Aiyar 2007
[54] Guha 1999: 52
[55] See *Manpower Profile in India 2005*: 303, table 6.12
[56] Ibid.: 25, table 1.1.17
[57] 1971; Wolf 1969
[58] For example, Attwood 1993
[59] The pillow end of a string cot, or *charpai*, is the side where the weaving of the coir is firm. On the other side thick ropes are drawn against the wooden frame to maintain the tension of the cot. This end is not comfortable as it has many gaps between the zigzag of ropes. In villages the pillow side is reserved for elders, and also, as I discovered, for guests.

14. CONCLUSION

[1] See *Report on Conditions of Work* ... 2007: 6
[2] Ibid.: 15

REFERENCES

Abbi, B.L., and Kesar Singh (1997): *Post-Green Revolution Rural Punjab:*
A Profile of Economic and Socio-Cultural Change (Chandigarh: Centre
for Research in Rural and Industrial Development).

Acharya, Shankar (2006): *Essays on Macro-Economic Policies and Growth*
in India (New Delhi: Oxford University Press).

Acharya, Shankar, Robert Cassen, and Kirsty McNay (2004): 'The
Economy: Past and Future', *in* Tim Dyson, Robert Cassen, and
Leela Visaria (eds.), *Twenty-First Century India: Population, Economy,*
Human Development and the Environment (New York: Oxford:
University Press, 2004).

Acton, John Emerich Edward Dalberg (1985): *Selected Writings of Lord*
Acton, vol. 1, *Essays in the History of Liberty*, Indianapolis, Liberty
Classic.

Aiyar, Swaminathan Ankelswaria (2007): 'Mystery of India's Economic
Growth', *Economic Times*, 10 Oct. 2007.

Anderson, Benedict (1991): *The Imagined Community: Reflections on the*
Origin and Spread of Nationalism (London: Verso).

Asian Development Bank (ADB) (2001): *Key Indicators of Developing*
Asian and Pacific Countries, vol. 32 (Delhi: ADB and Oxford
University Press

Attwood, Donald W. (1993): *Raisng Cane: The Political Economy of*
Sugar in Western India (Delhi: Oxford University Press).

Babb, L.A. (1998): 'Rejecting Violence: Sacrifice and the Social Identity
of Trading Communities', *Contributions to Indian Sociology* (NS),
vol. 32, pp. 387–407.

Bandopadhayay, Suraj, and Donald Von Eschen (1991): 'Agricultural
Failure: Caste, Class and Power in Rural West Bengal', in Dipankar
Gupta (ed.), *Social Stratification* (Delhi: Oxford University Press.

Bardhan, Pranab (1986): *Land, Labour and Rural Poverty: Essays in*
Development Economics (Delhi: Oxford University Press).

Basu, D.N, and S.P. Kashyap (1992): 'Rural Non-Agricultural

Employment in India: Role of Development Process and Rural–Urban Employment Linkages', *in Economic and Political Weekly*, vol.27 (Review of Agriculture), pp.A-178-A 189.

BBC News 2007 internet site: http://newsvote.bbc.co.uk/mpapps/print/news.bbc.co.uk/2/hi/asia-pacific/347695, dated 6 Nov. 2007

Beidelman, T.O. (1959): *A Comparative Study of the Jajmani System* (New York: Locust Valley).

Béteille, Andre (1965): *Caste, Class and Power: Changing Patterns of Stratification in a Tanjore Village* (Berkeley: University of California Press).

—— (1980): 'The Indian Village: Past and Present', in E.J.Hobsbawm, et al, (eds.), *Peasants in History: Essays in Honour of Daniel Thorner*, (Calcutta, Oxford Univeristy Press).

—— (1986): 'Individualism and Equality', *Current Anthropology*, vol. 27, pp. 121–34.

—— (1991): *The Backward Classes in Contemporary India* (Delhi: Oxford University Press).

—— (1996): 'Caste in Contemporary India', in C.J. Fuller (ed.), *Caste Today* (Delhi: Oxford University Press).

—— (2000): *Chronicles of Our Time* (New Delhi: Penguin Books).

Blair, Harry (1980): 'Rising Kulaks and Backward Classes in Bihar: Social Change in the late 1970s', *Economic and Political Weekly*, vol. 15, pp. 64–74.

Boas, Franz (1955): *Primitive Ar,*(New York: Dover).

Bose, Pradip Kumar (1991): 'Mobility and Conflict: Social Roots of Caste Violence in Bihar', in Dipankar Gupta (ed.), *Social Stratification* (Delhi: Oxford University Press).

Bougle, Celestin (1991): 'The Essence and Reality of the Caste System,' in Dipankar Gupta, (ed.), *Social Stratification* (Delhi: Oxford University Press)

Bourdieu, Pierre (1977): *Outline of a Theory of Practice* (Cambridge: Cambridge University Press).

Brass, Paul (1991): *Ethnicity and Nationalism:Theory and Comparison* (New Delhi: Sage).

—— (1997): 'The Politicization of the Peasantry in a North Indian State', in Sudipta Kaviraj (ed.), *Politics in India* (Delhi: Oxford University Press).

—— (1997b) *The Theft of an Idol: Text and Context in the Representation of Collective Violence* (Princeton, NJ: Princeton University Press).

Breman, Jan (1974): *Patronage and Exploitation: Changing Agrarian Relations in South Gujarat, India* (Berkeley: University of California Press).

Burra, Neera (1996): 'Buddhism, Conversion and Identity: A Case

Study of Village Mahars', in M.N. Srinivas (ed.), *Caste: Its Twentieth Century Avatar* (New Delhi: Penguin Books).

Business Week (2007): 'The Coming Boom', 23 Oct. 2007.

Census of India 2001, Slum Population, Series–I, vol. 1, (New Delhi: Office of the Registrar and Census Commissioner).

Chaddha, G.K. (2003): Rural Non-Farm Sector in the Indian Economy: Growth, Challenges and Future Direction (mimeo). Paper presented in the joint Jawaharlal Nehru University and IFPRI Workshop, *The Dragon and the Elephant: A Comparative Study of Economic Reforms in China and India*, held on 25-26 March 2003, at India Habitat Centre, New Delhi.

Chakravarti, Anand (2001): *Social Power and Everyday Class Relations: Agrarian Transformation in North Bihar* (New Delhi: Sage).

Chandrashekhar, C.P and Jayati Ghosh (14, Sept. 2005) 'The Burden of Farmers' Debt', Internet site: http://macroscan.com/the/finance/sep05/fin140905Farmers_Debt.htm

Chang, Ha-Joon (2008): *Bad Samaritan: The Myth of Free Trade and the Secret History of Capitalism* (London: Bloomsbury Press).

Chattopadhyaya, B.D. (1976): 'Origin of the Rajputs: The Political, Economic and Social Processes in Early Medieval India', *Indian Historical Review*, vol. 3, pp. 59–82.

Choudhary, Shiv Kumar (2006): 'Tamil Nadu Model of Reservation: The Myths and Reality', *South Asia Politics*, Dec., pp. 34–49

Cohn, Bernard (1987): *An Anthropologist Among Historians* (Delhi: Oxford University Press.

Compilation of Documents Submitted to the Supreme Court 2006 by the Solicitor General of India in the Matter of Ashok Kumar Thakur and the Union of India: New Delhi, In the Supreme Court of India, Extraordinary Civil Original Jurisdiction WP© No. 265/2006, vol. 1 (National Commission on Backward Classes Materials).

Cort, John (2004): 'Jains, Caste and Hierarchy in Northern Gujarat', *in* Dipankar Gupta (ed.), *Caste in Question: Hierarchy or Identity?* (New Delhi: Sage).

Deliege, Robert (1993): 'The Myths of Origin of the Indian Untouchables', *Man*, vol. 28, pp. 533–49.

Damodaran, Harish (2008): *India's New Capitalist Class: Caste, Business and Industry in a Modern State* (New Delhi: Permanent Black).

DeParle, Jason (2007): 'Jobs Abroad Support "Model" State in India', *New York Times*, 7 Sept. 2007.

Desai, I.P. (1976): *Untouchability in Rural Gujara*, (Mumbai: Popular Prakashan).

Desai, Sonalde (2007): 'Exploding the Myths about Private Schooling', in *Economic Times*, 27 July 2007.

—— and Amaresh Dubey (2007): 'Baniya, Babu and Borrowing Household Debt', *Economic Times*,3 October,2007

Deshpande, Partha (2002): 'Suicides by Farmers in Karnataka: Agrarian Distress and Possible Alleviatory Steps, *Economic and Politcal Weekly*, vol. XXX, pp. 2601–10.

Dhanagare, D.N. (1983): Peasant Mobilization in India, 1920–1950 (Delhi: Oxford University Press).

Dirks, Nicholas B. (2001): *Castes of Mind: Colonialism and the Making of Modern India* (Delhi: Permanent Black).

Djuknovic, V., and E.P.Mach (eds.) (1973): *Alternative Approaches to Meeting Basis Health Needs in Developing Countries* (a UNICEF and WHO study) (Geneva: World Health Organization).

Djurfeldt, Goran, and Staffan Lindberg (1975): *Behind Poverty: The Social Formation of a Tamil Village* (London: Curzon Press).

Dumont, Louis (1988): *Homo Hierarchicus: The Caste System and its Implications* (London:Weidenfeld & Nicholson).

—— (1956): *The Division of Labour* (New York: Free Press (paperback)).

Dwyer, Rachel, and Divia Patel (2002): *Cinema India: The Visual Culture of Hindi Film* (Delhi: Oxford University Press).

Economic Survey 2005-06: (New Delhi: Ministry of Finance and Economic Division, Government of India).

—— *2006-07:* New Delhi: Ministry of Finance and Economic Division,Government of India).

Economist (2007): 'India on Fire', 1 February.

—— (2007) 'A Himalayan Challenge', 11 October.

Elias, Norbert (1978): *The Civilising Process, vol. 1, The History of Manners* (New York: Pantheon).

—— (1983): *The Court Society* (New York: Pantheon).

Embree, Ainslee T. (ed.) (1988): *Sources of Indian Tradition* (New York: Columbia University Press).

Epstein, Scarlett (1973): *South India: Yesterday, Today and Tomorrow* (London:Macmillan).

ESCAP 2003 (Economic and Social Survey of Asia and Pacific) (New York:ESCAP).

—— *2004* (New York: ESCAP).

—— *2005: Dealing with Shocks* (New York: ESCAP).

—— *2006) Energizing the Global Economy* (New York: ESCAP).

Etzioni, Amitai (1995): *The Spirit of the Community: Rights, Responsibilities and the Communitarian Agenda* (London: Fontana Press).

Fay, Sidney B. (1951): 'Bismarck's Welfare State', in Herman Ausubel (ed.), *The Making of Modern Europe: Book Two: Waterloo to the Atomic Age* (USA: Holt, Rinehart & Winston).

Ferry, Jules (1946): 'On the Inequality of Education', in Justus Buchler,

K. William Kapp, and Robert S. Lopez, *Introduction to Contemporary Civilization in the West: A Source Book*, vol. 2 (New York: Columbia University Press).

Fertilizer Association of India 1988 *Report of the High Powered Committee on Fertilizer Consumer Prices* (Fertilizer Association of India, New Delhi).

Five Year Plan 2002–07 (New Delhi: Planning Commission, Government of India).

Folgar Robert W. (2007): Capitalism and Democracy in 2040: Forecasts and Speculations (NBER Working Paper Series 13184, June 2007). http://www. nber.org/ papers/w13184

Frankel, Francine (1988): 'Middle Classes and Castes in India Politics: Prospects for Politcal Accomodation', in Atul Kohli (ed.), *India's Democracy: An Analysis of Changing State Society Relations* (Delhi: Orient Longman).

—— (1989): 'Caste, Land and Dominance in Bihar: Breakdown of the Brahmannical Order', in Francine Frankel and M.S.A. Rao (eds.), *Dominance and State Power in India: Decline of a Social Order*, vol.1 (Delhi: Oxford University Press).

Friedman, Thomas L. (2007): 'No, No, No, Don't Follow Us', *New York Times* (Op-ed), 4 Nov. 2007

Galanter, Marc (1984): *Competing Equalities* (Berkeley: University of California Press).

Galbraith, John Kenneth (1987) *Economics in Perspective: A Critical History* (Boston: Houghton Mifflin).

Geertz, Clifford (1984): *The Interpretation of Culture* (London: Hutchinson).

Gordon, James, and Poonam Gupta (2005): 'Understanding India's Service Revolution', in Wanda Tseng and David Cowen (eds.), *India's and China's Recent Experience with Reform and Growth*, (Houndmills, Hampshire: Palgrave, Macmillan).

Gore, M.S. (1993): 'Social Movement and the Paradigm of Functional Analysis With Reference to the Non-Brahmin Movement in Maharashtra', *in* Yogesh Atal, et al. (eds.), *Understanding Indian Society: Festschrift in Honour of Professor S.S. Dube* (Delhi: HarAnand Publications).

Goswami, Omkar (n.d.): *Rural is Much More than Only Agriculture* (New Delhi: CERG Advisory Pvt. Ltd).

Guerard, Albert (1951): 'Saint-Simon on Horseback: The Economic and Social Policy of Napoleon III', in Herman Ausubel (ed.), *The Making of Modern Europe: Book Two: Waterloo to the Atomic Age* (USA: Holt, Rinehart & Winston).

Guha, Ramchandra (1999): *Savaging the Civilized: Verrier Elwin, his Tribals and India* (Delhi: Oxford University Press).

Gupta, Dipankar (1988): 'For a Sociology/Anthropology of Illness: Towards a Delineation of its Disciplinary Specificities', *International Sociology*, vol. 3, pp.403–13

—— (1996): *The Context of Ethnicity: Sikh Identity in a Comparative Perspective* (Delhi: Oxford University Press).

—— (1997): *Rivalry and Brotherhood: Politics in the Life of the Farmers of North India* (Delhi: Oxford University Press).

—— (2000): *Interrogating Caste: Understanding Hierarchy and Difference in Indian Society* (New Delhi: Penguin Books).

—— (2000b.) *Culture, Space and the Nation-State: From Sentiment to Structure* (New Delhi: Sage).

—— (2007): 'Explaining BSP's Victory: When the Caste Calculus Fails', *Economic and Political Weekly*, vol XLII: pp. 3388–96.

Gupta, Harmala Kaur (2004): 'How Basic is Palliative Care?' *International Journal of Palliative Nursing*, vol. 10: pp. 600-01

Guru, Gopal (2001): 'The Language of Dalit-Bahujan Politcial Discourse', in Ghashyam Shah (ed.), *Identity and Politics: Cultural Subordination and the Dalit Challenge*, vol. 2 (New Delhi: Sage).

Guthrie, Douglas (1958) *A History of Medicine* (London: Thomas Nelson and Sons

Handbook of Industrial Policy and Statistics, 2003-05 (New Delhi: Office of the Economic Adviser, Department of Industrial Policy and Promotion, Ministry of Commerce and Industry, Government of India).

Harriss, John (1982): *Capitalism and Peasant Farming: Agrarian Structure and Ideology in Northern Tamilnadu* (Delhi: Oxford University Press).

Harriss, Marvin (1989): *Cows, Pigs, Wars and Witches: The Riddles of Culture* (New York: Random House).

Hasan, Zoya (2000): 'Representation and Redistribution: The New Lower Caste Politics of North India', in Francine Frankel, et al. (eds.), *Transforming India: Social and Political Dynamics of Democracy*, (Delhi: Oxford University Press).

Himanshu (2007): 'Recent Trends in Poverty and Inequality: Some Preliminary Results', *Economic and Political Weekly*, vol. XLII, pp. 497–508.

Hobhouse, L.T. (1911): *Liberalism* (London: Williams & Norgate).

Hobsbawm E.J. (1988): *The Age of Capital, 1848-1875*: London: Cardinal).

Peoples' Union for Democratic Rights and Peoples' Union for Civil Liberties (1984): *Who are the Guilty*, (New Delhi: Peoples Union for Civil Liberties and Peoples Union for Democratic Rights).

Holmstrom, Mark (1985): *The Social Anthropology of Indian Labour* (Cambridge: Cambridge University Press (in Association with Orient Longman, Mumbai).

'IMA 2006 Research Strategy for 10th Annual Chief Executive Officers' Roundtable: Briefing Paper', New Delhi.

Inden, Ronald (1991): *Imagining India* (Oxford: Basil Blackwell).

India Key Data 2007: 2008: 2007: Incorporating Budget Analysis, The Red Book (Mumbai: Kal Nirnay, Sumangal Press).

iWatch, 2008 *Employment 1st,* Mumbai.

Jackson, Cecile, and Molly Chattopadhyay (1998): 'Identities and Livelihoods: Gender, Ethnicity and Nature in a South Bihar Village', in Arun Agrawal and K. Sivaramakrishnan (eds.), *Agrarian Environments: Resources, Representation and Rule in India* (Durham, Duke University Press).

Jaffrelot, Christophe (2003): *India's Silent Revolution: The Rise of the Low Castes in North Indian Politics* (Delhi: Permanent Black).

Jain, Meenakshi (1996): 'Backward Caste and Social Change in U.P. and Bihar', in M.N. Srinivas (ed.), *Caste: Its Twentieth Century Avatar* (New Delhi: Penguin Books).

Jain, Sunil (2003): 'Poor are Spending More on Education', *Business Standard,* 22 July 2003.

Jayaram, N. (1996): 'Caste and Hinduism: Changing Protean Relationship', in M.N. Srinivas (ed.), *Caste: Its Twentieth Century Avatar* (New Delhi: Penguin Books).

Jhabvala, Renana (2005): 'Work and Wealth', *in* Alyssa Ayres and Philip Oldenburg (eds.), *India Briefing: Take off at Last* (London: M.E. Sharpe).

Jodhka, Surendra S. (2004): 'Sikhism and the Caste Question: Politics in Punjab', in Dipankar Gupta (ed.), *Caste in Question: Identity or Hierarchy?* (New Delhi: Sage).

—— (2002): 'Caste amd Untouchability in Rural Punjab', *Economic and Political Weekly,* vol. 37, pp.1813–23.

—— (1998): 'From Book View to Field View: Social Anthropological Constructions of the Indian Village', *Oxford Development Studies,* Vol. 26, pp. 311–31.

Karanth, Gopal (1996): 'Caste in Contemporary Rural India', in M.N. Srinivas (ed.), *Caste: Its Twentieth Century Avatar,* (New Delhi: Penguin Books).

Karyokinesis, Kirata (1982): 'An Introduction to the Political Economy of Tribal Societies in North East India', in K.S. Singh (ed.), *Economies of the Tribes and their Transformation* (New Delhi: Concept Publishing House).

Kaviraj, Sudipta (2000): 'Democracy and Social Inequality', in Francine

Frankel, et al (eds.), *Transforming India: Social and Political Dynamics of Democracy* (Delhi: Oxford University Press).

King, Stanley (1963): 'Social Psychological Factors in Illness', in Howard E. Freeman, Sol Levin, and Leo G. Reader (eds.), *Handbook of Medical Sociology* (New Jersey: Prentice Hall).

Kolenda, Pauline (1978): *Caste in Contemporary India* (Menlo Park, California): The Bejamin/Cummings Publishing Co.

Kumar, Parmod (2006): 'Contract Farming through Agribusiness Firms and State Corporation: A Case Study of Punjab', *Economic and Political Weekly*, vol. XLI, pp 5367–75

Kumar, Vivek (2003): 'Uttar Pradesh: Politics of Change', *Economic and Political Weekly*, vol. 38, pp.3869–71

Kundu, Amitabh and Niranjan Sarangi (2007): 'Migration, Employment Status and Poverty: An Analysis across Urban Centres, *Economic and Political Weekly*, vol. XLII, pp.299–306

Lal, Deepak (1983): *Development Economics*, London: Institute of Economic Affaris and Hobart Paper Back, No. 16

—— (2005): *The Hindu Equilibrium, India c. 1500 B.C.–2000 A.D.* (Oxford: Oxford University Press).

Lampton, David (1977): *The Politics of Medicine in China: The Policy Process, 1949–67* (Kent, England: WM Dawson & Sons).

Leach, E.R. (1969): 'Introduction' in Edmund Leach (ed.), *Aspects of Caste in South India, Ceylon and North West Pakistan* (Cambridge: Cambridge University Press).

Lee, Derek Byer, Xianshen Dias and Chris Jackson (2005): *Agrarian Rural Development and Pro-Poor Growth* (Washington DC: The World Bank).

Lele, Jayant (1981): *Elite Pluralism and Class Rule: Political Development in Maharashtra, India* (Toronto: University of Toronto Press).

Lofland, Lyn H. (1985): *A World of Strangers: Order and Action in Urban Public Spaces* (Prospect Heights, Illinois, Waveland Press.

Madan, T.N. (1998): 'Secularism in its Place', in Rajeev Bhargava (ed.), *Secularism and its Critics* (Delhi: Oxford University Press).

Madduri, Sivaprasad D. (2006): 'The Ills of Corporate Medicine in India', *Hindu*, 10 September.

Manor, James (1997): 'Caste and Class in a Cohesive Society', in Sudipta Kaviraj (ed.), *Politics in India* (Delhi: Oxford University Press).

Manpower Profile in India 2005 Yearbook 2004 (New Delhi: Institute of Applied Manpower Research: Concept Publishing House).

Marriot, McKim (1955): *Village India: Studies in the Little Community* (Chicago: Chicago University Press).

—— (1959): 'Interactional and Attributional Theory of Caste Ranking', *Man in India* 39: 92–107.

—— (1976): 'Hindu Transactions: Diversity without Dualism in Transactional Meaning', in B. Kapferer (ed.), Philadelphia, Institute for the Studies of Human Issues

Marshall, T.H. (1950): *Citizenship and Social Class and Other Essays* (London: Syndics of Cambridge University Press).

—— (1975): *Social Policy in the Twentieth Century* (London: Hutchinson University Library).

Mckinsey Report (2007) 'Bird of Gold,: The Rise of India's Consumer Market', by John Albett, et al., May 2007, McKinsey & Co.

Micheluti, Lucia (2004): 'We [Yadavs] are a Caste of Politicians': Caste and Modern Politics in a North Indian Town', in Dipankar Gupta (ed.), *Caste in Question: Identity or Hierarchy?* (New Delhi: Sage).

Milner, H. (1994): *Status and Sacredness: A General Theory of Status Relations and Analysis of Indian Culture* (New York: Oxford University Press).

Ministry of Agriculture Website 2000-01: http://dacnet.nic.in

Ministry of Agriculture *Year Book 2003* (New Delhi: Government of India (in collaboration with All India Report on Agricultural Census and Fertilizer Cooperation of India and Agricultural Statistics at a Glance).

Misra, Rajiv, Rachel Chatterjee, and Sujatha Rao (20 *India Health Report* (New Delhi: Oxford University Press).

Mitra, Siddhartha, and Sangeeta Shroff (2007): Farmers' Suicides in Maharashtra', *Economic and Political Weekly*, vol. XLII, pp. 73-77.

Mitra, Subrata (1980): 'Norms and Modalities of Political Choice', *Contributions to Indian Sociology*, vol. 14 (NS), pp. 51–75.

Moffat, M. (1979): *A Untouchable Community in South India: Structure and Consensus* (Princeton NJ: Princeton Universtiy Press).

Mujumdar, N.A. (2002): 'Rural Development: New Perspectives', *Economic and Political Weekly*, vol. 37, pp.3983–87.

Murugkar, Milind, Bharati Ramaswami, and Mahesh Shelar (2007): 'Competition and Monopoly in Indian Cotton Seed Market', *Economic and Political Weekly*, vol. XLII, pp.3781–89

Nanda, Meera (2007): 'Secularism without Secularisation: Reflection on God and Politics in US and India', *Economic and Political Weekly*, vol.XLll, pp.39–46.

Nandy, Ashis (1998): 'The Politics of Secularism and the Recovery of Religious Toleration', in Rajeev Bhargava (ed.), *Secularism and its Critics* (Delhi: Oxford University Press).

—— (1989) *The Tao of Cricket: On Games of Destiny and the Destiny of Games* (New Delhi: Viking).

Narayan, Badri (2004): 'Inventing Caste History: Dalit Mobilisation and Nationalist Past', in Dipankar Gupta (ed.), *Caste in Question; Identity or Hierarchy* (New Delhi: Sage).

Narayanmoorthy, A. (2007): 'Deceleration in Agricultural Growth: Technology Fatigue or Policy Fatigue', *Economic and Political Weekly*, vol. XLII, pp.2375–77)

NASSCOM 2006 ITES-BPO Industry: *Fact Sheet* (New Delhi).

NASSCOM-IDC 2006 Domestic Services (IT-ITES): *Market Opportunity* (New Delhi).

National Agricultural Policy (2002): *Rural Labour Enquiry Report on Indebtedness among Rural Labour Households,* (New Delhi: Department of Agricultural and Co-operation, Ministry of Agriculture, Government of India).

National Commission for Scheduled Castes and Scheduled Tribes 1984-98 and Ministry of Statistics and Programme Implementation 2002 (New Delhi: Government of India).

National Commission for Scheduled Castes and Scheduled Tribes (2001): *Sixth Report* (1991–2001), (New Delhi: National Commission for Scheduled Castes and Scheduled Tribes).

National Council of Applied Economic Research (2002): *Quarterly Review of the Economy*, November (New Delhi).

National Council of Applied Economic Research (2002) *India: Market Demographics Research* (New Delhi).

National Health Policy 2002 (New Delhi: Ministry of Health, Government of India).

National Sample Survey (1999): *Notes on Morbidity and Treatment of Ailments* (New Delhi: Ministry of Statoistics and Programme Implementation, Government of India).

National Sample Survey (2005): *Indebtedness of Farmer Households* (January–December 2003) (National Sample Survey Organisation, Ministry of Statistics and Implementation, Government of India).

—— Press Note 2005 on 'Household Indebtedness in India as on 30.06.2002', released on 29 Oct. 2005 (New Delhi: National Sample Survey Organisation, Ministry of Statistics and Implementation, Government of India).

—— (2006): *Some Aspects of Operational Land Holdings in India, 2002-03* (New Delhi: National Sample Survey Organisation, Ministry of Statistics and Implementation, Government of India).

—— 2006 *Some Aspects of Operational Loan Holdings in India, 2002-03,* National Sample Survey Organisation, Ministry of Statistics and Implementation, Government of India

Nayar, Baldev Raj (2006): 'India's Globalization: Evaluating the Economic Consequences', *Policy Studies*, 22: Washington DC.

Newsweek (1997): 'India in the Sunlight', 4 August 1997.

NRI Realty News (2007): Internet site: nrirealtynews.com

O'Hanlon. Rosalind (1983): 'Maratha History as Polemic: Low Caste Ideology and Political Debate in Late Nineteenth Century', *Modern Asian Studies*, vol. 17, pp. 1–33.

OECD (2007): *Health at a Glance: Fact Book* (Paris: OECD).

Office of the Development Commissioner 2008, Ministry of Micro, Small and Medium Scale Enterprises, Ministry of Micro, Small and Medium Enterprises, New Delhi

Omvedt, Gail (2001): 'Ambedkar and After: Dalit Movement in India', *in* Ghanshyam Shah (ed.), *Identity and Politics: Cultural Subordination and the Dalit Challenge* (New Delhi: Sage).

—— (2004): 'Untouchables in the World of IT', *Contemporary Review*, vol. 284,, pp. 286–88

Panagariya, Arvind (2005): 'India in the 1980s and the 1990s: A Triumph of Reforms', in Wanda Tseng and David Cower (eds.), *India's and China's Recent Experience with Reform and Growth* (Houndmills, Hampshire: Palgrave/Macmillan).

Parsons, Talcott (1951): *The Social System* (Glencoe, Illinois: The Free Press).

—— (1959): *The Structure of Social Action*, New Delhi: Amerind Publishers

Parthasarathy, G., et al (1998): 'Determinants of Rural Non-Agricultural Employment: The Indian Case', *Indian Journal of Agricultural Economics*, vol. 53, pp. 139–54.

Phookan, Manjushree (2004): 'A Brief Market Report on the Cosmetics and Toiletries Market in India', *Customized Market Research, U.S. & Foreign Commercial Service and U.S. Department of State.* Email:manjushree.phookan@mail.doc.gov

Pochhammer, Wilhelm von (1981): *India's Road to Nationhood: A Political History of the Sub-continent* (New Delhi: Allied Publishers).

Polgar Stephen (1963): 'Health Action in Cross-Cultural Perspective', *in* Howard Freeman, Sol Levine, and Leo G. Reeder, *Handbook of Medical Sociology* (New Jersey: Prentice Hall).

Pradhan, Basanta et al (2000): 'Rural-Urban Disparities: Income Distribution, Expenditure Pattern and Social Sector', *Economic and Political Weekly*, vol. 35, pp. 2527–39).

Pushpendra (2002): 'Dalit Assertion Through Electoral Politics', in Ghashyam Shah (ed.), *Caste and Democratic Politics in India* (Delhi: Permanent Black).

Radhakrishnan, S. (1957): *Occasional Speeches and Writings (second series)*,

February 1956 to February 1957 (New Delhi: Publications Division, Government of India).

Radhakrishnan and Charles A. Moore, 1957, (eds.), *A Source Book in Indian Philosophy* (New Jersey: Princeton University Press).

—— (1958): *Indian Philosophy*, vol. 1 (London: George Allen & Unwin).

Ramaswamy, E.A. (1990): 'Indian Trade Unionism: The Crisis of Leadership', in Mark Holmstrom (ed.), *Work for Wages in South Asia* (New Delhi: Manohar).

Rao, N. Sudhakar (2001): 'The Structure of South Indian Untouchable Castes: A View', in Ghanshyam Shah (ed.), *Identity and Politics: Cultural Subordination and the Dalit Challenge*, vol. 2 (New Delhi: Sage).

Rao, Vijayendra (2007): 'The Technology of Cultural Change', *World Development Report* (Washington DC: The World Bank. Internet site: http://www. cuklutreandpublication .org/bijupdf/ TechChange.pdf)

Rasul., M.A. (1974): *A History of the All India Kisan Sabha* (Calcutta: National Book Agency).

Rawls, John (1971): *A Theory of Justice* (Cambridge, Mass.: The Belknap Press/Harvard University).

Reisman, David (1950): *The Lonely Crowd: A Study of Changing American Character*, (New Haven: Yale University Press).

Renan, Ernest (1990): 'What is a Nation?' in Homi K. Bhabha (ed.), *Nations and Nationalism* (London: Routledge).

Report on Conditions of Work and Promotion of Livelihoods in the Unorganised Sector 2007 (New Delhi: National Commission for Enterprises in the Unorganised Sector, Government of India).

Robins, Nick (2006): *The Corporation that Changed the World: How the East India Company Shaped the Modern Multinational* (Hyderabad: Orient Longman).

Rodrik, Dani and Arvind Subramanian (2005): "From 'Hindu Growth' to Productivity Surge," (Washington D.C.: *IMF Staff Papers*;, vol. 52, no. 2, International Monetary Fund.

Rudolph, Lloyd I. and Susanne Hoeber (1987) *In Pursuit of Lakshmi: The Political Economy of the Indian State* (Delhi: Orient Longman).

Russell, Bertrand (1950): *Unpopular Essays* (London: George Allen & Unwin).

Ruthven, Orlanda, and Sushil Kumar (2002): *Moving Mud, Shifting Soil: Change and Development in Wage Labour Livelihoods in Uttar Pradesh, India* (mimeo), Working Paper 176 (London:Overseas Development Institute).

Sahay, Gaurang Ranjan (2001): *Village Studies in India: A Case of Bihar*, (Jaipur: Rawat Publications).

—— (2004): 'Hierarchy, Difference and the Caste System: A Study of Rural Bihar', in Dipankar Gupta (ed.), *Caste in Question: Identity or Hierarchy?* (New Delhi: Sage).

Sahay, A., and S.K. Rai (2005): 'How Entrepreneurial are Youth of Varanasi', *Journal of Services Research*, vol. 4, pp. 195–203.

Sarvekshna 2000 National Sample Survey (New Delhi: Ministry of Statistics and Implementation, Government of India).

Sen, Amartya (1997): 'Tagore and His India,' *New York Review of Books*, vol. 44, no. 11.

Sengupta, Arjun (2007): 'Against the Grain', *Hindustan Times*, Edit. Page, 21 Aug. 2007.

Sengupta, Jayashree 2008 'No Respite from Price Rises: Help the Poor with Better PDS.' *The Tribune*, edit page 10.

Shah, A.M. (1996): 'Job Reservation and Efficiency', in M.N. Srinivas (ed.), *Caste: Its Twentieth Century Avatar* (New Delhi: Penguin Books).

Shah, Ghanshyam (2001): 'Dalit Movements and the Search for Identity', *in* Ghanshyam Shah (ed.), *Dalit Identity and Politics: Cultural Subordination and the Dalit Challenge*, vol. 2 (New Delhi: Sage).

Shanin, T. (1971): 'Peasants as a Political Factor, in T. Shanin (ed.), *Peasants and Peasant Society*, (Harmondsworth: Penguin Books).

Sharma, K.L. (2001): *Reconceptualising Caste, Class and Tribe* (Jaipur: Rawat Publications).

Sharma, K.L. (1997): *Rural Society in India* (Jaipur: Rawat Publications).

Sheth, D.L. (2002): 'Caste and Class: Social Reality and Political Perception', in Ghanshyam Shah (ed.), *Caste and Democratic Politics in India* (Delhi: Permanent Black).

Shils, Edward (1981): *Tradition*, Chicago::University of Chicago Press).

Shiva Kumar, A.A. (2007): At Your Service, *India Today*, 31 Dec. 2007: 114–15)

Siddiqi, Majid H. (1978): *Agrarian Unrest in North India: The United Provinces 1918-22* (Delhi: Vikas Publishing House).

Simmel, Georg (1978): *The Sociology of Georg Simmel*, trans. and ed. Kurt H. Wolff (Glencoe, Illinois: The Free Press).

Simmons, Colin, and Salinder Supri (1995): 'Participation in Rural Non-Farm Activity in India: A Case Study of Cultivating Households in Jalandhar District, Punjab', *International Journal of Punjab Studies*, vol. 2, pp. 133–53.

Singh, K.S. (ed.) (1982): *Economies of the Tribes and their Transformation* (New Delhi: Concept Publishing Co.).

Singh, Shivani, and Amit Mukherjee (2004): 'Private Hospitals to Fill Gap', *Times of India*, 28 July 2004.

Smith, David 2007 *The Dragon and the Elephant: China,India and the New World Order* (London: Profile Books).

Smith, Harvey L. (1978): 'Two Lines of Authority: The Hospitals' Dilemma', in Howard D. Schwartz and Cary S. Kart (eds.), *Dominant Issues in Medical Sociology*, (Massachussets: Addison-Wesley).

Srinivas, M.N. (1987): *The Dominant Caste and Other Essays* (Delhi: Oxford University Press).

—— (1996): 'Introduction', in M.N. Srinivas (ed.), *Caste: Its Twentieth Century Avatar* (New Delhi: Penguin Books).

Starr, Paul (1982): *The Social Transformation of American Medicine* (New York: Basic Books).

Statistical Outline of India 2006-07 (Mumbai: Tata Services Limited; Department of Economics and Statistics, Mumbai).

Stiglitz, Joseph E. (2003): *Globalization and its Discontents* (New York: W.W.Norton)

Stromquist, Nelly P. (1998): 'NGOs in a New Paradigm of Civil Society', *Cultural Issues in Comparative Education*, vol. 1, pp. 62–67 (New York: Columbia University Press).

Taeube, Florian A. (2002): 'Structural Change and Economic Development in India: The Impact of Culture on the Indian Software Industry', pp. 1–10. *Development by Design*, Think Cycle (Bangalore: Internet address: taeube@wiwi.uni-frankfurt.de).

Third Census of Small Scale Industries Sector (2002): (New Delhi: Ministry of Commerce and Industries, Government of India).

Trevelyan G.M. (1951): 'The Great Days of Reform', in Herman Ausubel (ed.), *The Making of Modern Europe*, Book Two, *Waterloo to the Atomic Age* (USA: Holt, Rinehart & Winston).

Tully, Mark 2002: *India in Slow Motion* (London: Viking)

—— (2007); 'Living in a Material World', *Hindustan Times*, Edit. page, 20 June 2007

US Census Bureau (2005): *Statistical Abstract of the United States* (US Federal Highway Administration Annual. Internet site:http://www.fhwa.dot.gov/policy/ ohpi/hss/hsspubs.htm).

—— (2005): *Current Housing Reports, Series H150/05, American Housing Survey in the United States* Internet site: http://www.census.gov/hhes/www/housing/ ahs/nationaldata.html

UNCTAD (2004): *Handbook of Statistics* (Geneva: United Nations).

—— (2007): *World Development Report* (Geneva: United Nations).

Upadhya, Carol (2007): 'Employment , Exclusion and "Merit" in IT Industry', *Economic and Political Weekly*, vol XLII, pp, 1862–68.

Vaidyanathan, A. (2001): 'Poverty and Development Policy', *Economic and Political Weekly*, vol. 36, pp.1807–14.

Van Damme, Wilfred (1996): *Beauty in Context: Towards an Anthropological Approach to Aesthetics* (Leiden: E.J. Brill).

Visaria, Pravin (1995): 'Rural Non-Farm Employment in India: Trends and Issues for Research', *Indian Journal of Agricultural Economics*, vol. 50, pp.398–409.

Vora, Rajenda (2004): 'Decline of Caste Majoritarianism in Indian Politics', in Rajendra Vora and Suhas Palshikar (eds.), *Indian Democracy: Meanings and Practices* (New Delhi: Sage).

Wagle, Naren K. (1998): *Customary Law Among Non-Brahman Jatis of Pune* (mimeo.), Toronto University, Centre for South Asian Studies.

Washbrook, David (1989): 'Caste, Class and Dominance in Modern Tamilnadu', in Francine Frankel and M.S.A. Rao (eds.), *Dominance and State Power in Modern India: Decline of a Social Orde*, (Delhi: Oxford University Press.Website: www. buyusa.gov/india)

Weiner, Myron (2002): 'The Struggle for Equality: Caste in Indian Politics', in Atul Kohli (ed.), *The Success of India's Democracy* (Delhi: Foundation Books).

Wilkinson, Steven I. (2004): *Votes and Violence: Electoral Competition and Ethnic Riots in India* (Cambridge: Cambridge University Press).

Wiser, W.H. (1969): *The Hindu Jajmani System: A Socio-Economic System Interrelating Members of Hindu Community* (Lucknow: Lucknow Publishing House).

Wolf, Eric (1969): *Peasant Wars in the Twentieth Century* (New York: Harper & Row).

World Bank (2007): *Human Development Indicators* (Washington: The World Bank).

World Trade Report (2006): (Geneva: World Trade Organization).

Xaxa, Virginius (2001): 'Protective Discrimination: Why Scheduled Tribes Lag Behind Scheduled Castes', *Economic and Political Weekly*, vol. 36, pp.2765–72.

—— (1999): 'Tribes as Indigenous People of India', *Economic and Political Weekly*, vol. 34, pp. 3589–95.

Yadav, Yogendra (2001): 'Understanding the Second Democratic Upsurge: Trends of Bajhujan Participation in Electoral Politics in the 1990s', in Francine Frankel, et al (eds.), *Transforming India: Social and Political Dynamics of Democracy* (Delhi: Oxford University Press).

Young, Michael, and Peter Willmott (1973): *The Symmetrical Family: A Study of Work and Leisure in the London Region* (London: Routledge & Keagan Paul).

Zelliot, Eleanor (1970): 'Learning the Use of Political Means: The Mahars of Maharashtra', in Rajni Kothari (ed.), *Caste in Indian Politics* (Delhi: Orient Longman).

INDEX